MAXIMIZING HAPPINESS THROUGH INTIMATE COMMUNICATION

COMMUNICATION
3rd Edition

MAXIMIZING HAPPINESS THROUGH INTIMATE COMMUNICATION

Self-Help Relationship Advice, Marriage Solutions, Couples Therapy, Great Sex, & More!

3rd Edition

Marshall L. Shearer, MD
Marguerite R. Shearer, MD

Fresh Ink Group

Roanoke

MAXIMIZING HAPPINESS
THROUGH INTIMATE COMMUNICATION
Self-Help Relationship Advice, Marriage Solutions, Couples Therapy, Great Sex, & More!
3rd Edition

Copyright © 2003, 2004, 2011

Fresh Ink Group
An Imprint of:
The Fresh Ink Group, LLC
PO Box 525
Roanoke, TX 76262
Email: info@FreshInkGroup.com
www.FreshInkGroup.com

Edition 1.0	2003
Edition 2.0	2004
Edition 3.0	2011

Book design by Ann E. Stewart

Cover design by Joe Posada

Cataloging-in-Publication Recommendations: Non-Fiction; Self-Help; Relationships (Self-Help); Communication (Self-Help); Marriage Counseling (Self-Help); Couples Therapy (Self-Help); Sex Problems (Self-Help); Personal Counseling (Self-Help); Divorce Prevention (Self-Help); Dating (Self-Help); Sex (Self-Help); Intimacy (Self-Help); Relationship Experts (Self-Help)

Library of Congress Control Number: 2010940773

ISBN-13: 978-1-936442-01-0

We dedicate this book to our readers

Table Of Contents

Acknowledgements

We are grateful to our many friends and colleagues who contributed in so many ways, including our workshop participants, reading groups, and book club members for their indulgence and excellent feedback.

We especially want to distinguish the contributions of these individuals who looked beyond simply working with us to complete this project, people who shared our goal of helping others learn to nurture their loves and achieve the happiness we all deserve:

The late Charles Kramer, MD, for his careful reading and many wonderful suggestions,

David Logan, MD, for his thoughtful critique of the addictions material,

Michael Rudy, MSW, for his review and invaluable advice,

Paula Christensen, for her substantial contributions in the area of abused women,

Thomas Overmire, PhD, for his excellent editorial organization of our many drafts, and

Stephen Geez, MA, for his unflinching critiques and exhaustive editing.

We also thank Joe Posada for the poignant cover art, Patsy LaFave at The Write Place for manuscript preparation and indexing, plus Ann Stewart of The Fresh Ink Group, LLC, and the site management staffs at:

www.DocShearer.com

www.FreshInkGroup.com

Preface

This book teaches how to improve communication in intimate relationships. These include marriages, "significant others," gay partnerships, close friendships, and in the long-run relationships with your children. Enjoying the greatest rewards of being together requires only that you both respect the other's values, feelings, desires, and needs. You must care deeply about each other's happiness.

The ideas and examples we offer are gleaned from more than four decades practicing as a psychiatrist and family physician. Our experience includes advising readers of our syndicated newspaper column about sex-related problems; leading seminars on relationship issues for groups ranging from university students to church congregations; providing intensive singles and couples therapy for patients facing more serious challenges; and training other professionals in the field, including two years with the Masters and Johnson Institute. In all, we've found that what most people want is confidence that whatever life brings you, the two of you will face it together. These are the couples who learn, and never stop learning, their own strategies for intimate communication.

Whether your relationship is in serious trouble, or you face nagging problems that seem to defy solution, or you'd simply like to add some rich icing to your cake, this book is for you. It is not a "one size fits all" telling you what everybody else should do, but rather a means to becoming the experts of your own relationship. Through principles, examples, and understanding, we will show you how.

You can explore these ideas on your own, but it's best if you and your partner take turns reading one chapter at a time, then discussing it—just the two of you, or with a therapist. Try to avoid the teacher/student authority pattern of one reading and explaining to the other. Instead, make the commitment that you will do this together: giving yourselves the gift of mutual happiness that you both want and deserve.

This book will get you started, but it is your communication that will do the rest. Become your own relationship experts, and you'll discover all the magic of growing that ultimate, most meaningful love.

Marshall L. Shearer, MD
Marguerite R. Shearer, MD

Section I
Basic Assumptions

This section describes our philosophy and basic assumptions that form the core for this book. Chapter 1 deals with our assumptions about the goals of people in committed relationships.

Chapter 1:   Happiness

CHAPTER 1
HAPPINESS

Mutual happiness is the primary goal of an intimate relationship. People enter into committed relationships to enhance their own happiness first, and their partner's happiness second.

Happiness is an ongoing emotional state, with peaks and valleys like joy, sexual arousal, sadness, wonder, surprise, and hurts, and of messages of being valued and loved. The peak experiences flow into and out of the underlying state of happiness in ways similar to how waves flow in and out of the sea.

Enhancing happiness doesn't mean guaranteeing happiness. Rather, it means adding to the richness, enjoyment, and fulfillment of the total experience of living. People bond together in friendship, sexual relationships, or marriage for many reasons:

- To maximize their own happiness
- To maximize their partner's happiness
- To have children
- To gain financial security
- To have sex
- To gain social acceptability

It makes a difference, however, whether the success of an intimate relationship is measured by the emotional state of happiness or by the increased quality or quantity of sex, materialism, or social position. In our medical practice we have often heard, "He doesn't care about me as a person; all he is interested in is sex," or, "I'm just another possession to impress her friends."

Part of the function of courtship is for people to judge if the necessary ingredients for their own happiness and their potential partner's happiness are compatible and likely to be realized in marriage or some other form of committed relationship.

Self-Interest versus Selfishness

Our society reacts differently to the words "self-interest" and "selfishness." Self-interest is looking out for oneself and maximizing the good things in life. Self-interest is honorable. Selfishness is self-interest without regard to the effects on others. Selfishness is generally viewed as bad—bad in others, and especially bad in oneself. Selfishness is something to be avoided.

√   ***Seeking one's own happiness is not a selfish attitude. It is valid self-interest.***

In daily living, the distinction between selfishness and self-interest often becomes confusing. Selfishness may at times hide under the guise of self-interest, which adds to the general confusion. To clarify this important difference, the following three levels need to be distinguished.

> **Level I** is your intent or attitude as you act to maximize your happiness— to be considerate of the possible effects on others or to disregard the potential effect on others. This level is entirely subjective. No one else knows your intent better than you do.

> **Level II** is actual effect of your action(s) on others. This is the level of unintended consequences, accidents, negligence, and recklessness. It ranges from stepping on your partner's toes while dancing, to unintentionally embarrassing another by telling a story or joke at a party. This level is also the level of the effect of a hurt you intended. Your action is objective. The effect may be objective and might be observed by witnesses, or the effect may be subjective, only in the mind of the person affected.

> **Level III** is the creation of an agreement between you and another person to inform each other as soon as either of you feels hurt or put upon.

These positions are consistent with the Golden Rule: "Do unto others as you would have them do unto you." Confucius stated the same principle in negative form: "Do not do unto others what you would not have them do unto you." This is also consistent with the Second Commandment of Jesus: "Love thy neighbor as thyself." All these statements seem to say the standard of love for another person is self-love. In all these statements, the standard of action is within the one acting.

√   ***Do unto others as you would have them do unto you—under the circumstances as you understand them.***

In an effort to avoid being selfish, too many people go to extremes, placing ourselves on watch for other people's feelings to be sure we don't hurt them inadvertently. This attitude places an undue responsibility on us because it requires us to judge our partner's reaction and to guess which of our actions has triggered the negative response. To do this you must be constantly on alert, which takes a great deal of mental energy, plus it stifles spontaneity and contributes to feelings of insecurity. "Was our guard vigilant?" "Did we do the best thing?" Seldom do we consider that our partner's negative reaction might have been triggered by someone else or even by a memory. Your partner will become aware of this scrutiny and most likely will adopt it reciprocally, with results that you, in turn, will be under similar observation. By taking the responsibility to inform your partner when any slight, hurt, or imposition occurs, you can both drop your vigilant safeguarding and be free and spontaneous.

√ *By saying "Ouch!" you protect yourself from being hurt and also protect your partner from being selfish.*

With the "Ouch!" procedure (See Chapter 7) either individual can be alerted to the partner's hurt and can examine her/his action in regard to self-interest versus selfishness. Continuing the action that generates the hurt would be to act selfishly.

People generally know when they feel slighted—a red bulb lights up on the mental dashboard of the one who is hurt. Each individual instantly becomes aware of discomfort, which should be communicated as promptly as possible by a non-accusatory message such as "Ouch!" For example:

"My alarm just sounded 'Ouch!' I felt slighted by that. Please stop." Avoid saying, "You hurt me," for that would trigger your partner to go on guard.

One wife we saw in therapy informed her husband:

She: Whenever you call me by the nickname 'Kitten,' it hurts me.

He: I've been calling you Kitten at times for twenty years.

She: Yes, and for twenty years it has hurt on those occasions.

He: But your father called you Kitten.

She: That's why it hurts. He hated cats. He was mean and cruel to them— just as he was to me at times.

Risk

Avoiding needless risk or the possibility of hurting one's partner, children, or someone else is yet another dimension to the healthy distinction between self-interest and selfishness. Risk also often involves a violation of trustworthiness and openness. An example is: "I'll misappropriate this money temporarily, and invest it short term in this sure thing. Then I'll repay the money and keep the profit. No one else will know."

√ *Unless you protest, expect the same hurts to keep recurring.*

Another example is violating one's commitment to be sexually faithful: "I'll take the risk of my partner not finding out about it. What she/he doesn't know won't hurt him/her."

Even when an affair doesn't come to light, it *does* hurt the relationship by reducing trustworthiness and openness, and by lowering one's resistance to violating that commitment again.

Love

Romantic love is a many-splendored thing. The components vary from one relationship to another, and within the same relationship over time, perhaps from moment to moment. Romantic love, like happiness, is an underlying steady state within which there are highs and lows and, at times, even anger. Romantic love is expecting that many of your needs and desires—including sexual ones—will be met, and it is the willingness to meet your partner's needs and desires. In American culture, sexual passion is expected to be a major component of romantic love.

A couple may be in a loving relationship that is sexually gratifying without necessarily being "in love." In such relationships, the elements of attraction and passion may be low or absent. This type of relationship may be found in arranged marriages that are still common in some parts of Africa, the Middle East, and South Asia.

√ *Love is caring about the other person's happiness almost as much as your own happiness—and sometimes more.*

Passionless relationships also occur in the United States for various reasons such as the desire to have children. With some frequency, divorcees, widows, and widowers in relationships may describe them as loving, but without being "in love," that is, without sexual passion. Healthy love is punctuated by the needs for a separate identity, autonomy, time with other friends, opportunities for personal growth, and solitude. Such relationships, as well as arranged marriages, are often very stable. They are built on respect, devotion, commitment, caring and compassion, and mutual needs, including sexual needs; e.g., financial and social needs, and the need to have the partner be a mother or father figure in the household.

Being "in love" has all the components enjoyed by the loving couple described above, plus attraction and passion. People's concepts of love are individually determined. Essentially, they are either (1) the best—the most psychologically satisfying—relationship that person has experienced, or (2) that plus the one or two aspects that were felt to be missing in the relationship. Many people's concept of love grows and develops with progressively healthier relationships. (See Chapter 12)

Sometimes there is a passion to be together and to share thoughts, moods, emotions, and bodies. One's loins can ache for the loins of the lover.

Romantic love includes an admiration of the other that honors, protects, and cherishes him/her above all others. The feeling of being cherished is especially meaningful. To be so loved is pure joy. It is so very precious and yet so very fragile. This joy bounces between the partners, moving to increasing heights. Love communicates caring and compassion in attitude, feeling, thought, and action in both little and big ways, day in and day out, year after year.

Unfortunately, hurts that go unresolved can also resonate between the partners, creating a downward spiral. Preventing or reversing that spiral is what this book is all about. Love and passion often continue within a committed relationship well into the declining years. The urgency and impatience of youth passes, as well as the component of sex and intercourse as a defining or confirming experience of self-identity. Yet, still there is a strong need to be together emotionally, psychologically, and physically, and to connect in deeper and more meaningful ways with your lover and partner of all those years.

Passion can be maintained—or rekindled—by variety and some unexpectedness in your psychological and physical approaches to each other. There is still a need and desire to "get into each other," for the two of you to once again become one, culminating in that moment of an oceanic feeling of absence-of-ego boundaries at orgasm. In a happy, fulfilling relationship, intercourse has gradually, perhaps imperceptibly, become a sacred ritual. (See Chapter 26)

People are shaped by who and what they love. In a loving relationship, you are shaped by your actions and reactions to your partner, just as your partner is shaped by her/his actions and reactions to you.

Happiness is loving and having that love reciprocated. Reciprocated love generates a mutual commitment of steadfastness, devotion, and dependability. *"All the world loves a lover."*

√ *People are shaped by who and what they love. They are also shaped by who loves them. When both of these influences are combined in the same person, the effect is greater than the sum of them individually.*

Reciprocated love and commitment expands into trust—trust that you won't be hurt deliberately or ridiculed as you express your needs, desires, and your innermost hopes and dreams. These elements of love create the underlying steady-state of happiness and increased self-esteem. It is this radiance of happiness and increased self-esteem that is so apparent to the world. See Chapter 13 for a discussion of trust and self-esteem as essential factors in the growth of love. □

IN BRIEF

Happiness is an underlying emotional state that is made up of many other pleasant and unpleasant emotions over time. In large part, happiness is the result of managing our own self-interest without hurting anyone else. Self-interest without regard to hurting others is selfishness. This distinction is traced in daily living. Count on your partner for prompt, accurate feedback, and reciprocate with the same quality feedback to avert selfish behavior.

YET TO COME

There are many important implications to the assumption that people form bonds to increase their own happiness first, and their partner's happiness second. The following chapters deal with these implications: the word "I," misunderstood words, vulnerability, the way to handle differences of opinion, feelings are facts, and the way to handle hurts and anger. These provide building blocks for much of our approach.

Section II
Verbal Communications

Verbal communication is the backbone of our program. Taken together, the chapters in this section form a complete, functional system. These communication principles continue to reappear throughout the book in various applications and complex situations, including making love.

CHAPTER 2
USING THE WORD "I"

Most people have heard the admonition to use "I sentences," but they don't, probably because "I sentences" are not adequately understood. I sentences don't necessarily sound different to the speaker, but they can make a world of difference to the receiver.

Almost all couples at times have some degree of difficulty with communication. The simplest and most effective rule we know to keep those difficulties to a minimum is to start all sentences with the pronoun **I** as the subject. For example: "I feel," "I think," "I want," "I hurt." This has the effect of eliminating "you" as the subject. The difference may not seem much when you say it, but it can make a world of difference when you hear it.

Analyze your own reaction to the following: "I am hurt by that" versus "You hurt me." The human reaction to the first statement is compassionate. "Where?" "How?" "What can I do to help?" The second statement creates a defensive reaction of either "No, I did not" or "You had it coming."

Try applying this to sex play: "Your touch is too rough" versus "I need a gentler touch." The first implies something is wrong with the toucher, even though that was not the intent of the speaker. The latter is simply a statement of preference. Again, "Don't do that" versus "I'm not ready yet" or "I need more _____." One statement can be heard as taking control and giving orders. The other leaves room for the partner's desires. Some people may call this selfishness—we call it self-interest.

Another example: "A group you like is coming to town for a performance next weekend." The speaker thinks she/he has made a request to go. The hearer takes it as just information input. They don't go. One feels rejected and ignored; the other is mystified by that reaction. This is contrasted with "That group I like is coming to town next weekend for a performance. I would like us to go."

There is no misinterpreting the speaker's meaning of "I didn't hear you." But the meaning of "What did you say?" is dependent upon the inflection and the interpretation of the inflection of the speaker. Frustration about something else can be heard as hostility and as a challenge.

If you feel you have to be careful what you say to avoid your partner becoming upset or angry, then make a habit of using "I sentences." It is the surest way to avoid giving offence and being misunderstood.

√ *It is virtually impossible to be heard as hostile, accusatory, or*

dominating when the speaker uses I as the subject of every verb.

Contrast "I love you" with "You love me" or "Let's love each other" or "I want to be your friend" with "Be my friend."

"You" probably has to be the subject when questions are asked: "Where do you want to eat tonight?" We recommend that such a question always be preceded by a position statement: "I would like to eat there. What is your preference?" This gives a position, and it shows consideration for the other's desires or feelings. This avoids the familiar contest of "I'm more polite than you are."

But what if your partner is not considerate? Suppose the response is "I don't care where you want to eat." Then the hurt is ten times worse than if we had never stated a preference. This is called vulnerability—a major subject in itself. Due to fear of vulnerability, some people choose to hide behind politeness. (See Chapter 4)

"I am all for me" is completely self-centered. "I am for us" describes what we feel most relationships are about. "I am in this relationship to enhance my happiness and to enhance your happiness. I am for us." This is a statement, a declaration: "Here I stand." It is a statement of vulnerability because it opens the self to the hurt of rejection to a greater degree than would result from rejection without the statement.

"I think" in front of a "you" phrase is not an **I** sentence. There is no difference between "You are an S.O.B." and "I think you are an S.O.B."

When asking for an **I** sentence, don't say, "You didn't use an **I** sentence." Even if said with the kindest of feelings toward the partner, that sentence can be heard as an "I got ya." Rather, say, "I would like to hear that as an **I** sentence." You also can use non-verbal invitations when requesting **I** sentences, such as touching your eye, or some other agreed-upon signal.

I sentences are also useful in other relationships:

> ■ *A faculty wife always felt uncomfortable at faculty wives' functions because other women were obliquely putting her down all the time: "Oh, how nice—you've worn your blue flowered dress again." She was advised to reply, "I hear that as both a compliment and a put-down. What were your intentions?" That put a stop to such digs.*

There are basically only four strategies people can employ to get their needs met by someone else:[1]

- One is a simple statement or request. "I would like _____ " or "Would you please do _____ for me?"

- The second is to barter or make a deal. "I will do this for you if you will do

---

[1] We are indebted to Michael Rudy, MSW, for this categorization.

that for me." This might include taking turns in some area of decision-making.

- The third way is through manipulation, convincing the other person that some statement is true or partially true so she/he will want to do what the first person wants.

- The fourth way is through coercion or intimidation.

In a caring, intimate relationship, only request and barter are appropriate. Both of these can begin with **I** sentences.

To use **I** is to become more real and authentic. It is a commitment statement. This is where I am. **I** is a statement of self-respect. **I** sentences may be awkward at first. Give yourselves time to feel comfortable using them. We firmly believe that if a couple will diligently use **I** sentences for two weeks, the benefit to the relationship will be so rewarding that neither will ever give up using **I**. □

IN BRIEF

Using "I" as the subject of every verb is the best way to represent yourself while minimizing the likelihood of being heard as offensive.

YET TO COME

I sentences are only the first step of a communication system. The system is expanded in the remainder of Section II.

CHAPTER 3
MISUNDERSTOOD &
INFLAMMATORY WORDS

The common connotation of a word or phrase is often much more narrow than its definition. A word is first heard in its connotations, which often is not what the speaker intended to be heard.

We all use a number of common words that probably would be best not used at all. They are ingrained in our speech patterns from our earliest years, but any success we have in eliminating them will be to our distinct advantage. These words include: "why," "should," "ought," "let's," "always," "never," and all negative terms in general.

Why

We advise all of our patients to eliminate the word "why" from their vocabulary. *Why* has a connotation that "I have prejudged you as having done something wrong, but I am willing to listen to an excuse." Parents ask, "Why did you fail the test?" But who asks, "Why did you make an A?" Or we ask, "Why didn't you put gas in the car?" but never, "Why did you put gas in the car?"

Why is often used in berating someone. *Why* is heard as coming from a superior position and directed toward a subordinate. This is not always the way the sender intends the message to be heard. The word *why* can mean "I am curious," but such a meaning is often apt to be misconstrued, especially if there is ill will in the relationship.

If you are curious, then simply say, "I am curious about that," or, "I am curious how you came to that conclusion." Avoid using *why*.

Should & Ought

The words "should" and "ought" need to be used sparingly, especially in daily speech. These words belong only in moral statements such as the Ten Commandments and in contractual relationships!

If moral obligation is intended, well and good—then go ahead and use *should* or *ought*. If not, don't use them. Their use in everyday speech implies, "I am the authority. I shall tell you what is right or moral, what should be." Again, it is a message from a superior to a subordinate. The natural response to someone else saying "You should" is to dig in your heels, resist, and resent it.

Should and *ought* serve to program listeners to feel guilty, even when you use them about yourself. For example, you might say to yourself, "I should cut the grass tomorrow." If you don't cut the grass tomorrow, you are very apt to feel guilty, perhaps just because you used the word *should.*

We submit there is nothing moral about cutting the grass. You could say, "I want to cut the grass tomorrow," but that is not true if you don't like to cut the grass. What you like is the result after the grass is cut. That appearance is worth the effort. Hence, you might say, "It is in my best interest to cut the grass tomorrow." Now if you don't cut the grass, you have simply made the judgment that spending your time some other way—such as watching a ball game or going fishing—was in your better interest or gave you more pleasure than cutting the grass. In the latter example, the question has become "Which was in my overall best interest, both long-term and short-term?"

√   *"You should..." violates two rules: (1) it implies superiority in setting moral standards, and (2) it is not an I sentence.*

There is an old-fashioned word that fits here: "behooves." "It behooves me to cut the grass tomorrow."

√   *"Should" and "ought" carry the connotation of moral superiority.*

Let's

Likewise, the word "let's" is best eliminated. *Let's* is preemptive; it doesn't invite the other to express any opinion. It works well with children: "Let's pick up our toys now," or, "Let's go to bed." It isn't that the other person can't express an opinion, but a negative statement is almost always called for first. We find this frequently from the "big, protective, loving" husband talking to the "little woman" and smothering her in the process.

Negatives

"No," "not," "don't," and other negating terms need to have only limited usage. It behooves both you and your partner to be very sparing in the use of negating terms, and to always follow the negating sentence with a positive statement. "I don't want that" really isn't much information. It implies that you should know what really was wanted. There is a superior attitude conveyed in "Try guessing again, and then I may tell you if you are correct this time."

Contrast the above with "I don't want that; I prefer this." This sentence conveys the necessary information while accepting the listener's lack of knowledge. Most of the time the single sentence "I prefer this" is all that is necessary, and it avoids the possibility of the listener feeling rejected by the negating term. Consider "I don't want intercourse tonight," as opposed to "I don't want intercourse tonight, but I would like to snuggle." It is much harder to hear personal rejection in the latter statement.

To illustrate just how little information is conveyed with a negating sentence, consider the following negative directions for driving to our office:

1.   Do not go to Toledo.

2.   Do not go to Detroit.

3.   Do not turn left at the second traffic light.

4.   Do not go eight miles.

Negating sentences should be avoided for emotional reasons. The emotional mind cannot encode a negative. Hence, "I do not want intercourse tonight" is often heard as "I have been rejected" or something else before it enters the emotional or unconscious mind. The negating term exists only in the intellectual part of the mind.

■   *Sigmund Freud illustrated this point with the example of a patient who dreamed of a figure standing at the foot of the bed with a knife ready to stab the sleeper. Freud asked the patient to think of the figure in the dream and then ask himself who came to mind. The patient replied, "Well, it was not my mother."*

But, of course, it was. The thought of "mother" began in the patient's unconscious mind, but because that thought was unacceptable it was changed to its negative when it came to full consciousness.

Similarly, it is virtually impossible for anyone to draw a single picture for which a caption containing a negating word (e.g., "no," "not," "never") would be appropriate. It may be done with a series of drawings or with an overlay. An example of the latter is a left-turn sign that is overlaid with a red line through the picture, providing the negation of the turn.

A dog may be depicted as "friendly," from which it may be inferred that it will not bite. To be non-verbally depicted as communicating "I will not bite," the dog would need to be shown in the second picture with its mouth around the human's arm or leg, then in subsequent pictures having removed its mouth without biting.

Always & Never

"Always" and "never" are often used when the meaning would be more appropriately expressed in other terms. For example: "I need a lot more hugs from you" is a better statement than "You never hug me anymore" or even "It seems like you never hug me anymore."

When Pat says, "You always/never do _____" during a heated discussion, the words *always* and *never* are inflammatory. Chris is apt to take offence and to recall the one or several exception(s) to the statement. The point Pat was trying to make is lost in the discussion (or argument) of the minor exceptions, and there are now two arguments instead of one. In addition, Pat's intent is usually to psychologically hurt Chris, and it is recognized as an attempt to hurt or put down Chris.

√   *"You always..." or, "You never..." means the discussion has moved from the issue to a deliberate attempt to hurt the partner by generating feelings of guilt or inadequacy. It means the speaker is out for character assassination.*

The use of *always* or *never* in a discussion is an indication that a critical shift has occurred; the original issue has become secondary to the intent to hurt or engender guilt. *Always* and *never* in an argument should be taken by both parties that "the fat is in the fire." It is time to disengage until feelings cool, then readdress the original issue later. □

IN BRIEF

- *The connotation of "Why?" to the hearer is "Justify yourself to me, the judge."*

- *"Should" and "Ought" belong only in sentences that are truly moral statements. "You should" or "You ought" implies that the speaker is the moral authority directing the listener.*

- *"Let's" tends to pre-empt the other's expected position, which might be different. Let's is often used with children.*

- *Negative words convey minimal information. Negatives are absent from the emotional mind. When used, negative statements need to be followed by a contrasting positive statement.*

- *"Always" and "Never" are inflammatory words. As such, their use is an indication of moving from the specific issue under discussion to general character assassination.*

YET TO COME

Vulnerability is a major component of a loving relationship.

CHAPTER 4
VULNERABILITY

"Can I trust you not to ridicule my hopes, dreams, and self-felt weaknesses if I share them with you?"

Vulnerability is an individual's openness to being hurt. (Our discussion will be limited to psychological hurt, as opposed to forceful, physical hurt.) We become vulnerable to other people in direct proportion to our love or respect for them, not their love for us. For example, if a perfect stranger says, "You're stupid," we generally disregard the statement completely. Rather, we think there is something wrong with the stranger. But if someone we love or respect says we are stupid, it hurts. And the depth of the hurt is in direct proportion to how much we value her/his opinion of us—how much we love or respect her/him.

Another example is the misguided but loving mother who says, "You are wrong" or, "That is not the way it is" to a teenager who replies, "I don't care what you think." The parent is usually more hurt than the teenager because during the middle teen years parental love, however miscommunicated, is generally greater than the love from teen to parent.

√ *The strength of a relationship is directly proportional to the mutual vulnerability in the relationship.*

Unilateral Vulnerability Is Equally Troublesome

Being vulnerable to someone is granting him/her the power to hurt you, to ridicule or make fun of you. There is some minimal vulnerability in the expression of any feeling or opinion. Without sharing this much of yourself, there is no chance for a relationship. A deeper, more meaningful intimacy and vulnerability is the sharing of your past and also your hopes, fears, dreams for the future, and your self-felt weaknesses. The other person may take advantage of your vulnerability by belittling your dreams or by deliberately trying to hurt you in an argument by throwing your past up to you. When vulnerability is unilateral rather than mutual, it breeds resentment in the person who feels more vulnerable. This resentment can destroy a relationship.

■ *A young woman working in a hospital was intensely attracted to an over-confident, over-assertive young male resident surgeon. She maneuvered to be as near him as possible. Ultimately they married, as she had hoped. She felt, however, that she had caught him via her many efforts, as if she had tricked him into marriage versus his really being attracted to her. She felt vulnerable. She had no idea of what he valued in her.*

During therapy, the surgeon related to us that he felt he had chosen his wife freely. When asked what he particularly liked about her, he replied, "She makes my life complete. I am comfortable in the hospital setting, but I could never initiate the social function with friends that she does, and that I thoroughly enjoy." He had never told her this. He realized the power that the imbalance of vulnerability gave him over her; he enjoyed that power and was unwilling to let her know what she meant to him.

When she divorced him, he was devastated. He expressed and showed that he was hurting. After the divorce was finalized, they began dating again. This time he let her know all she had meant and did mean to him. In time she realized that he was as vulnerable to her as she was to him, and they remarried each other.

√   **People who lack legitimate power in a relationship may resort to manipulation to get their needs met, or they may leave the relationship.**

The relationship between love/respect and vulnerability is a two-way street. That is, either aspect can and does influence the other. Increasing vulnerability and not having it taken advantage of will increase trust, love, self-esteem, and respect. Similarly, increasing love increases vulnerability. Hence, it behooves Chris to protect Pat's vulnerability, not only to increase Pat's happiness, but also in order to maximize Pat's love of Chris. Part of the difficulty is that Chris doesn't always recognize when Pat is being vulnerable, or perhaps doesn't recognize just how vulnerable Pat is being. There are two basic reasons for not spelling out our vulnerability clearly and openly: (1) a belief that we shouldn't have to, and (2) the fear of being hurt.

She/He Should Already Know

Many people believe that if their partners truly love them, they will automatically know their wants and vulnerabilities. This belief is partially true. People who are around each other a significant amount of time, and who pay attention to each other, can read each other's moods fairly well. This is especially true if the mood is protracted over a period of time, and if there is no effort to hide it. However, it is one thing to read someone's mood; it is quite another matter to guess the perceptions and thoughts that gave rise to the mood. Consider this example:

■   *A man is late getting home one evening. The family is already eating dinner, and after greeting everyone, he sits down. The next thing he hears is his wife asking, "What's the matter? Don't you like the food?" Surprised, he answers,*

"What? No. The food is fine, I guess. I haven't tasted it. What prompts you to ask?" She says, "Well, you were staring at the food on your plate and shaking your head 'no.'" The muscles in his neck tell him he had been shaking his head, and he remembers looking at his plate. "I wasn't thinking of the food. I was thinking of something that didn't go well at the office. Psychologically, I was not home yet." She accepts his explanation, and they have a good evening.

The wife reads his mood and incorrectly guesses at the cause, but she checks out her guess. Further, she checks it out in a timely manner. If she waits till after supper, or even two minutes, her question will be coming from left field, and it is doubtful that her husband will be able to recall shaking his head and looking down.

Let's take this example one step further. Suppose the wife is hurt by what she surmises is his not liking the food, but she says nothing. Chances are she will be frosty most of the evening, and the husband will have no clue as to the cause. Her action involves "reading and checking it out." If she doesn't say anything, it will be "reading and guessing."

Salespersons, physicians, lawyers, and negotiators may be very good at reading moods and even at guessing contents. There is an advantage in these more formal situations in that timing can usually be relied upon to a much greater extent than in sexual or platonic relationships because the attention is focused on a limited number of known issues. But it is still guessing.

Casual relationships can have both a winner and a loser, but in committed relationships there are either two winners or two losers. There is no need to guess in a committed relationship. Even if an individual feels she/he is accurate 80% of the time, why take the risk with the remaining percentage? And by asking, there is less chance of the other person feeling manipulated.

The belief that "If you love me, you will know what is wrong without my having to say anything to you" often has another deeper root, which usually goes unrecognized. It is the mistake of confusing divine love with human love. God is presented as omniscient, all-knowing—just as Santa Claus is supposed to be. Then we hear that "God is love." At some other time we learn that the word that characterizes a close, ideal relationship is "love." Hence, the feeling: "If she/he truly loved me, she/he would know."

But this is equating divine love with human love and attributing the powers of divine love to the partner. Human love is *not* omniscient. A person can be loved deeply, but to communicate maximally, thoughts, feelings, and desires must be actively represented.

Fear

Instead of being completely open, fearful individuals often expose only a small part of their vulnerability. Then their partners don't recognize it as vulnerability and, unknowing or carelessly, step on the vulnerability. Pat thinks, "Ah ha, I knew I shouldn't trust Chris. I won't be vulnerable that way again." At other times when anger and hostility are high, one partner might succumb to the desire to hurt the other by taking advantage of that knowledge, even if the issue is not part of the current dispute that triggered the anger. This compounds the hurt and decreases the other partner's future willingness to be vulnerable. Either way, some portion of the love dies.

Open vulnerability seems to be almost universally respected. Two buck deer fighting over a doe don't fight to the death. The fight stops when one becomes ultimately vulnerable by turning his side to the other's antlers. Similarly, dogs stop fighting when one dog stretches its neck, exposing its jugular veins, or rolls on its back, exposing the vulnerable underbelly. On the playground today, fights usually stop when one signals or says, "I give up."

Having weapons available often changes this pattern. The pattern also changes when an individual is fighting for her/his group (gang, family, country) rather than just for himself/herself.

Vulnerability, when expressed openly, almost always stops an attack. The majority of exceptions to this statement are situations in which the hurt is incidental to the partner's goals, such as hurt received from an addict partner who is trying to make sure his/her next "fix" is available. (See "The Meaning of Hurts," Chapter 7) Examples of these exceptions are described in Section IV, "Understanding Stubborn Problems," Chapters 14, 16, 18, 19, & 20.

√   ***When you first meet a person, you put your best foot forward, quite understandably. Eventually, though, you must put your other foot forward, too.***

Another danger is that the partner may be sadistic—an extremely rare situation—and both individuals may have to face the fact that one actually does enjoy hurting the other. To reach this as a valid conclusion, the couple will need to work through some of the principles to be discussed under *Anger*. (See Chapters 7, 14, 15, 16, & 17) Ultimately they must make a choice: tolerate the situation or leave it. □

IN BRIEF

Vulnerability is an essential ingredient of intimacy and love. It is "letting your hair down" and exposing your dreams and self-felt weaknesses to your confidant and lover. It behooves you to protect your partner's vulnerability.

YET TO COME

The next chapter is a discussion of feelings. Differences can be resolved by a discussion of depth and intensity, which will be addressed next. The differences will also be addressed under the topic of Anger. (See Chapter 15)

CHAPTER 5
FEELINGS ARE FACTS

In an intimate relationship, statements of one's feelings are very vulnerable statements that deserve the utmost respect and consideration. A major aspect of love is the emotional aspect.

Feelings are facts—emotional facts. As such, they are very important to a relationship. Emotional facts are not necessarily logical or rational. For example, you can feel scared in a graveyard at night, yet your thoughts tell you—and you know!—there is nothing to fear. If your sister were there with you and told you there was nothing to be afraid of, you would agree. But, her statement wouldn't change the feeling.

√ **Feelings are out of our direct willful control; therefore, there should be no value judgment placed on feelings.**

A "feeling" arises from all that is our past, plus some current trigger. It is not uncommon to fail to recognize what caused it. Feelings are not right or wrong; people are not adequate or inadequate based on how they feel in a given situation. However, their actions based on the feeling are subject to value judgment.

Of course, our emotions usually match what we think and know. And there are times when mentally recognizing the logical, rational facts can and does change a feeling. However, most of us have experienced times when we felt unloved, even though we had no rational basis for the feeling and when, in fact, we were loved.

Most people will acknowledge that their feelings are not always rational and logical. With such an acknowledgment, there is no way an individual can expect her/his partner's feelings to always be rational. Most people will also acknowledge that they can simultaneously experience opposing feelings that do not cancel each other out. This is called *ambivalence*.

It behooves us to protect our partner's vulnerability about the feeling statements. To ridicule such statements or deal with them in some strictly logical manner is to cause the partner to stop making feeling statements. Anyone who has to be on guard, to the extent that each feeling has to be subjected to a logical rational analysis before it can be communicated, will resent the obligation, and will stop making those communications. Such couples lose a considerable amount of psychological intimacy.

Psychological intimacy is the sharing of hopes, dreams, self-felt weaknesses, and feelings. It is being vulnerable. It is the ability to be at ease and spontaneous without having to watch what is said. The language of love is not necessarily logical or rational.

"I feel rejected" is best responded to with "Hey, I love you" and a move to be close rather than "I did not reject you" or even "Where did that feeling come from?" One of the most efficient responses is "What can I do to help (you deal with your feelings)?" The person with the feeling has a better idea of what is most likely to help change her/his feeling.

Feelings cannot be changed by will alone. A person cannot change a feeling by saying, "I shall no longer feel sad; I shall feel happy," then throw some mental switch and have the feeling change. Of course, willpower can affect thoughts, actions, and interactions, which can change feelings. In this way, willpower can indirectly influence feelings.

Since we cannot directly control our feelings, we are not responsible for how we feel at any given moment. But we are totally accountable for choosing to concentrate or dwell on those feelings and, especially, for choosing to act on the basis of those feelings. This includes what we do to increase the chances of changing those feelings in the desired direction.

Don't ask or expect your partner to change your feelings for you. Your partner may assist you, but should never take charge or assume the responsibility. Each person is responsible for dealing with her/his own feelings, both positive and negative. You can ask for assistance from your partner.

In medical practice a distinction is made between requesting a consultation or referring the patient who has a puzzling condition. In either case, the patient is seen by the specialist. With a consultation, the responsibility for the patient remains with the first physician, who now has the benefit of the specialist's thinking and recommendations. The primary physician may follow all, part, or none of the specialist's recommendations. On the other hand, if a referral is requested and accepted, the patient becomes the responsibility of the specialist.

In dealing with your negative feelings, it is acceptable to request a consultation, but never a referral. Likewise, never accept a referral about someone else's feelings. The only job description for taking the responsibility for changing (or creating) someone else's feelings was the Court Jester. His job was to make the king feel merry. The Jester became known as "the fool."

It is even more important that, as a partner, you *not* take charge with an attitude of "I will fix it for you." This is useless, often making the other feel little and ineffectual in addition to the original feelings. "Do something with me to help change my feeling. I don't want to be done to; I want to be done with!" is the cry.

√ *It is fun to be a giver. It is fulfilling.*

Many childhood fairy tales involve a maiden in distress and a Prince Charming who comes riding up on a big white horse to make everything fine. The lady and the prince get married and live happily ever after. Some husbands are so indoctrinated with similar fairy-tale-like dynamics that any negative concerns expressed by their wives create a feeling of obligation to fix them. When a husband finds he can't, he still feels he should have been able to, which makes him feel inadequate and resentful of the burden. Sensing this, his wife quits communicating. This wife cannot use her husband as a sounding board to bounce ideas around with. She can't use him to explore alternatives without him making the selection for her.

In a different way, a woman can take on a similar responsibility for the husband:

■   *A wife senses by the way her husband enters the house that something is wrong. She assumes he has had a bad day. She takes it as her responsibility to change his mood. She thinks, Should I speed supper up to give him something in his stomach, or should I delay supper and sit and talk with him? Should I bring the kids in to distract him, or send the kids outside so he has peace and quiet?*

She begins on Plan A. In a few minutes she realizes that it is not working, so she shifts to Plan B. Then she sees that Plan B is not working and shifts to Plan C. By this time she is becoming annoyed that he is not responding to all her loving kindness, and he is beginning to feel guilty since she is trying so hard.

√   **For there to be a giver, there must be a receiver.**

Instead of all this convoluted thinking, the wife might simply say, "Looks like you had a bad day. What can I do to help?" Chances are, he will come up with something she would never think of. "Those new shoes hurt my feet, and I was walking most of the day. I want to go soak in the tub and drink a beer."

The point is, the helper is only the assistant who can make suggestions, but never takes charge of the job. Their reply can be shortened to simply "I've had a hard day. I would like to soak in the tub with a beer." He should not need to appear haggard and in pain for the partner to accept it.

√   **In spite of love and good intentions, trying to change someone else's feelings single-handedly is a nearly impossible job.**

Some people feel it is demeaning or begging to ask for something such as a touch or a hug. If the partner doesn't have the right to refuse, she/he will hear the request as being bossy or ordering. If the partner doesn't intrinsically care, doesn't have her/his own happiness entwined with the other's happiness, then it is begging.

One end of the continuum is begging, whining, supplicating, and crawling; the other end is ordering, demanding, and controlling. The narrow center range provides information. For example:

"Since you are not a mind reader, let me tell you what I think I would like. Of course, it is your choice to give it or not, but I will enable you to make an informed choice instead of guessing. I do not intend to limit your choices—that approaches ordering—nor do I intend to lie at your feet, giving you all the choices or the chance to walk on me."

Picture the wife who, after a number of years of marriage, is able to say, "Sometimes I need to hear you say you love me when we start to make love." Most husbands don't realize the depth and intensity and vulnerability of that request. Nor do most wives recognize the vulnerability, openness, depth, and intensity when, after a disappointing sexual encounter, a husband says, "I need you to rest your hand on me somewhere."

Never presume that you *know* what another is feeling. Guessing in an intimate relationship compares to electing a shortcut across a minefield instead of staying on the road! This was illustrated by the vignette of the man who was late for dinner. (See "She Should Already Know," Chapter 4)

In love we want to enhance our partner's happiness, but we are not mind readers. We desperately need information about what would enhance our partner's happiness.

√ **The more intimate the request, the more valuable and the more fulfilling the gift.**

The more personal the information we seek, the more we need it, and the greater the likelihood that it is available from only one source: our partner. Our partner is obligated, in love, to provide that information. We are obligated, in love, to protect that vulnerability. We are also obligated, in love, to provide the same information to our partner. That is being vulnerable. But in a most intimate way we are allowing the partner to give. For the partner to give, we must receive; there can't be a giver without a receiver. The partner needs the fun and enjoyment of giving as much as we do. Periodically, this opportunity adds to intimacy and strengthens the relationship. Both parties need to be able to give as well as to receive. □

IN BRIEF

Feelings are facts—emotional facts. Feelings are not always logical. A major component of love is the feeling component. Feeling statements are vulnerable statements that let your partner in. When both of you make feeling statements, it adds to intimacy.

YET TO COME

Simply labeling and identifying a feeling is usually, by itself, not adequate communication. How strong is the feeling?

CHAPTER 6
DEPTH & INTENSITY

*Sometimes the depth and intensity of a feeling or a position is critical informa-
tion that you both need in order to make the best decisions for a relationship.*

Communication has only begun when an individual makes a position statement
using an **I** sentence. The depth and intensity of a position often will make a world of
difference. Contrast "I have a positive regard for you" with "I love you." For those
really in love, the first statement may seem insufficient. It is the depth and intensity of
love that leads people to carve on trees, make radio announcements, compose poetry
and songs, or borrow "sweet nothings" from another's compositions.

√ *The difference between "I have a positive regard for you" and
"My love for you knows no bounds; it is as deep as the ocean"
is the depth and intensity.*

There will be many times when the individuals in a relationship have different ideas
on a topic. The resolution of differences is not for one or the other to give in, but to
measure the depth and intensity of the feelings they each have about their respective
positions. This usually requires several paragraphs. The interchange of information of
"what it means to me" should continue until one individual says, "I can see you have
stronger feelings about this than I do. We will do it your way."

We all know intrinsically how deeply we feel; we don't, however, automatically
know the depth of our partner's feelings. Both sides must speak up if the couple is to
accurately judge who has the stronger feeling.

■ *A couple goes to the movies. Chris says, "I would like to sit up front." Pat
says, "I want to sit in the last row." Communication has just begun. Each has an
obligation, in love and to the relationship, to say what it means to sit in the back
or the front. First, let's assume Chris says, "I left my glasses at home; I won't be
able to see unless I sit up close." Pat says, "I tend to get restless and fidgety. I get
up for a drink after I finish my popcorn, and I don't like to disturb others."*

We would assume that both individuals would conclude that Chris had the greater
need, and Pat would acknowledge it and willingly sit up front, probably on the aisle to
minimize disturbing others.

On the other hand, the conversation could be like this:

Chris: "I feel more a part of the action when I sit up front and don't see the edges of the screen."

Pat: "To tell the truth, I get claustrophobic unless I'm right back near the exit where I can get out. I'm afraid if I sat up close, I would be so anxious that I couldn't enjoy the picture and that I might disturb you and others."

Under such circumstances, we would assume that Chris would acknowledge that Pat had the greater need or desire, and would say so.

Let's assume that Chris's glasses were inadvertently left at home and that Pat is claustrophobic. This situation of deep intensity for both individuals is rare, but is certainly possible.

Chris: "How would it be for you if we sat right under one of those emergency exit signs up front?"

Pat: "I don't know; maybe it would work. I'm willing to try it, but I might have to move to the rear."

Chris: "That would be okay. If you get anxious, say so and I'll move with you."

Under these circumstances both would feel that their desires were being considered, and that the best alternative for the relationship was selected. Suppose, however, the reply to the question of sitting under the exit sign was "I've tried that. It doesn't work for me." What are some alternatives?

- Sit separately

- Go home to get your glasses and see a later show

- Do something else that evening

The depth and intensity that each person feels about these alternatives also needs to be weighed. Sometimes a much better alternative becomes apparent. Consider:

Pat: "I would like to eat at this restaurant."

Chris: "I like the atmosphere of the one across the street much better. It looks cozy. What is it that appeals to you about this restaurant?"

Pat: "I would like to get a drink. I doubt the one across the street offers drinks."

Chris: "Let's go see. If it doesn't, how about going here for a drink or two, then going across the street to eat?"

The 1-to-10 Scale

Some couples find that the use of an arbitrary scale is helpful in measuring depth and intensity. Consider a situation where one individual wants to go to a play, and the other wants to stay home. Assume their discussion has not clarified who has the deeper desire, in spite of many precise statements from each about what the alternatives mean.

Under such circumstances many couples find a scale from **1** to **10** useful. Scaling one's felt need or desire enables each individual to be more specific—if somewhat artificial—in describing the potential benefit of weighing depth and intensity.[2] For example:

Chris: "I want to go to the play at about an **8**. What is your number to stay home?"

Pat: "I'm at a **6**."

If the couple goes to the play, the emotional return of **8** and emotional cost of **6** results in an emotional profit of **2** to the relationship.

■   *A wife says she wants to get a new couch, which is on sale for $1,600. The husband says, "We don't need a new couch. This one isn't showing wear, and it goes well in this room." The sale lasts for a month, and the above statements are repeated several times, but the couple does not press on to a conclusion. Then the husband says, "You have brought this up several times. I'm getting the message that a new couch is more important to you than I realized. On the scale of 1 to 10, how much do you want the couch?" She replies, "At a 7." He says, "For goodness sake, go buy it; I'm at a 3 or 4."*

Or another example:

Pat: "Where would you like to eat tonight? I don't feel strongly about it."

Chris: "I don't really care. Johnny's Restaurant comes to mind, but I'm only at a **2**."

---

[2] We tend to use the depth of intensity scale in our own marriage more frequently in regard to issues at the low end of the scale.

Pat: "I was thinking of the Pikeville Grill, but only at a **1**."

However, don't do what you feel will be overall negative for you and the relationship. Some situations don't offer any good choices. Here the goal is to minimize emotional losses. Consider:

Chris: "I can see you have a real strong desire to do that. I'd like to be with you, but that doesn't interest me. I'd be bored, and I fear that I would be a wet blanket on your enjoyment. So how would it be if I do my thing while you do yours?"

This moves from "what is better for the relationship" to "what is best." We assume that if the individuals agree to do something together, both believe that potentially the activity will enhance the relationship. It also means one individual does not have the right to go begrudgingly, playing the long-suffering martyr.

We have yet to see an individual who we feel was taking advantage of the partner in the use of the 1-to-10 depth and intensity scale. However, if this is a concern, the individuals can write their numbers simultaneously.

Not all activities live up to their assumed potentials. If people are disappointed, that disappointment needs to be communicated. For example:

"This play is not what I had expected. It disturbs me. I want to leave. If you want to stay, I'll meet you in the lobby after the play is over."

Some couples agree to taking turns in deciding how to spend time together (e.g., going on a skiing vacation this year and to a warm climate next year).

Sometimes a second issue is added to the first. Let's assume that a disagreement occurs regarding eating at different restaurants. Each expresses the desire, represented by a **4** for him and **6** for her. He acknowledges his wife's desire is deeper and they go to that restaurant, only to find upon entering that the place is full of women and there is not another man in sight. This would not be significant for many men, but it disturbs this man. (Remember: Feelings are facts.) Now, his cost increases from a **4** to an **8**, and he should say so.

We have been describing relatively simple, straightforward differences of desire, not the compounding of an issue with other psychological issues—perhaps old hurtful ones, the "You always get your way" kind of thing. Often the depth and intensity of this "always" issue is much greater than the depth and intensity of the original issue. Often the "always" issue is itself a **10**. (See "Always & Never," Chapter 3)

Compound anger will be dealt with later. (See Chapter 17) For now, try out the system of depth and intensity with the simple non-compound issues. Get some familiarity with the system and feedback. Realize that on simple issues your partner (1) cares about your feelings, (2) will listen, and (3) is willing to maximize the emotional return to the relationship. □

IN BRIEF

There have been position statements using I sentences, and what each option means to each person. Resolution is reached when one realizes and acknowledges, "You feel stronger about this than I do." As long as both believe that their own feeling is the stronger, they continue to communicate depth and intensity. Each needs to continue to clarify what the meaning of each alternative is for him/her, and to elicit the partner's comparable response. Sometimes using a scale of 1 to 10 is helpful to communicate depth and intensity.

YET TO COME

The meaning of hurts and how to deal with them.

CHAPTER 7
THE MEANING OF HURTS

"Ouch!" is a very valuable four-letter word for every intimate relationship.

There will be times when you or your partner is hurt by the other. In good relationships, hurts are rare and of low intensity. One test of a relationship is how the hurts are dealt with.

Remember, the basic assumption is, "I made a commitment to my partner to enhance my own happiness first, and to enhance my partner's happiness second." Hence, any hurt you receive must have been for one of the following reasons:

- **Accident/Carelessness:** One or both of these arise from not thinking through the implications and/or ramifications of the act. An apology is in order.

- **Miscommunication:** Your partner failed to communicate clearly, or you simply misunderstood. Immediate clarification is important.

- **Retaliation:** Usually this will be for an unacknowledged hurt received earlier. Perhaps the earlier hurt was all or partially outside conscious awareness.

Other situations can also give rise to the dynamic of a hurt originating outside the individual's awareness:

- **Domination-control:** Your partner needs to dominate or control you in order to avoid being hurt, either by habit that began in childhood or specific intent in regard to you or to the issue. "The best defense is a good offense." (See "Put-Downs," Chapter 9, and Chapters 18 & 19)

- **Identity or Autonomy:** The issue giving rise to the hurt might be one of feeling the need to keep from being "swallowed up."

- **Superiority:** The hurt arises from your partner's need to feel smarter or morally superior, especially when that need is tied to his/her identity.

- **Neurotic Reaction:** These arise from your partner's unconscious past experiences, and are triggered by the current situation. Often, even your partner will be unaware of the source. (See "Neurotic Reactions," Chapter 16)

There are other possible motivations for your partner to hurt you intentionally:

- **Addiction:** Your partner hurts you out of an overwhelming need to maintain an addiction. (See "Addictions," Chapter 20)

- **Sadism:** Extremely rare, this means your partner inflicts hurts in order to enjoy watching you struggle with them. Do not assume this to be the true motive unless you have worked through the principles discussed under "Anger." (See Chapters 7, 14, 15, 16, & 17) If this is the cause of your partner hurting you, ultimately you must choose between tolerating the situation and leaving it.

Ouch!

We suggest that you or your partner say, "Ouch!" when either of you feels psychologically hurt.[3] *Ouch!* will stop the ongoing interaction and mark the point when the hurt was first recognized. It often enables the partner to hear the words just spoken as they "linger" in the air. Otherwise, after a few minutes pass that mental echo may be gone, and all the speaker remembers is what was intended.

When *Ouch!* is used promptly, the message in question very often can be immediately clarified by the sender. The listener can compare the two statements and realize the ambiguity in the first, then accept the second as the intended message. The listener has (1) acknowledged the sender as the ultimate authority on the message's intended meaning, and (2) received a revision to replace the first concept with its perceived put-down. In this way, the whole incident is resolved.

Saying *Ouch!* is more crucial with verbal hurts than with physical hurts because your partner is less likely to realize you have been hurt. It is not a question of whether or not your partner should have realized you were hurt.

One of the best aspects of saying *Ouch!* or otherwise giving your partner prompt feedback that you have been hurt is that it relieves your partner from having to be perfect, and from being sure she/he never steps on your psychological toes. No one can dance if there is constant concern about stepping on toes. Similarly, no one can be spontaneous in a loving relationship if she/he is always on guard not to inadvertently cause a psychological hurt.

> √ *An agreement to say Ouch! and the understanding that people can mis-speak or mis-hear means you will always have the opportunity to correct the message, thereby resolving the hurt without any detrimental effect.*

---

[3] If someone steps on your toe, you usually immediately say, "Ouch!" The other person recognizes the situation and apologizes. Both of you assume it won't happen again.

Reluctance To Say "Ouch!"

Some people, especially men, are reluctant to use *Ouch!* because it doesn't fit with their masculine image of themselves. "Real men" don't hurt. These men need to remember that they gave their partners the power to hurt them by their love for their partners. (See Chapter 4) By their love, they let their partners inside their usual defenses. It is the concept, not the wording of the communication, that is important.

Acknowledging to yourself that you have been hurt may take personal courage, and it calls for confrontation of the partner by verbalizing the hurt. Some people fear such confrontations. Some believe confrontations are not "nice." An individual may say something like "I'm not sure how you intended me to hear that. Somehow, I heard a put-down. That isn't what you meant, is it?"

The message of the hurt, regardless of the words used, needs to be delivered without anger or sarcasm; deliver your message with a hurt tone or with curiosity as to why you were hurt. One of these emotions in your voice will greatly enhance your chances of receiving a caring response.

√   *It is an obligation on your part, in love and to the relationship, to give your partner accurate and prompt feedback whenever you are hurt.*

Responding To An Ouch!

The model for responding to your partner's statement of a hurt is the same as responding to your partner's physical hurt. Consider your likely response to your partner falling from a ladder at home. Chances are you will rush to your partner, maybe verbalizing, "Oh no!" You have displayed the most crucial element of your response: concern. The second and third elements of your likely response—in either order—are most likely to be "Where are you hurt?" and "What can I do to help?" if it isn't obvious. By this time the responder has usually made some assessment of the severity of the hurt. Usually, the couple doesn't begin to consider the how and why this accident occurred until later.

Unfortunately, some people respond to the partner's statement of being hurt as though it had been said as an accusation, e.g., "Why didn't you see I needed help and hold the ladder for me?" On receiving such a message, whether it was intended in that tone or not, the partner is apt to respond defensively, perhaps with stoicism. Men in particular often become silent and stone-faced, turn their backs, and leave the room or the house. Any of these responses tends to infuriate the partner. It is often interpreted as not caring, which constitutes an additional hurt and generates an urge to lash out in anger. A downward spiral has been set in motion.

When you hear an *Ouch!*, it behooves you to respond by giving your full attention to your partner, and with some mixture of concern and curiosity to ask, "Where are you hurt? How can I help you deal with this hurt?"

Even when the original message of the hurt is sent with resentment, hostility, and accusations, you need to respond with concern and curiosity. The basic assumption is that your partner is in this relationship to enhance his/her happiness first and your happiness second.

A response of concern tends to be heard as a loving message, and it reduces anger. Then the two of you can jointly address the other issues associated with the hurt, which further demonstrates concern and cooperation. It focuses attention on the hurt and prevents it from progressing to secondary complications for the relationship. This process of jointly addressing a hurt also engenders feelings of cooperation, of caring, and of being cared for, all of which result in feeling close and having some control and mastery over your future.

√ *It is the partner's responsibility, in love, to listen, to hear the hurt, and to be genuinely concerned.*

Remember the Goal

As couples learn to enhance their communication with techniques such as saying "Ouch!" it is important that each partner keeps foremost in mind their mutual goal: improving the relationship. Messages such as "Ouch!" need to be delivered without resentment, conveyed simply as information. For the first and second round of interchange, the hurt can be assumed to be caused by poor communication. However, regardless of the care with which the message is sent, it can be mis-heard. Often the distortion is caused by hostility. The difference can be as subtle as failure to use an "I Statement": "You hurt me" versus "I was hurt by that." Tone of voice and body language add other critical dimensions.

Two couples in therapy come to mind as examples of this problem:

In one, the husband delivered all of his messages as accusations. It sounded like he was keeping score, tracking who gave whom the most hurt messages, which encouraged her to respond with similar messages. They would follow our suggestion for one sentence, then regress to their old communication habits. Unable or unwilling to break this cycle, they ultimately got divorced.

In the other, the wife complained that her husband was saying that he was hurt "all the time." It became a control issue. Our effort to get him to let the smaller hurts go by never succeeded. In this case, we identified the husband's need to be in control even of the therapy. We recognized we were not helping. It seemed that the man was competing with me to be sure the therapy did not succeed. I pointed out the competition several times to no avail, then finally recommended ending therapy. They agreed.

Be Aware of Your Hurts

Small hurts may be safely overlooked if you recognize that your partner is under unusual physical or mental stress. Allowances can be made for hurts that occur when your partner is already irritable, cross, or frustrated. However, be wary of making excuses for your partner, especially with the rationalization of "she/he didn't mean it."

Some people are so afraid of feeling hurt or its consequences that they have turned down their sensitivity until they don't even register slight hurts. Some seemingly turn their sensitivity off, and they may not recognize hurts at all. Unfortunately, people can't turn down sensitivity to hurt without also turning down vulnerability, their affection, and other positive feelings. The valleys of potential hurt cannot be reduced or eliminated without also reducing the peaks of joy. (See "Vulnerability," Chapter 4) To maximize affection you need your hurt receiver turned "on." Equally, you both need your partner's hurt receiver turned on.

√ *People who, through past experience, expect to be hurt usually turn down their level of sensitivity, vulnerability, and affection.*

Sometimes a hurt is not recognized until sometime after the hurt has occurred. A hurt needs to be communicated as soon as it is recognized. "I just realized I got hurt a while ago. It was when _____." By discussing a hurt as soon as you recognize it, you and your partner will come to recognize a hurt sooner, and in time will recognize a hurt while it is occurring. Be aware of your hurts; it is part of being alive.

Minimizing Hurts

When you have communicated the fact that you have been hurt, don't tolerate any response from your partner that minimizes your statement of hurt. One common minimizer is: "You are too sensitive."[4] A person may be too sensitive for her/his own potential happiness. Often this is due to having a "bad day" and is called *irritability*. But there may be other responses, too:

> "*I am too sensitive for whom? Not for myself. Are you saying I am too sensitive for you? I expect you to respect my sensitivity. Feelings are facts. It is a fact I am hurt. Do you care?*"

Or,

> "*Yes, I am more sensitive than usual. I have had a hard afternoon. I hope you will be supportive of me instead of being critical, without my having to provide a reason.*"

---

[4] Notice that this violates the **I** sentence concept, so one reply could be: "I need to hear that in an **I** sentence."

Another minimizer of a hurt statement is:

> *"I was doing this (e.g., telling these jokes) before I met you. There is nothing wrong with them. Other people like them. You even used to like them."*

The reply could be:

> *"So what? Those jokes offend me now. I feel put down and humiliated by them. My feelings toward them seem to be increasingly negative every time you tell them. I find I am beginning to hate you at those times as much as I hate those jokes. Obviously, it is your choice whether you tell them or tell a different set of jokes. I need to let you know how much those jokes cost me and our relationship."*

Or,

> *"Are you saying I am too sensitive to you? If I reduce my sensitivity to you, I will also be reducing my caring about you and, consequently, reduce my love for you. Is that what you are asking me to do?"*

However, if you find yourself making frequent ouch statements, recognize they can be heard as controlling—dominating—not loving. With these circumstances we recommend you scale your hurts from 1 to 10 in intensity and only communicate the hurts of a high number. Don't try to rush headlong to your ideal relationship; let it grow. When you can talk and resolve the high number hurts you do communicate, then you can lower your threshold one or two points on your ouch scale to be communicated.

Resolving Hurts

As long as the basic assumption is true, then the first hurt doesn't fit any of your expectations. The first hurt was likely a miscommunication—word, action, or failure to act. Hence, it becomes very important to verify or check out that first hurt. Saying *"Ouch!"* is one way to begin to do so. Another way is to say something like "I heard you say _____. Is that what you meant?" Or, "I saw you do _____, and I interpret it as _____ (a hurt). Is that the way you intended me to receive it?"

Any message or action that results in a hurt becomes an important relationship transaction. It should be checked out, and it deserves verification just as the airport control tower requires pilots to repeat landing instructions for verification.

Often the partner will reply, "That's not what I intended; what I meant to say was _____." Only the tape recorder is an authority on what was said. Consequently, don't get caught in the argument: "You said _____." "No, I did not. I said _____."

Sometimes people do mis-speak, and people can also mis-hear another's statement. Don't get hung up on fixing blame; in regard to past miscommunication, go with the present restatement. The important thing is that the receiver receives the same message the sender intended to send. Always try to believe what your partner says she/he intended to say. If you have trouble accepting the restatement, say so and give the reason: "I heard what you said, but for me it doesn't fit with _____."

√ *Each individual is the world's absolute authority on what she/he intended to say. Likewise, each individual is the world's authority on what she/he heard.*

Effects of Unresolved Hurts

If hurts persist over several hours or recur frequently over several days, it becomes increasingly essential to label them as hurts and discuss them. All serious hurts, especially frequent or repetitive hurts that are not resolved, undergo transformation to another set of thoughts and feelings that will result in serious problems for the individual and for the relationship. (See Chapter 14)

√ *People who experience their current relationship as unfair or unjust over an extended period of time are apt to go outside the relationship—either temporarily, with an affair, or permanently, with a separation or divorce.*

Unfortunately, some partners refuse to seriously examine a hurt when requested to do so. This refusal itself is a secondary hurt. It is a message of not caring. It is also a message that the partner is not taking any responsibility to help the individual resolve her/his feelings of hurt. Under these circumstances, you might struggle with the question of, "What could I do to avoid a similar hurt?" Perhaps the answer is not to be so vulnerable, or to avoid the other person entirely.

In spite of the resulting decrease in vulnerability and affection, the question and its answer are appropriate when you have little or no hope of influencing your partner's behavior in a way to prevent a hurt. Without the concern from your partner about your hurt, your attitude becomes "I will change what I am able to change, and not waste energy on what I cannot affect. If I cannot change the other person, it will be a waste of energy theorizing what she/he could have done differently. Still, I will keep the invitation open by periodically repeating the statement of my hurt."

When you are willing to settle for what the relationship is, it is useless to ask only the question "What could my partner do differently?" This is very close to asking,

"What should the other person do?" The psychological result will be the same as asking, "Who is to blame?" and answering, "Her/him." This answer results in feelings of being unjustly wronged or being a victim or martyr, and it generates feelings of anger, helplessness, or self-righteousness. These feelings, in turn, lead to a sense of the other person owing homage, extra consideration, or compensation, usually without the actual price being spelled out. These feelings and thoughts are in themselves a transformation of the hurt.

When you resolve hurts mutually, it increases trust, self-esteem, and the sense of being loved and of being in control of your life. Vulnerability is also increased. In this way, the concept of the best possible relationship grows. (See Chapter 13)

For a discussion of what can happen to hurts that are not resolved, see "Transformation of Hurts," Chapter 14. □

IN BRIEF

A couple needs to jointly address moderate or deep hurts suffered by either of them. Examples of possible dialog include:

1. *Some form of the statement "I'm hurt."*

2. *"What I heard or experienced was _____. Is that what you intended, or is that the way you wanted me to take it?"*

3. *The other's reply of clarification.*

4. *Acceptance of the clarification statement, or a statement of the reasons for difficulty in accepting the revised statement.*

YET TO COME

Ahead in Section III, the maintenance manual for intimate relationships.

Section III
Relationship Maintenance

Like everything else in life, relationships require maintenance. Without it, they coast in the same direction as everything else: downhill. Not all investments yield the expected payoff, but none has better potential for high return than an investment in your intimate relationship. This section assumes that you are familiar with the principles and suggestions in the preceding sections.

CHAPTER 8
THE LARGER ISSUES;
AVOIDING PROBLEMS

Be aware of the larger picture—time, consideration, openness, communication, trustworthiness.

During courtship each person devotes considerable time, energy, and creative thought to the relationship. With commitment and "settling in," it receives less attention. This is natural and understandable—so long as it is not overdone, and if both people "buy in" to the way their time, energy, and other resources are being spent.

In terms of human activity, there are seven different types of time. However, for some people the last two types mentioned— *Solitude Time* and *Reverence Time*—may be identical. Theoretically, we all need some of each type in our weekly activities. The amount of time individuals need for each varies widely.

Human life is characterized by cycles: our hearts beat in cycles, we breathe in cycles, and our brain waves are in cycles. We eat, eliminate waste, and sleep in cycles. We exert ourselves physically and rest in cycles, and we make love in cycles. We live and die in cycles. We need to expect and encourage cycles in the way we spend time, which includes cycles of work and play.

The Times of Your Life

There is a human need for different kinds of time:

- **Couple Time:** By *Couple Time* we mean quality time with your one and only.

- **Achievement Time:** Hopefully, *Achievement Time* coincides with making a living. Creative hobbies are another outlet for *Achievement Time*, a chance to "see what I/we can do."

- **Buddy Time:** This is usually with the same gender. *Buddy Time* can double with *Achievement Time*. Clubs, sports, civic activities, charities, etc. usually fill this need.

- **Family Time:** The primary emphasis is on relationships within the family. This may be fun- or work-centered, as long as the emphasis is kept on the relationships rather than the work. It is assuring that everyone feels loved and shows concern for each other's needs and enjoyment.

- **Alone Time:** We all need occasional time when no interaction is expected. No one is to intrude into our thoughts. Some people can be "alone" in a crowd of strangers; others need to experience more control over possible intrusions into their space.

- **Solitude Time:** Solitude may coincide with *Alone Time* or with *Reverent Time*. Or the individual may need *Solitude Time* that is distinct from the other two.

- **Reverent Time:** Where and how individuals find their own *Reverent Time* has the widest variation from one person to another. Someone may find it alone or in the company of others, or both at different times. Some find it chiefly in prayer and other acts of worship; others find it in acts of kindness. Some find it in nature or in reading or in art. Others find it within themselves. Some find it primarily in intimate relationships. And others can't find it anywhere.

Couple Time

The purpose of *Couple Time* is to engender feelings of closeness. *Couple Time* may be spontaneous, or it may involve time set aside to be with each other, which in turn may include a planned activity or not. Of course, not all time designated for togetherness results in closeness, just as all other types of investments sometimes fail to yield the hoped-for results. *Romantic Time* is a special type of *Couple Time*.

Time spent together talking is a simple, inexpensive, and at the same time very meaningful way to spend *Couple Time*. The freedom to express ideas and feelings without any concern of being ridiculed or having your statements belittled adds to intimacy. We saw a number of women who complained their men seldom talked about what was going on in their minds, especially about their feelings and thoughts. In the absence of this information, the women tended to feel insecure. Listening attentively to what your partner has to say is very meaningful to the speaker. Usually there is also trust that your partner will use discretion in what she/he repeats to others, and will keep a confidence if you request.

The amount of time a couple needs for togetherness varies. We have found that most couples need to spend about one to one-and-a-half blocks of time a week to maintain a good relationship. A block of time is three or four hours, or one "date night" a week. The half-block of time could be spent attending church service or lingering at the table after a meal or relating before and after making love (as well as during love-making). All may comprise quality *Couple Time*.

The primary focus and interest of both individuals needs to be on each other, not on accomplishing some goal. Some couples, on occasion, may feel close working together when neither resents doing the task or feels pressured. If they go sailing together for *Couple Time*, winning the race should take a second place to togetherness, unless both are highly competitive. When doing something with another couple, the primary interaction needs to be between the two partners. If the primary interaction is between the two men in the front seat and the two women in the back seat, consider it *Buddy Time*.

It is possible to have too much time together. Busy couples who look forward to having time together on a vacation or during retirement often find that initially they enjoy each other, but before long, one or both become irritable. If they don't recognize the irritation as an indication of the need for some other type of time, they are likely to really get on each other's nerves.

√ ***Irritability with each other indicates the need for some time apart.***

In his essay on marriage in *The Prophet*, Kahlil Gibran[5] says, "Let there be spaces in your togetherness." This wisdom applies equally to other intimate relationships. Create this space with the simple statement "I think I need some distance. I'm going shopping with so-and-so. I'll be back about nine." Or, "I need a change of scenery. I'm going to shoot pool and watch the ball game on TV. I'll be back about ten." Or, "I am going over to my friend's house for an hour or so."

The question "How would it be for you if I went to _____?" can be inserted in any of the above examples. This phrasing doesn't feel like asking permission, as many other forms of phrasing might, but it does elicit your partner's attitude of "not controlling and not allowing you to walk on me." (See "Feelings of Rejection-Control," Chapter 19) Then take the time away guiltlessly! If your partner is the first to make this type of statement, hear it as the rhythm of life, not as rejection.

The need for togetherness and for *Alone Time* is influenced by the amount of time spent during the working day in intense interpersonal interaction. Chris, who works as a customer representative in a complaint department, will need a different kind of time when away from the job. Chris's time needs will contrast sharply with those of Pat, a computer programmer who works alone or with low-intensity interpersonal interaction. Chances are high that at the end of the day Pat will need human interaction while Chris will want time alone. (See Chapters 16 & 17 for other examples)

This difference in needs should be recognized for what it is, without either partner taking the disparity as rejection or lack of caring. One of the virtues espoused by the ancients was: "Everything in moderation."

Value your partner's friends, and in general don't begrudge times she/he spends with them. It is part of the space in togetherness that gives your partner validation, a sense of autonomy from you, and it increases a sense of self-esteem. When each of you value your own and your partner's identity, integrity, and uniqueness, there is little

---

5 Gibran, Kahlil: *The Prophet*, Alfred A. Knopf, New York, 1951, p15

danger of being swallowed up. It behooves each of us to protect our own and our partner's potential for personal growth.

Trustworthiness-Trust

Mutual trust is extremely important in a relationship. The complementary (supporting) attitude to your partner's trust of you is your own trustworthiness. It is your trustworthiness in your partner's eyes that supports and sustains this trust. Similarly, it is your partner's trustworthiness that supports your trust.

√ *Each of us has complete control over our own trustworthiness, which is the foundation for our partner's trust.*

Trust is not "all or nothing." It may grow or decline. Trust within a relationship may vary with the activity area. For example, trust may be high in regard to sexual matters, but low concerning money due to impulsive buying or gambling. Perhaps the area of trust that is most significant for most people is trusting that your partner genuinely cares about you as a person—your identity, the integrity of your autonomy, and your overall happiness. This implies that your partner won't deliberately hurt you. In families, this trust extends to counting on one's partner to be kind and supportive of the children.

Trustworthiness is judged in part by the level of openness, which has two components: (1) being honest and forthright, and (2) giving information that you think your partner would like to know. This includes telling your partner of your plans *before* they are scheduled to take place. Doing this often avoids the burden of after-the-fact explanations, and it maintains or increases your credibility and your partner's trust. This is being forthright. Do this even if it requires an extra five minutes of explanation.

√ *Love unites and tends to make two people one. Anger separates and individuates.*

Manipulation has no place in an honest and forthright relationship. Manipulation is defined as deliberately misleading your partner by presenting inaccurate facts or by omitting pertinent facts with the belief that the misrepresentation(s) will lead your partner to the conclusion you desire—different than might be made if all the facts were known. Manipulation, once recognized by the partner, severely compromises future trust in similar situations. Little fibs, if they are discovered, erode integrity and trust. "Where does my partner draw the line on little fibs?"

Increased vulnerability—from being honest, open, and forthright—results in increased intimacy and trust. It also helps you paint an accurate picture of yourself, which precludes your partner from guessing, and it reduces the likelihood of unwarranted suspicions, concerns, or jealousy.

Being open and honest is natural when your heart is in the right place—that is, focused on your partner. That loving heart means that you can trust your motives and your intents, and it frees you to be more spontaneous, more playful, and non-defensive, all of which invite your partner to be the same.

High Passion

Passion is high in many courtships, infatuations, other sexual adventures, and affairs. The unknown aspects add to excitement, which in turn, add to passion. Some couples have an extra high need for passion in their courtship. These couples often play affection and jealousy games with each other to test the other's love and, more importantly for them, to keep the level of suspense, excitement, and passion high. They do so with real or feigned hurts, with anger or emotional withdrawal, or even with fights, followed by passionate reconciliation.

√ *Caring and respect for the other person are essential for genuine love.*

The motivation for these alternating messages of closeness-distance lie on a continuum from genuine love and hurt to conscious manipulation. These relationships can be surprisingly stable. The partners have varying degrees of insight into their need for high passion and their pattern of achieving it.

Others with a constant need for high passion may create it by developing infatuations that lead to intercourse with new sexual partners, or by having ongoing affairs. Affairs heighten excitement by their furtiveness and illicit nature, and by their inherent risks. They often involve unnecessary risks; for example, by using a bed one of them shares with a committed partner.

Infatuation

Being in a committed relationship does not mean the individual won't be attracted to others. If the attraction occurs on first meeting, it is clearly infatuation. If the attraction persists over a number of encounters, the individual may be confused as to whether it is love or infatuation. Passion may be high in both conditions, or may even be higher in infatuation, especially if the sexual aspects of the committed relationship have become boring or otherwise unsatisfying.

The sexual desire of infatuation is narrowly focused and easily gratified. The aspects of respect and caring for the other person are usually minimal or absent. The need to be together and know each other is usually expressed only in physical and sexual ways.

√ *Love has staying power.*

Sexual desire based on a person's social position or prestige (e.g., politician, prom queen, football hero, movie star) rather than individual traits is a hallmark of infatuation. Intercourse motivated by this is for self-definition and aggrandizement. There is an immaturity and impulsiveness in the need to have whatever you want whenever you want it.

Infatuation can progress and grow into love by the development of mutual respect, mutual vulnerability, and genuine caring about the other person as an individual.

Fidelity

A number of factors keep a person faithful in a mutually committed, monogamous relationship. Two of the most important are: (1) valuing the relationship so much that you are unwilling to risk hurting your partner or the relationship, and (2) not being willing to destroy the trust at all the levels. Infidelity renders you less able to trust yourself or to be as open and honest as before, even if the infidelity is not discovered.

Around the time of commitment, the partners need to convey the following message: "Fidelity is expected, and infidelity would be regarded as a serious breach of trust and loss of respect." This message is in contrast to other messages that say, "I don't care if you have sex with others as long as you don't embarrass me and don't bring home any sexual diseases," or, "I can tolerate almost anything except infidelity. If I learn that you've had sex with someone else, that will be the end of our relationship."

This latter message is often heard as a challenge—the "One Forbidden Thing." This message of an absolute line not to cross may concern other issues: "Don't ever take money from our savings account without telling me first." Or, "If I ever find you are taking drugs, we are through." Tales of violations of the One Forbidden Thing are found throughout literature, including the Biblical account of Adam and Eve in the Garden of Eden. This message also grants almost ultimate power to those who choose to use it, and it creates the question of "Can I get her/him to love me enough *not* to follow through with that threat?"

If the relationship is to continue after infidelity is known, a new foundation of trust will have to be established, which will begin with understanding: (1) what the unfaithful partner felt was missing in the relationship, and (2) the history of miscommunication or the absence of communication about unfulfilled needs and/or unresolved hurts. Sometimes the known infidelity also results in a complete loss of respect for the partner.

Self-Respect

Periodically, we need to look inside ourselves to discern which aspects we like and those that we wish to change. The individual who never looks inside—for whatever reasons like fear, lack of awareness, or self-loathing—develops a distorted and inconsistent view of the self.

Hopefully, what we each like about ourselves includes a wide range of traits, skills, ideas, and values. Almost invariably, the self-assessment will include one's lovability and a warm heart that is expressed in action. The foundation for the sense of intrinsic lovability comes from experiencing unconditional love from our parents and other significant adults during our childhood. It is reinforced by our lovers.

Self-assessment also includes an evaluation of the skills and capabilities we each have or are in the process of developing. It is the favorable traits from self-assessment that the teenager puts on display for validation by peers. Both the display and validation of one's lovability and capabilities are based on interpersonal skills. Whether we are teenagers or adults, our sense of lovability expands by having a sweetheart or lover who reciprocates the feeling of love.

Teenage romances are notoriously unsteady, partially due to their immaturity. Some teens are "looking to do better." There may be a constant tug-of-war between being "myself" and changing to be that person everyone— or someone who is especially admired—likes or thinks is cool. The teen who is deserted in the romance suffers a gross insult to self-esteem and sense of lovability. That is why it hurts so much.

Ideally, we present our true selves in courtship, and our potential partner is attracted by many of those same traits that we value in ourselves. When this process is reciprocated, some kind of bond usually forms. Finding our soul mate reinforces our sense of self-worth and respect, as well as love of the partner. There is validation all around.

As two people become a couple by forming an intimate relationship, they each need to retain a sense of individual self throughout the relationship. Spending time alone and with buddies, and having some separate and independent interests, help to maintain a sense of self.

To disregard one's sense of self and to define the self chiefly by a partner's evaluation is to become psychologically dependent on continuous positive feedback from the partner. It is to lose all sense of autonomy—to be swallowed up. Further, in time such an attitude will cause a loss of respect by the partner. The exception is the partner who needs to provide nurturing to someone who seems incapable or who is wandering about without a sense of direction. (See "The Need to Give," Chapter 12) Outsiders tend to see this kind of relationship as submission and domination.

The feeling of being swallowed up, with its accompanying loss of self-esteem, can precipitate anger or a severe argument in order to regain some sense of autonomy. (See Chapter 18)

Respect for Partner

During courtship, people put their best foot forward. If a relationship develops, the individual presumes—correctly or not—that the other person respects and is attracted by those traits. If one individual senses that the partner is losing interest, then she/he will tend to accentuate those same traits. A person is also respected because she/he expects or even demands to be respected. If that respect is not given by the potential partner, the individual will likely withdraw from the relationship. Respect can be about a wide variety of issues.

We will divide respect into three general areas. Others may categorize respect differently. One area consists of the desires, values, and deeply held beliefs. These are part of the individual's identity. An example is a marriage between people of different religious values who both continue to worship in different ways. Each respects the other's religious activities, even though they don't personally agree with the other's values. Another aspect of respect for the partner merges with characteristics that one individual finds attractive in the other, e.g., artistic ability, reliability, being fun to be with. Sometimes the partner is respected for what she/he brings to the relationship—a talent or skill, or some need that provides the other with meaning in life. Sometimes it is something the individual wishes she/he possessed—sort of an alter ego. Our third category consists of values that are often taken for granted: the partner will not become addicted, has some ambition, and will fulfill the roles of breadwinner and child caretaker that the couple has agreed upon.

Often the equality is spelled out in intellectual sparring that ends in a near draw.

√ ***Without respect for yourself and respect for your partner, there can be no love.***

The following example illustrates hurts and loss of respect on multiple levels:

■ *Bob already lost considerable money on an investment that was questionable. His wife, Donna, suspected the deal was fraudulent from the beginning. In spite of her vigorous protests, Bob made the investment. In a short time they not only lost their money, but were faced with additional liability. The couple had to declare bankruptcy.*

After ten years or so, they are able to build their dream house. Then comes another business deal. The wife is very critical and suspicious of this one, too. She refuses to sign the papers for the debt. Nevertheless, he secures financing without her signature and persists with the investment. Within a year the deal turns out to be a sham, and again the couple loses their home and faces bankruptcy.

Her biggest hurts are his disregard of her opinion and his persistence in spite of her strenuous objection. "Like we weren't a partnership, yet the loss cost us and the children our house. I was part of that."

Having been through two similar business deals, she feels he has not and will not learn from the experience. She has lost all respect for him. She doesn't want him to touch her. He moves out, and a divorce follows. □

IN BRIEF

We need to be aware of our human need for activities in each of several types of time, and to see that our individual needs are met. We also need to recognize that our partner has the same needs, but perhaps in different proportions.

The single most important dynamic that keeps most individuals faithful is an unwillingness to put the relationship at risk. Of course, the better the relationship, the less likely the individual will put it at risk.

YET TO COME

It is the little things of day-to-day living—year in and year out—that determine the true quality of a relationship.

CHAPTER 9
LITTLE THINGS MEAN A LOT

The most attractive thing that either partner can wear is a smile.

Chances are, the first thing you did when you first met the person who eventually became your partner was to smile. Keep it up! Make a habit of smiling each and every time you see one another. When you return home and your partner is already home, go to your partner first thing. If your partner is already asleep in bed, snuggle. Even if your partner doesn't awaken, that message of affection will have some effect, though subliminally. If your partner is awake, a smile on first eye contact will set the tone for what happens next, especially if it is followed by an embrace and a meaningful kiss. Making eye contact conveys a positive message, supplementing whatever is being spoken.

Appearance

There is never any excuse for poor hygiene. Good hygiene is fundamental for self-respect and good health. Poor hygiene will turn your partner away and will erode respect. Grooming is secondary to hygiene. Sometimes one of you may grow lax in your grooming, perhaps while you are off from work or overwhelmed by caring for children.

Tell your partner about your reaction if you find yourself backing away due to hygiene, grooming, or other issues of appearance. Find out if there are circumstances that alter your feeling or the feelings of your partner about these issues. It is your obligation to the relationship to speak up. Remember, silence on any issue is grounds for the other to believe that what is occurring is acceptable to you. Use **I** sentences:

- "I have always thrilled to your touch, but when I see your fingernails like they are now, I don't want to get within touching distance. I would like for us to clean up before we continue."

- "I find myself distracted by your breath. I would like for us to take time out to brush our teeth and use a mouth wash before we continue."

- "You have such a handsome face that I enjoy looking at you, but when you don't shave, I can't help but feel like you don't think I'm worth the effort. I know that's not what you intend, but that's the way it registers with me."

Don't confuse poor grooming with being disheveled. A disheveled appearance can be alluring on occasion, especially during physical activity.

One partner may put on weight when a couple starts living together and preparing their own meals. There is a tendency to divide the food equally between them, despite of the fact that one person may be several inches taller and weigh considerably more. People who habitually eat everything on their plates may be puzzled by a smaller partner's weight gain until they analyze where the calories are coming from. Learn which little things mean a lot to your partner—and any variation about those things—then pay strict attention to those issues.

Children

In most families the mother takes the major responsibility for the baby. The father needs to step up to take over some of the chores that she had been doing. Older children need some one-on-one time with their mother, too. Without it, they are apt to feel that Mother loves the baby more, and become jealous and perhaps hostile to the baby. Father needs to take care of the baby while mother is spending time with the older children.

One of the most meaningful things the father can do is also spend more quality time with the older children. It helps the other ones accept their younger sibling. Fathers can and should change diapers, too. Don't be squeamish about getting your hands dirty. The human skin—in this case, hands without cuts or abrasions—is one of the most versatile substances known, and it is easily cleaned with soap and water.

Often the most stressful time in a household with a new baby—with or without older children—is just before supper. So much is going on! Talk about what the two of you can do to ease any time period in which either of you feels pressured.

A woman needs to be sure that her husband learns of her pregnancy from her, *not* from the husband of one of her friends. Most women need emotional support from their lover about their appearance and continuing lovability during pregnancy and afterwards. The woman needs to watch her weight gain and to exercise to retain her muscle tone, especially to compensate for the tendency of middle-age spread. The new father needs to be aware and appreciative of the physical and emotional impact having a baby puts on his lover.

√ *Make sure your children experience your joy in their achievements and in their happiness. Doing so will strengthen their self-esteem.*

Children's Love

Guide and train your children to show thoughtfulness and love to your partner. Doing so in little everyday ways and on special days will pay big dividends for all of you, especially since the children are likely to carry this behavior over into adolescence and adulthood.

√ *The more one loves, the more potential one has to love.*

Realize that it is only in regard to romantic or sexual love that we want exclusive love from the other. A child's love for one parent doesn't reduce its potential love for the other parent. Nor does a parent's love for one child decrease love for the child's siblings. Parent-to-child love and child-to-parent love is not a limited quantity.

Parents

In general, each of us has a greater depth and intensity about issues involving our own parents than we have about our partner's parents. Each of us needs to be the lead person during any discussion with our partner in regard to our own parents. This is true even when one or both partners experience a set of parents as being intrusive, demanding, or controlling. Discuss the issues with each other. Jointly work out the position(s) you want to present to the parents. Then jointly decide on the best way to represent your relationship to the parents. Generally it is wise not to be the lead person in presenting an issue to your partner's parents, but sometimes doing so is the least stressful for the two of you and the most effective. Do so only after careful consideration, and with your partner's full endorsement.

In the actual discussion, hold to the position you two agreed to. If the parent(s) present new information, take a recess from the discussion: "We weren't aware of that. The two of us will talk it over and get back to you." Your position may be a depth and intensity of something that has been said before: "We can't and won't tolerate your undermining our discipline of our children. Please stop it." Usually it is more effective not to specify the action you plan to take if the parents don't change. Do not make advance threats, e.g., "We have a duty to protect our children from whatever we think will be damaging. We judge the effects of this issue to be damaging." Similar statements can be made about any objectionable behaviors that are a burden to you or that tend to disrupt the household. You can speak of your love or respect for them, as long as you hold to the position the two of you decided on.

Put-Downs

Avoid making snide comments or put-downs. Some people are very kind and considerate of their partners in public, yet engage in nasty put-downs in the privacy of their home. Other people are just the opposite. They are kind and considerate of the partners, except with a group of friends. That's when some men play to the gathering by putting down "the little woman." Likewise, some women take swipes at their partner in a gathering when the couple has previously been in an unresolved argument. Avoid put-down jokes. No pot shots!

√ *Without feedback, any change is random.*

Don't make hurtful little swipes under the guise of being funny. Your partner may be hurt, but not able to object without being in the awkward position of making a major issue out of it and being considered a poor sport.

But the hurt individual has an obligation to communicate the hurt in some form:

- For some partnerships, this can be a look.

- Another non-verbal and private message in a group is to go to the partner's side and unobtrusively pinch her/his arm.

- The next level of response might be saying, "I'd prefer you not tell that type of joke." Or, "I take that as a put-down. Is that the way you meant it?"

If public put-downs become repetitive in spite of **I** and "Ouch" statements, then a confrontation at home is in order: "I've told you I feel hurt and put down by your 'humor.' Apparently I didn't convey my depth and intensity clearly enough. It really bugs me. It is at a **10** to me."

The following needs to be said with a tone of sincere curiosity, not with an edge to your voice: "Do you want to hurt and embarrass me? What do you get out of it, some kind of admiration from your friends? Do you care more about what they think of you than what I think of you? Or do you get some kind of enjoyment out of hurting me? I want you to know that's the way I'm taking it."

If you don't think you can say all of this before being interrupted, then write it. Maybe mail it as a letter.

√ *In love, your partner is the person whose happiness you have committed yourself to maximizing. This doesn't mean you can't be upset or angry with your partner; it does mean that it behooves you to keep your anger focused on the issue.*

Your partner is the person you love. If you have an issue to work through together, do so, or put it on hold until the two of you can work it through. It makes no sense to insult your partner for the sake of scoring, or to impress the audience at her/his expense.

Reaction to Partner's Errors

Assume that your partner is dealing with each situation in the best way she/he knows. Some couples enjoy the same activity until they engage in some form of competition as teammates. Criticism of a partner during activities like playing cards can become so vitriolic that the partner refuses to play as a teammate. If both continue the enjoyment of cards, it is with different partners—and surprise!—mistakes by the new partner are treated with a tone of civility.

√ *Anyone who needs to step on someone else's ego in order to feel adequate or important is only putting her/his own smallness and selfishness on display.*

If your partner had known a better way to deal with the situation at the time, she/he would have done it that way. Further, your sterling suggestions for improvement are not retained. In other words, it is the very expression of anger when combined with instruction that often precludes your partner from learning the material that is so important to you. Remember, the two of you are doing this for togetherness and fun!

A somewhat similar situation occurs when a couple is late leaving home for a significant appointment and, five miles down the road, one of you realizes that an important item has been forgotten. As you turn around to get the item (and lose more time) there is no need for anyone to be berated. The forgetting was not purposeful; the individual is already feeling bad about having forgotten. A put-down or explosive yelling will have no benefit currently or in the future. In love, these situations call for silence, if not support.

√ *Being criticized by an angry person often mentally jams your ability to remember.*

Your Own Errors

Acknowledge your own errors as soon as you become aware of them. Apologize if it is appropriate to do so. When in doubt, apologize anyway. There is no weakness in apologizing.

√ *Apologizing requires strength of character and self-confidence.*

Sometimes restitution is called for, even with a committed partner. The restitution could be apologizing to those people who heard your verbal attack on your partner. However, once you have done so, forgive yourself and get on with your life. Don't get hung up ruminating, "If only…" Rather, face the future with increased knowledge and perhaps wisdom for the next time.

√   *Every time you find yourself thinking, "If only _____," shift your thoughts to "next time."*

Support

So much for the elimination of negatives.

Now look for ways to bring positives to your relationship. The opposite of a put-down is a compliment. Give compliments freely, but genuinely. Look for things for which to thank or compliment your partner. Support her/his endeavors, whether educational, career, charity, hobbies, interests, or friends. By support, we mean being available to listen, to assist, to free up time for the partner to spend on the endeavor. It also includes trying to make adequate financial support available without placing any reservations, debt, obligation, or guilt on the partner. Acknowledge her/his achievements and help her/his friends and others recognize them.

Realize that achievement and recognition of that achievement are major sources of self-esteem and self-respect. The other major source is feeling loved. Supporting your partner nurtures these sources and, in turn, engenders her/his respect and love for you.

Talking and Listening

Sometimes the primary intent of the speaker and perhaps the listener is enjoyment of the relationship. The words are of secondary importance. Perhaps it is just saying your lover's name repeatedly. Perhaps it expands into a string of compliments. Maybe it grows into a love song, even one composed by someone else. A serenade is an elaborated extension of this concept. Listening to the sound of your lover's voice often is very meaningful. "Sweet nothings in the ear" enhance a relationship and love-making.

Some talking is information exchange. "The car's gas tank is nearly empty, so you will need to get gas before you go to _____." Or, "You pick up the dry cleaning on the way home and I'll get groceries."

■   *One wife complained her husband seldom talked to her. Near the end of the therapy session, we suggested he talk to her more. The next week she again complained he wasn't talking to her. He replied, "I did talk to you every night; I read the paper to you!"*

Serious talking or problem-solving falls into subgroups. One form is: "I need a sounding board. I don't want advice. I first need a thoughtful and intelligent listener who can point out possible contradictions and ask questions to help me clarify my own thinking." Or, "I can envision this situation unfolding in several different ways. I need your help in thinking through each scenario and considering the various choices." Without this preamble, many partners are apt to take charge of the problem by giving advice or feeling some obligation to *fix it*. The speaker shows attention by talking. The other aspect of "talking" is listening. Listeners, too, need to be attentive. Listeners show attention by frequent eye contact, and by not fidgeting or being distracted. Don't try to have a serious conversation while the TV is on. Turn the TV off, go into a different room, or postpone the conversation.

An exception to the above advice occurs when the topic is very emotional for either of you. Under these circumstances, you might have your conversation while doing something else such as fixing dinner. This tactic is very useful with elementary-school-age children and adolescents.

Conversation should continue as long as either of you has follow-up questions, questions of clarification, or questions that logically extend topics to peripheral areas. The conversation should continue until both of you are satisfied with ending the conversation for now. There are some exceptions, such as running out of time due to other obligations. When this happens, always set a time to resume the discussion.

> ■ *One unrefined, rather unattractive man from Appalachia, 42 years old and bald, told me, his psychiatrist, that he never had any difficulty "getting" women, i.e., having sexual intercourse with most any woman he wanted. When asked how, he said, "We will be sitting around in a bar, and I will pick the woman I want to have sex with. I will listen and hang on her every word, making frequent and prolonged eye contact. She has my full attention, even if someone else is talking. Women are starved to be listened to by a man."*

Some individuals don't want to confront relationship issues. To avoid these discussions, they may appear irritated or angry. In this situation, you might try saying, "I hear irritation—or anger—in your voice. If I am correct, where did it come from?" Your tone of voice will be just as important as the words, or even more so. Don't have an edge in your voice, only curiosity. You may ask, "Where is your hurt or irritation?" or, "I'm getting the message you don't care (or want to be bothered) about my feelings or my need for clarification. Am I right in this interpretation?"

√ **If you are in love and your partner isn't happy (and is not hiding the fact), then you can't be happy, either.**

As a rule, when dealing with a partner who is reluctant to address some issues, you will do best with short comments—one- or two-liners. Do not expect a verbal response. "That hurts." "I don't think I had that coming." "When you feel like telling me how I hurt you, I'll be glad to listen."

This is a campaign. Don't expect any behavioral change until after numerous comments. Even then the change may be only in frequency and/or the intensity of the anger.

Difficult Times

One indication of the strength of a relationship is whether the couple turns toward or away from each other in times of difficulty. Take the time—and perhaps the embarrassment—to explain the difficulty. Your eye contact is apt to be extremely intermittent if you feel sheepish or embarrassed about the contents. You are relating by speaking. The listener needs to convey attentiveness by keeping her/his eyes focused on you almost constantly. The more serious the subject, the more constant the listener's eye contact needs to be.

Expect acceptance and support and, perhaps, even understanding. In an intimate relationship nothing happens to only one person. Everything affects both of you, either directly or indirectly. Together, consider the alternative courses of action, including other individuals with whom the two of you might consult.

> √ *In times of difficulty, turn toward each other, regardless of whether or not the difficulty involves one or both of you.*

Your partner is the person who is committed to enhancing your happiness, second only to her/his own. Your partner is on your side. □

IN BRIEF

Give your partner compliments and many little messages of her/his importance to you. When your partner acknowledges an error, be forgiving and supportive. When you make an error, apologize, if appropriate, and forgive yourself. Tell your partner whether you are asking for (1) a sounding board to help clarify your thoughts, (2) advice, or (3) action, as in "Please take care of the problem." Listen attentively, with frequent eye contact.

YET TO COME

The next chapter deals with the differences between work and play.

CHAPTER 10
WORK & PLAY

A happy healthy life includes the ability and willingness to both work and play. Play and work are part of the cycles of life.

Sigmund Freud said, "Good mental health is the ability to work and to love." Despite elaborate attempts by government agencies, presidential commissions, and research committees to define mental health, Freud's statement remains one of the best available. It may make this concept a little clearer to contrast the work mode and the play mode, realizing that "to love is to play."

- **Play is loving— always.** When play isn't loving, it is called "toying," as a cat toys with a mouse. Toying merges with a form of teasing, of power and domination or exploitation.

- **Loving is not always play.** One can show love by doing a task; for example, nursing a loved one who is sick.

- **Tough love is work** with a long-term future goal for the other person; it carries the risk of short-term anger or resentment from the other party.

Work and *Play* are different mental states that require different mental attitudes. Workaholics tend to approach everything as work, frequently to the partner's consternation. These individuals may be extremely efficient at their jobs, but they may have difficulty playing. Some can't play at all. If they go on a hike, it has to be for some goal, perhaps to prove fitness in the way of a 20-mile army hike. Often the workaholic even approaches love-making as work. On the other hand, playboys and playgirls of the world can party at the drop of a hat, but may have trouble keeping jobs or completing tasks. Some can't do a lick of work. They approach life on a whim.

There is a phenomenon at the beginning of a social party that is referred to as "breaking the ice." This happens when people have shifted their mental attitudes into the play mode. It may be very difficult, if not impossible, for the guests to be in the play mode if the host and hostess are still in an active work mode, scurrying around and attending to last-minute details.

√ *The coping mechanisms to enhance play are increased emotional involvement and increased spontaneity, not increased effort.*

Work is characterized by effort, thought, worry, consultation, concentration, and steadfastness of purpose. It is distinguished by having a goal and end point or end product. Usually, the result is easily judged or graded—"Good job!" These results may be obligations and responsibilities to others. If a goal is difficult to achieve, sub-goals can be established and effort can be doubled. If that isn't adequate, then the effort can be redoubled.

■   *In sexual therapy we often ask the couple to take turns being a toucher and a touchee. The touchee is to be passive until the roles are reversed. With one couple, the man, a physician, was so "hung up" on his professional identity role that when he touched his wife he couldn't enjoy fondling her. He gave her a physical exam.*

One characterization of play is the absence of a goal. Play is free, whimsical, and spontaneous. It is valued for the enjoyment of the moment. Play can unfold or develop as one pleasurable moment unfolds into another. A lot of play is exploring to see what you like or if you still like it.

There are appropriate—as well as inappropriate—times for each mode. For example, the man who tries to balance his checkbook while in the play mode can end up with bounced checks. On the other hand, the mother who is consistently in work mode when feeding her child may be generating an eating problem in the child.

People tend to find the most efficient ways of working, then use what they've learned as a model for achieving similar goals in the future. These learned insights are called routines or procedures.

If play becomes a routine, however, it tends to lose some of its pleasurable attributes. A joke that is laughed at in the morning may produce only a smile when repeated in the afternoon, and may fall flat if told again that evening. Few people want to eat the same food prepared the same way, night after night, regardless of how much they like it initially. For the couple who has intercourse every Sunday morning, whether they feel like it or not, the forced results aren't always satisfying.

There are areas in which work and play tend to merge or blend. Many games (e.g., cards, golf) are good examples. They are played for enjoyment (fun), but they often involve skill, analysis, and strategy. Creativity often involves playing with components for insight, followed by the work of shaping the idea to be complete or useful.

A person often is work-oriented while getting ready to play. Cooking a meal can be work, as can be decorating the house or planning what to take on a picnic. Although this cooking, decorating, or planning is work (and not necessarily enjoyable itself), it can increase the enjoyment of the play activity that follows. And there can be the added bonus of anticipating the fun while working.

Unfortunately, our language often adds to the confusion between the work and play modes. The phrase "to try" is ambiguous. Using "try" in the effort sense of "If at first you don't succeed, try, try again" relegates it to the work mode. Used in the sense of exploring, as in "Try on a jacket or a pair of shoes" or, "Try the taste of this food," it belongs in the play mode.

Another example: "to make" belongs in the work mode when used in the sense of force or coercion. If used in the sense of creating or "being on the make," it is in the play mode.

When the phrase "to look" is used in the "looking for" sense, it belongs in the work mode, i.e., "to seek," "to hunt," "to pick out," "to find." By contrast, the phrase belongs in the play mode when used in the "looking at" sense, i.e., "in regarding," "discerning it with the eyes," "admiring." The French and Spanish languages both have entirely different words for these two meanings of "look."[6]

√ **Our society speaks of Sex Play. We do not speak of Sex Work.**

Sex belongs to the play mode. Using coping mechanisms that are effective in enhancing play, e.g., whimsy, exploring, and doing what feels good at the moment, will sabotage work. In turn, using coping mechanisms effectively in the work mode, e.g., planning, effort, persistence, and goal origination, may result in the sabotage of play.

Every now and then men have come in for therapy, leaned over the desk, and said in a low, confidential tone: "Doc, tell me how to touch a woman." What they want is a routine, mechanical procedure—with guaranteed results!—such as "Touch her there for thirty seconds; then move to another area for a minute and a half," etc.

Both men and women can discern the difference between their partner's touch "to turn them on" versus the touch for enjoyment. Most adult women say they can feel the difference when a man is in the play mode, looking at them admiringly, and when he is in the work mode, mentally undressing them.

■ *A couple from a small town has lived a fairly staid, solid, predictable life. The man, an accountant, has been impotent about 90 percent of the time for the past ten years. One night, on the spur of the moment, the man and his wife drive to the city for a different type of meal than they are used to: knockwurst, dinkle-brau, and bock beer. Afterward, they go to a nightclub and listen to a Greek combo— again, something they had never done before. When they get home, they have intercourse spontaneously on the living-room floor. The next night they return to the city, eat the same meal, and hear the same music, but nothing happens at home. Over the next six months they repeat the trip, meal, and combo, but never recapture the same sexual magic.*

---

[6] Spanish uses MIRAR "to look at," BUSCAR "to look for." In French the words are REGARDER and CHERCHER.

The couple is failing to realize that it was their own mood that had put the magic in their night on the town. Their spontaneity and whimsy had allowed them to explore new things. The trip to the city on their first night was undertaken with a sense of adventure. They had enjoyed the meal and then the combo in the same way, each for its own experience. They approached touching each other in the living room with the same attitude of exploring for enjoyment.

The next night they had shifted to the work mode by turning the activities into a procedure with the expectation of success—intercourse—in mind. The whole evening was geared to that goal. Sexual enjoyment was lacking because it had become sex effort, rather than sex play. □

IN BRIEF

With work, the emphasis is on the goal, the achievement. With play, the emphasis is on the moment-to-moment enjoyment of the process. Sex is play.

YET TO COME

Accentuate the positive.

CHAPTER 11
ROMANCE

"Keep the love light burning."

Romance starts with kindness and consideration from each to the other. Politenesses like "please" and "thank you" need to continue throughout the relationship. "Thank you" can be sent non-verbally with a touch, a glance, or a smile. Two very meaningful ways to send this message for many couples are a lingering hug and by holding hands.

√ *Romance is a continuing message of "You are the most important person in the world for me."*

Thoughts and feelings of romance predominate during courtship, but too often they receive little cultivation after a couple lives together for a few months. The usual pattern of behavior—especially as presented by television sit-coms—is the "boy meets girl" format. The couple mentally joust and get to know each other psychologically, then sexually. Past generations heard much the same story—and it ended with "…and they got married and lived happily ever after."

Of course, the long-term commitment to a relationship also contributes to taking each other somewhat for granted. Furthermore, most couples invest their high energy in other areas such as jobs, children, home, financial security, and community. The problem is that in doing so they often allow the relationship to slide—sometimes too far.

At the end of a busy day a direct sexual approach that is not accompanied by psychological closeness is very likely to be received as unromantic or, perhaps, even without affection. It is as though after commitment the couple suddenly switched to a foreign language that is devoid of valued romance. Yet each expects to be understood as well as before.

All couples need some ongoing romance injected into their relationship, at least from time to time. Some of that can be on a low level, but once in a while it behooves each partner to spend a significant degree of thought and creativity to send that all-important message: "You are very special to me; I love you." The message doesn't have to be sent in words. But on the other hand, why not send it in words, too? Those words engender a sense of self-worth for both the hearer and the speaker.

√ *Few investments yield a more satisfying return than investments in romance.*

Romance is related to sexuality, and both are related to excitement that has within
it some element of surprise or suspense. The timing of the message and its form or
medium are all variables that can add to excitement. Messages need to be sent in your
own individual way, of course, but always keep one eye on how your partner will
receive them. If one is not received as a loving message, it won't generate the feeling of
being loved.

The loving message is at best a gift, a free gift without strings, often a surprise gift
given to please both the receiver and the giver. This pleasure is grossly diminished or
negated if it is given as a duty or an "ought." For example, one partner reluctantly says,
"Okay, yes, I'll go to visit your mother and father with you," then goes begrudgingly.
Such an attitude may meet an obligation and avoid a hurt, but there will be little delight
or closeness.

Individuals receive validation of self-worth from others in their life space—from
bosses, co-workers, friends, and those they are involved with in the community. The
validation that comes from a partner-lover is very special. The less validation an
individual receives from outside the relationship, the more she/he needs from the
partner.

Romantic messages enhance self-esteem for both the giver and receiver. Added
emphasis is placed on birthdays and special occasions. Anniversaries of meeting and
making a commitment, engagement, or moving in together can be celebrated, too. One
of the first things to do when you get a new calendar is to enter the dates that are
personally important, just as the publisher-noted holidays.

Sometimes the giver feels the expectation as an obligation. This may result in forgetting or giving a gift given begrudgingly. The receiver feels hurt by the begrudging
attitude, and resentment increases in both partners.

Many women are starved to hear "I love you." Some husbands can't say it because
they were brought up to believe that expressing emotions is unmanly. And when their
partners express a need to hear "I love you," they tend to feel boyish—"being told by
Mommy to do the proper thing." These men need to send loving messages frequently,
in their own way, and sometimes to send a big "I love you."

√ *"I love you" is the most vulnerable sentence in the English language.*

The lack of feeling of romance is further exaggerated by a shift of the social chair-
person role from the man (before living together) to the woman (after living together).
Often she misses the feeling of being pursued, with the accompanying sense of being

desired, valued, and loved. She also lacks the little surprises of what the man has thought up for the next date; hence, she lacks the evidence he has been thinking of her.

Again, each partner needs to communicate that she/he desires, and values, and loves, and is actively thinking of the other. Each partner needs to plan some outings or dates. Don't leave this to one partner; this is not a wise division of responsibility.

A joint date-business eating-out event doesn't send a very strong loving message. Consider making some evening at home special, perhaps with candles and your kind of music. Arrange for the children to be elsewhere.

√ *Romance is playful and fun; therefore, it needs to be whimsical and spontaneous, which at times may border on silliness. It often involves little, brief, spontaneous touches.*

The element of little pleasant surprises needs to be kept in mind. The husband might add to the suspense by not telling his wife exactly what he has planned. Of course, he will need to ask her to keep the time free and tell her the appropriate type of dress. He also needs to plan something he really believes she will enjoy. As with most advice, this statement has its limits. Surprises that involve major commitments of time/money—such as a vacation—may threaten the partner's feelings of autonomy and participation, and may backfire.

■ *A woman casually remarks to her husband: "It would be fun to take a month or two and tour the western United States in a motor home." Six weeks or so later, when they are experiencing some emotional distance between them, the husband buys a motor home for 75% of a year's income without consulting his wife. He expects her to be pleased and loving, but she is hurt and furious about the costs and her lack of input in the decision. She yells, "This was just a fantasy, a daydream. It never occurred to me that you would be so irresponsible as to act on it."*

It can be very meaningful when either of you sends little quick messages during the day that say, "I have been thinking of you. I love you." One way is a telephone call with no other intent than sending that message. If that is not possible, send an e-mail or a hand-drawn valentine marked "Personal." Inserting a love note in the other's clothes to be found by the partner when dressing is another way to send a loving message. □

√ *Romance may also be thoughtful, creative, and elaborate enough to require planning and work. Romantic messages may be outlandish.*

IN BRIEF

Don't let the love light die! The fire of love needs more fuel added frequently in the form of pleasant surprises. They may be whimsical and spontaneous, or ones that are thoughtful, creative, and require effort.

YET TO COME

The range of dynamics that people consider love. If you believe that the romance in your relationship has languished, we suggest that after reading this chapter you be sure to read Chapter 24, "Rebuilding a Relationship."

CHAPTER 12
WHAT PEOPLE CALL LOVE

The dynamics of a relationship that a person calls love are either those of the most satisfying relationship she/he has ever experienced, or that relationship plus whatever was felt to be lacking in that relationship.

Many people's concept of love grows and develops with progressively healthier relationships.

Recognize Me

Some people are starved for acknowledgment of their existence and presence: "Just speak to me—say 'Hi' or 'Hello' as you pass me." These individuals have not just been ignored; they have been shunned. When they find human recognition, they may call that love.

There are other people who don't want to be recognized; previously they decided to withdraw from most social action to avoid the hurt(s) of being rejected, ignored, or shunned. Nonverbally they signal their non-sociability and often won't respond to any form of recognition.

Pay Attention to Me

Other people need more. They crave attention; even negative attention is better than being ignored. These people need the confirmation that someone has taken an interest, however slight, in who they are or what they do. Chances are that as children these individuals did not receive the attention they craved from their parents. Perhaps their parents didn't receive much attention from their own parents. Other parents place a higher value on their own endeavors such as (1) working late at night "for the family," or (2) golf on the weekends "to maintain business and personal contacts," or charities, volunteer work, and bridge clubs. These activities may have left little time for parent-child interaction.

Negative Attention

Children from such families are apt to settle for negative attention, especially if it is the most meaningful attention they receive from their parents. These children and teens in particular know they can always get their parents' attention by getting in trouble at school or with the police, or by acting out sexually. Some may even prefer to be abused than to be ignored because it means someone cares. Even when acting-out episodes contain major elements of hostility directed at the parents, they are also tests of love. The children get some reassurance from the fact that their parents do interrupt their scheduled activities to pay attention to their urgent needs. The reassurance is worth the hassle and the negative attention. For them, negative attention may be taken for love.

Positive Attention

Some people take positive attention to be an expression of love. As children, their parents did spend some enjoyable time with them and did consider their wishes. Most sweetheart relationships through high school begin as positive attention. Meeting and talking between classes, five phone calls a week, a Coke date after school—all may be taken for love. This and other positive-attention relationships are characterized by giving and receiving positive attention by both parties. Some relationships don't progress beyond positive attention. To the independent observer, this attention can be scant, indeed.

What is received as positive attention by one person may be thought of as simply being helpful by the other, such as routinely giving someone a ride to school or work, or being a counselor or sounding board for the other person.

Let Me Give To You

There are other positive-attention relationships in which one person is motivated by the attention received and the other is motivated by the need to give. Many people have a deep need to give something of themselves and may interpret the validation of someone receiving from them as love. A love relationship may be motivated by each person having a need to give and by having found a willing and validating recipient in the other. Usually they give each other different "things." We call this a mutual need-to-give relationship.

There are one-sided need-to-give relationships. For example, a tutor is working with his/her student. The student takes the relationship as receiving instruction for payment, even though it could be considered positive attention. However, the tutor may take the relationship as an opportunity to give, and she/he may call it love. In this set of dynamics, the opportunity to give may be the best relationship the tutor has ever experienced: "I have never been considered to have anything of value to give anyone else. No one has said, 'You have something to give; you can make a contribution.' No one has ever asked anything of me."

Typically these people grew up in good middle-class, materialistic homes where they had all the conveniences. They had never been made responsible for any part of it.

All parents know that initially any job is easier to do yourself than letting a child do it. But never asking something of a child may create a serious inferiority complex. In these families, the children's job has been to go to school, to do the best they can for their own sake, and perhaps to clean their rooms.

The first time some women are really asked to give, they may be asked to give happiness by sharing their bodies sexually.

People with a "need to give" may form relationships that exploit the other person. Whether or not exploitation exists in a given relationship depends on the balance of respect each has for the other. For example, it is laudable to want to help others. Giving to someone who is downtrodden psychologically, socially, or even physically for the sake of matching one's ego ideal and feeling superior is exploitation. It is to be contrasted with giving that is motivated by genuine respect and concern for *this* individual.

Exploitation may generate feelings of superiority. Giving can occur on a more sophisticated level, with domination being "love given," and with gratitude and dependency being "love returned." Giving can also be subtle, even outside of conscious awareness. One person may be giving continually by going along with what the other prefers, which may be thought of as always giving **2–4** points on the 1-to-10 scale of depth and intensity. Then when a comparable issue arises that is honestly represented at an intensity of **8–10**, the partner may feel that reaction is outside the usual pattern and bounds of the relationship, and feel surprised and confused. This dynamic is portrayed in the movie *Runaway Bride*. Only as she approached the altar for the wedding does she realize—at some level—that she had not been honest with herself and, as a result, had not been honest with her intended.

√   *It is natural to want to give. Having a recipient can be mistaken for love.*

These dynamics may be the basis for some relationships between people of entirely different social classes. Further, these dynamics may also occur on an all-encompassing level: "Let me tutor you, you poor ignorant you," or, "Let me introduce you to the finer things in life, you poor peasant you." In the extreme, this reaches the proportions of the "kept man" or "kept woman" who is supported financially and sexually. Or, "Let me marry you and support you financially through school, you pauper you." Then after graduation there is a divorce and the individual wonders why. Maybe it was because the partner needs a chance to give a little, too, despite the fact that the other still needs to play "parent." The graduate may be called an ungrateful slob as though, if she/he continued to be grateful and dependent, it would still be love. (See "Unilateral Vulnerability Is Equally Troublesome," Chapter 4)

This need to give may extend to a person who is physically or mentally handicapped, and the giving may be called love. The recipient often regards the other's giving as love. Perhaps the downtrodden were not adequately given to, or were given to begrudgingly or with hostility. The need and willingness to be given to may be obvious, as with a physical handicap, or may be obscure or even below one's conscious awareness.

The individual who has had several committed relationships with one alcoholic after another is an example of this. Often it is not clear what attracted the individual to the alcoholic or alcoholic-to-be. Perhaps the trait the giver detects in the other is a difficulty dealing with stress, or a lack of directness. (See "Psychological Factors" and "Co-Dependency," Chapter 20)

These individuals may have had a childhood in which one parent took care of the other. Both alcoholism and co-dependency with alcoholics runs in families. Alternatively, the family background of the person who needs to give may have been modeled by the parents in their genuine altruism with patients or charities. Often the family background of the need-to-give individual combines parental modeling with philosophical and religious ideals of loving and giving to others.

Accept Me

This next concept of love is "accept me," where the individual desires: "Accept me for the person I am. Don't try to change me. Don't push me to get a better-paying job, to go to church, or to change the way I dress."

These individuals have the family childhood experiences in which nothing was ever quite right. "I would make four A's and one B at school, and all I would hear about was that B." It can be pretty great to really feel that you measure up to someone else's expectations, to be accepted as you are, without being asked to change this or that about yourself. This may be confused with love.

Admire Me

Others will settle for admiration, calling it love. They have never been in the limelight, never had much prestige, and never made any team, let alone the football squad or the homecoming court. These people like to receive flattery even when they suspect it is not completely genuine. It is great to be thought of as "cool." Some will even challenge authority or engage in risky behavior for the admiration of others.

These individuals have backgrounds that are similar to those who desire to be accepted, but they want more than just acceptance; they want to be looked up to.

Understand Me and Believe In Me

The desire for the partner to "understand me" and "believe in me" are not prerequisites for love; rather, they are indications of the depth of love. They grow as the love grows.

To what extent will you believe in your partner if, for example, she/he quits a job "on principle?" The decision can probably be accepted and respected, and that is enough for love. But will you, can you, understand why she/he had to? And, furthermore, will you also believe in her/him?

Our Definition of Love

Love is caring almost as much about the other person's happiness as you care about your own. In some moments, we would expect the individual to care *more* about the other person's happiness than his/her own. It is easier to be heroic and endanger one's self for another in some dramatic moment than it is to be really caring in the little everyday things, day after day, week in and week out, year after year.

√ *Let your heart take the lead and set the pace, but use your head to set the direction and distance you want to go.*

Time can prove whether feelings are based on love or simply sexual attractiveness. Part of mature love is the sharing of hopes and fears and sadness and happiness. You may commit yourself to someone with whom you can relate on many levels, someone you can trust and whom you can trust to love you.

Thinking about and discussing these issues is important, but don't analyze all the pleasure and spontaneity out of your relationships. Lead with your heart, not your head. But at some point in a relationship, stop and use your head to decide if you should give your heart full play. □

IN BRIEF

Too often people mistake having a fundamental need met as feeling loved. Those who crave recognition, acceptance, someone to receive what they have to give, or admiration are missing their potential for a fuller and more encompassing love. Love is caring almost as much about another's happiness as you care about your own. Love returned is experiencing the other's caring about your happiness as his/her own. It goes far beyond and is more meaningful than having one's need to be admired met.

YET TO COME

How love grows and declines.

CHAPTER 13
THE SPIRAL OF LOVE—
GROWTH AND DECLINE

How you can nurture the love in a relationship; how love grows or declines.

Love and intimate friendships can grow or decline. The change in love occurs in a cycle. Each cycle is visualized as one turn on the vertical dimension; hence, "spiral" is a more apt analogy.

Movement in either vertical direction is possible. A cycle of increasing love would be one turn upward on the spiral. Decrease in love is represented by a downward turn. These changes along the vertical are incremental changes, which means that the spiral continually adds to or subtracts from the quantity of love between the couple. We will describe the spiral with clearly delineated steps, which are most easily recognized at the beginning of a relationship, as most romance novels demonstrate. In relationships of longer duration the steps are not as discrete, though they are still easily recognizable. We will describe a negative spiral later. The next page shows the outline of a positive spiral:

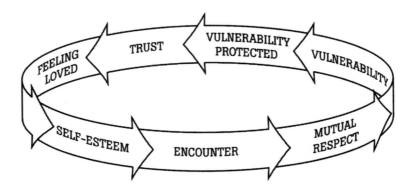

Each of the seven elements of the spiral leads to the next element of the spiral. In a long-term stable relationship, the incremental change is often imperceptible.

Description of the Steps of a "Spiral"

Self-Esteem: Self-esteem is one's feeling of self-worth, a general overall feeling of confidence. Two of the chief components of self-esteem are one's sense of skills and competence, and one's sense of lovability. The latter is the result of experiences of parents' love or love from parent surrogates, as well as past sweethearts and lovers. Self-esteem also is a function of one's appraisal of how others view you on multiple dimensions—your reputation. If yours is favorable, and if you think it is genuine rather than a façade, your self-esteem will be enhanced. Self-respect is a part of self-esteem.

    Role in the spiral: People with high self-esteem feel they deserve loving-caring relationships with elements of respect, protection of vulnerability, and trust. People with low self-esteem usually fear rejection, so they won't risk meaningful encounters like asking for a date, especially if they feel the other person is too good for them. People with high self-esteem have the confidence to create an encounter with a stranger whom they admire or find attractive, even at the risk of rejection.

An Encounter: Whether on first meeting or in an established relationship, an encounter is any interaction: a glance across a crowded room, a meeting, a request for a date, a gift, an expression of a preference for an evening's activities, a request for sex. It may also be any expression of an opinion, an offer of a favor, an act of consideration, or a conversation. Sometimes an encounter is not intentional, such as being assigned to work together or some other coincidental circumstance.

    Role in the spiral: Without an encounter, there is no spiral, no movement in the relationship. In an encounter, one or both individuals want to impress the other in some way and to gain or augment his/her respect.

Mutual Respect: Respect must be mutual or quasi-mutual. The respect a fan has for an entertainment superstar doesn't constitute a relationship. Respect generated by an adversarial relationship can turn to friendship or love. The respect or admiration each has need not be based on the same trait(s). Sometimes a relationship begins with banter and repartee that often ends in a "draw." People work together for extended periods of time without any special interest; then a relationship begins when something occurs that creates significant respect between them.

    From a beginning relationship to one that has existed for years, the role of respect is the same. The traits admired by a partner may shift, e.g., from valuing dare-devilish actions and beauty, drive, and ambition in a new relationship to valuing reliability, stability, and competence as a parent.

    Role in the spiral: The depth of respect is a major indication of the importance of the relationship to the individual. One of the individual's attitudes, perhaps outside of full awareness is: "If I want the other's respect, I need to say or do something impressive, which means being vulnerable." This accounts for much of the klutziness of some people who have recently fallen in love.

Vulnerability: Vulnerability is being open to being hurt. Vulnerability is the inevitable result of psychological intimacy, which in turn is the sharing of one's inner thoughts and feelings; it is sharing secrets, hopes, fears, embarrassments, expectations, both physical and psychological handicaps, and self-felt weaknesses, e.g., "I have had cancer and had a breast (or testicle) removed. I accept this, and most of the time it doesn't bother me, but there are times I don't feel like a whole woman (or man)." An "I need _____" statement, whether expressed in words or behavior, is a vulnerable statement. Not every request, desire, or complaint needs to be agreed with; rather, each statement needs to be accepted and given serious consideration, weighing it with or against your own desires or complaints.

Intimacy is allowing the other person access to parts of the self that can be hurt. Vulnerability is the result of letting the other person inside your usual defenses. Usually when two people recognize that the relationship is becoming serious, they share background information, including how each has been hurt before.

In the beginning of a relationship, vulnerability may be one-sided. But for the relationship to bloom, the vulnerability must be mutual. One-sided vulnerability breeds suspicion and resentment. A refusal to be vulnerable can doom a relationship. There are times that being honest will require being vulnerable. In an ongoing relationship, the scope and depth of vulnerability will be greater, and the partner will feel more secure that nothing of importance is being withheld. Increases in vulnerability flow from an increase in the sense of being loved. (For a more comprehensive discussion of vulnerability, see Chapter 4)

Role in the spiral: Vulnerability is directly proportional to psychological intimacy. Inherent in the decision to reveal personal information to another is the expectation that it will be kept confidential—that is, be protected.

Vulnerability Protected: Because confidentiality is already expected, protecting the other's vulnerability does not further enhance the other's respect or trust of you. However, to reveal that information would be a major hurt and result in a decrease of the other's respect and trust. The hurt can be experienced as a betrayal. Failure to protect the other's vulnerability turns a spiral negative. Some people are not sensitive about who knows of their sexual activity, or prior marriages, or criminal record; others are very sensitive about that information. You are free to ask if the other person wants that information kept confidential. If there is any doubt in your mind about your partner's attitude, don't reveal the information. In an argument, *never* throw up a vulnerability of your partner in an effort to hurt him/her. Each individual needs to feel secure that his/her vulnerabilities are and will be protected by the other, even in an argument.

Another category of protection is being ready to protect your partner from others. This can be someone who has knowledge of a vulnerability, e.g., a parent, sibling, or former lover, or perhaps someone without knowledge who nevertheless happens to be causing a hurt in some way that your partner is vulnerable. Don't move in so fast as to usurp your partner making his/her own stand. Rather, take your cue from some signal from your partner.

Role in the spiral: Failing to protect your partner's vulnerability will change the direction of the spiral, making it one of declining love or a withdrawal from the relationship. When vulnerabilities are not protected, further disclosure of vulnerabilities will likely cease, at least for a while—perhaps until there is a sincere apology and a realistic expectation that in the future one's vulnerabilities will be protected. Your protection of your partner's vulnerability is assumed, and has resulted in an increase of respect and trust.

Trust: Trust means counting on your partner not to hurt you deliberately or carelessly, either physically or, more importantly, psychologically. "You have protected my vulnerability. I can trust you. It is safe to love you."

Role in the spiral: The incremental change in trust, increase or decrease, is one of the payoffs of the prior steps of the spiral. It affects the amount of residual good will and expectations for the future.

Feeling Loved: The spiral has moved upward. There is an increased sense of loving and being loved. This is the payoff. It generates a growing sense of closeness, and of being valued for who you are. When the physical intimacy of sexual intercourse is combined with psychological intimacy, the resulting closeness is an even greater sense of loving and being loved. Each wants even more, and each understands that the other has the same needs for psychological intimacy. The result is usually more psychological disclosures that increase vulnerability.

Role in the spiral: Couples who together achieve a sense of being loved want to meet each other's needs, constantly demonstrating their love and their worthiness to be loved. This results in mutually increased self-esteem, respect, protection, and trust, plus more vulnerable disclosures and an even greater sense of being loved.

Self-Esteem: In an ongoing relationship, the level of self-esteem is a reflection of the accumulation of all the spirals of love that have transpired between them during their time together. If the relationship has been good, both partners' self-esteem is high and they are willing to make requests of each other easily. They expect their partner will want to fulfill the request and will be willing to go out of the way to do so. If the relationship has been continuous bickering, they half expect the partner to remind them of one of their shortcomings, or to receive a put-down of some sort. They expect an emotional rejection, even if the partner fulfills the request. When a relationship is so good that it enhances both partners' self-esteem, it leads to greater intimacy, vulnerability, trust, and momentum upward in the Spiral of Love.

The Spiral Repeats Again and Again

The incremental changes of love from a given spiral vary depending on the emotional importance of that spiral. This incremental change is represented by the vertical distance covered as a relationship moves up or down the spiral. If the change is minimal, the spiral can be pictured as tight, covering minimal distance. If the change is substantial, the spiral is spread out on the vertical dimension. Large incremental changes are more common in courtship and new partnerships. With every request and every expression of a desire, with every complaint and every hurt, a new vulnerability is presented and the love will grow or shrink.

In the preceding chapter, "What People Call Love," we described the dynamics of different levels of love. These levels can be represented as ranges on the vertical axis in the model of the spiral.

How Love Grows from One Level to the Next

There is some growth or decline in love in every spiral. As positive spirals become routine and habitual, especially in the relative absence of negative spirals, expectations develop that upward movement will predominate in the future in spite of some minor negative spirals from time to time. Each partner begins to want to give and to receive more. This generates ever-increasing levels of self-esteem, respect, vulnerability, trust, sense of loving and lovability, and in time a higher level of what they consider to be love.

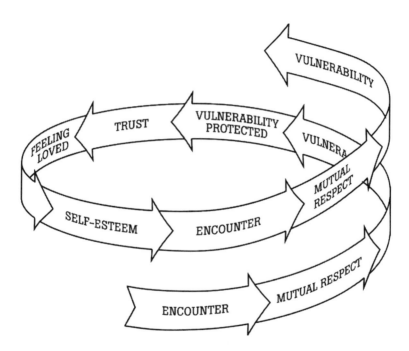

As a relationship grows, each element pushes the next one to a higher level, thus creating an upward spiral. The rate of growth in a successful (rewarding) relationship is usually faster at the beginning of the relationship. The rate slows down as the relationship becomes stable and predictable.

Consider a couple who has taken positive attention to each other as the primary basis of this friendship. Their previous relationships with parents, friends, or sweethearts is apt to have been based on attention, some positive, some negative, and some episodes of feeling ignored. As the two of them give each other positive attention, they increasingly eliminate instances of ignoring, they grossly reduce episodes of negative attention, and they feel freer to give positive attention by doing things for the partner. Positive spirals are accumulating.

In the Spiral of Love, requests are also considered an encounter with the partner, and the partner making the request is being vulnerable. The other may ignore the statement, resulting in a hurt, or may express resentment or frustration while complying with the request. Alternatively, the partner may decline, stating her/his own desire or reasons for not fulfilling the request. The couple may weigh the depth and intensity of each individual's position with honesty, caring, and concern. Even when the request is denied, the weighing of the desires of each and the caring and concern expressed are protecting the other's vulnerability, which contributes to love growing from one level to the next. The other alternative is that the request is fulfilled. As the number of requests that are addressed without hurt increases, there is an increasing accumulation of positive spirals. This results in increased feelings of lovability, self-esteem, and love. Each person comes to value the opportunity to do things freely for the other.

When giving and receiving becomes the predominant mode of meaningful interaction, the couple has moved up from positive attention to the next higher position on the spiral: the need to give.

Negative or Declining "Spirals"

A spiral becomes negative with an unresolved hurt. Hurts may be small or large, and the decline in love will be proportional. They give rise to expectations of more hurts and perhaps a feeling of hopelessness. Early in relationships, hurts tend to result in withdrawals from the relationship. The highest rate of divorce is in the first year of marriage because expectations for love and happiness are high and so is the potential for hurts.

A spiral can become negative at any step.

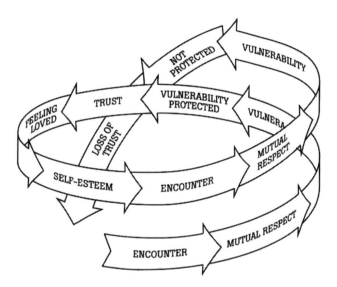

Each element has the potential to change the upward-downward direction of the elements that follow. These shifts may occur as a result of factors originating outside the relationship, or from the actions of either partner. In this example, one person increased his/her vulnerability, and then felt betrayed by the partner, triggering the downward shift.

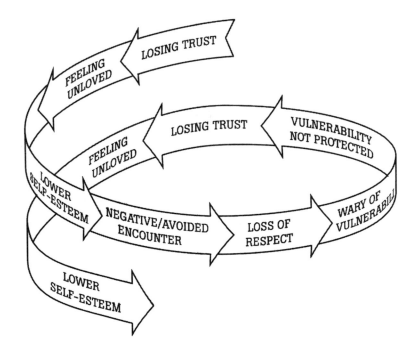

Once the relationship turns downward, the spiral is apt to continue in that direction unless the triggering hurt is resolved. Downward momentum may increase significantly over a short time interval. To reverse the direction, the partners may need to make a serious recommitment, and to consciously practice the communication and relationship principles described here.

If both people are being honest and open about their thoughts and feelings, there is no way a spiral can be increasing in love for one person and declining in love for the other. Examples of one person being deceitful about feelings in the relationship can be found in "Ambivalence," Chapter 16, and "Respect for Partner," Chapter 8.

Following are some of the common traps that cause couples to shift into a downward spiral:

Respect: The basic form of the message of non-respect is: "I don't give a damn about you or what you want." Two specific examples:

- One person initiates sex; the other turns his/her back and withdraws.

- A couple has just moved in together in the country. The man is watching sports at a friend's house. His wife calls: A rainstorm has caused some flooding. She asks him to hurry home to help her divert the water. He refuses to come home early.

Not to respect the partner or the partner's desires, needs, or fears is to send the spiral in a negative direction. It fails to protect vulnerability, shatters trust, reduces self-esteem, and diminishes feelings of being loved.

Vulnerability: Some people are so afraid of being hurt (or hurt again) that they do everything they can to keep their vulnerability to a minimum.

- A friendship is beginning, but one individual refuses to reveal anything about his past, even where he is from, because he once served a prison term. He knows the next question will be "What were you in for?"

- A husband refuses to discuss having a child, but doesn't feel safe revealing that he is afraid he would imitate his own parents' devastating dealings with him if he became a father.

- A request for a personal loan is turned down because the proposed lender refuses to be that vulnerable to his friend.

These spirals have turned downward. A relationship may progress despite this lack of vulnerability, particularly if the refusal to be vulnerable is limited to a specific area. Sometimes the refusal to be vulnerable causes more difficulty in the relationship than the original issue would have.

Vulnerability Not Protected: You need to protect all your partner's vulnerabilities. There are a number of different ways and reasons for not doing so. Not being aware your partner expected you to keep those facts confidential is one. Carelessness or lack of attention is another. Sometimes a person may get so "carried away" by the group conversation that she/he surrenders the partner's protection to the competing desire to be the center of attention in a group discussion at a party. Also, violating a confidence directly or indirectly may be deliberate and calculated.

- One person requests the partner pick up the dry-cleaning while in town. The partner agrees, but returns without it. There are different scenarios:

    The other's hurt can be minimized by an apology and/or an offer to go get the cleaning.

    Or the partner might say, "I just forgot," and hear the reply, "You only think about yourself and what you want. How hard is it to remember dry-cleaning?"

    Or the partner might say, "The cleaners was closed by the time I got there," and hear the reply, "You knew what time they closed. You knew I needed that suit for my job interview tomorrow, and there won't be time to get it in the morning. You know how important that interview is to me— to us."

- An argument has moved to deliberate attempts to hurt the other by throwing up sensitive issues from the other's past that were shared in closeness. Knowing that the other served thirty days for a second offence as a young adult, the partner calls him/her a "jail bird."

- At a gathering with friends, one spouse mentions that the partner spent time in a psychiatric hospital. The partner is hurt and furious: "You had no right to tell that about me. I told you that in confidence. I thought you had a right to know, but our friends didn't have that right."

    "You didn't ask me to keep it confidential."

    "I assumed you had some sense of propriety and two ounces of common sense."

Other than beatings or betrayals, perhaps the two most devastating hurts to a romantic relationship are being ignored or ridiculed.

Trust: A spiral may turn negative at any of several steps for lack of respect, lack of vulnerability, failing to protect vulnerability, or violation of trust. Regardless of the step of the downturn, trust is eroded and the feeling of being loved is reduced. "My partner doesn't love me enough not to have hurt me that way." These thoughts in turn reduce self-esteem.

■ *"I see you got new drapes for the house. They look nice, but where did you get the money?" "I took it out of our savings account." "That was money we agreed to save for a vacation next year. We agreed neither of us would touch that money without consultation with the other. You violated that agreement. How can I trust you? You are a self-centered sneak!"*

Outside Factors Affecting the Spiral

When something bad happens, both of you have two different but intertwined goals: to deal with the problem and its subsequent issues as best you can, and to prevent them from affecting your Spiral of Love. The outcomes of these goals are often independent of each other.

We will discuss some of the common ways couples fail to protect their spirals, then offer alternative coping strategies. Consider these examples, the odd-numbered ones showing couples who successfully protect their Spiral of Love, the even-numbered ones portraying couples whose efforts are inadequate:

1. *A couple's home is completely destroyed by fire. Besides the initial shock and suddenly becoming homeless, they also have to deal with insurance issues, the salvage operation, and all the aggravation associated with the design and rebuilding of a new home to their satisfaction. Still, they succeed in protecting their Spiral of Love by communicating, openly sharing their feelings and holding each other.* A couple's home is their castle, but together they can shut out problems in the world even if they temporarily have no home.

2. *A couple inherits a large sum of money. One wants to splurge on luxuries and things both have always wanted. The other wants to develop an overall plan, even though neither has any experience with investments at this level. As a couple, they have always been popular with family and friends, which contributes greatly to their self-esteem. Now friends and relatives are coming by either for a handout or loan, or with a proposal for some "sure thing" investment. These requests stress both partners, but each differs on how much to accommodate them. The cold reactions from those who are denied reduces both partners' self-esteem. In frustration and anger, one calls the other "miser," and the other counters with "irresponsible spendthrift." All the money in the relationship had been considered "our money," but as their respect for each other erodes, that is no longer assumed.* Their trust in each other declines, which reduces feelings of love and being loved, replaced more and more by feelings of hurt and anger.

3. *The 16-year-old daughter of a two-career couple becomes involved with alcohol. Realizing they need to provide more parental supervision, they discuss which parent can afford to spend more evenings at home with the least "cost" to the family. These frank discussions include weighing depth and intensity so they can implement their choices without resentment.* Remember, in terms of the spiral, a discussion is an encounter, so these two are finding ways to accommodate a problem, meet their changing needs, and work out a solution without damage to their Spiral of Love.

4. *A new gambling casino opens near the office of a woman who had previously struggled with a gambling problem. Her partner worries that she might begin gambling again. When he asks about her urges, she assures him they are minimal and easily controlled. He continues asking, even with no basis for concern except the location of the casino. His obsession about the possibility of her giving in is greater than her compulsion to gamble.* Noting his low level of

trust in her, she begins to feel more monitored than loved and supported, which leads to reducing her feelings of being loved.

5.   *Shortly after the birth of their first child, the husband unexpectedly becomes legally blind. They develop strategies for accommodating this change, then go on and have two more children.* They protect their Spiral of Love by refusing to let this challenge damage it. It is not the severity of an outside factor that matters as much as how well a couple protects their spiral from whatever consequences it brings.

6.   *A man invests with a con artist and winds up losing the house he shares with his wife and two children. His wife stands by him, and after four years they have a new home and a third child. Then they are offered another investment opportunity by a different person from a different firm, but the wife recognizes its similarity to the earlier swindle. What she sees as a scam, he considers a golden opportunity. She protests vigorously, but still he makes the investment—and loses their second home.* In therapy, she discovers she has lost all respect for him because he failed to show any respect for her and her opinion. His proceeding without her support reduces her feeling of being part of a team, which reduces her feeling of being loved.

7.   *A couple allows one of their mothers to move in on a permanent basis. The older woman begins a pattern of getting into battles of will with the couple's three-year-old daughter. The parents talk to the mother about this repeatedly, but even though she keeps agreeing to back off, it becomes clear that emotionally this is not possible. Agreeing that further talks would be futile, the couple chooses to protect their daughter by asking the child's grandmother to leave.* Unable to accommodate the outside factor, they remove it rather than let it damage their Spiral of Love.

8.   *A woman who is known for harping about drunk drivers has a few drinks at a baby shower, then decides she is okay to drive herself home. She is arrested and spends the night in jail. Mortified and fearing for her reputation, she begs her husband never to tell anyone what happened. He agrees, but then winds up telling his best friend, who tells his wife, who makes a comment to the woman who had been arrested. She is hurt that her husband betrayed her vulnerability, so she loses some trust in him. She withdraws, becomes depressed, and refuses to get close to him psychologically or physically.* Because he failed to protect her vulnerability, the resulting loss of trust reduces her feelings of love and being loved.

9.   *A man suffers multiple small strokes following heart surgery. He suffers loss of memory and impaired judgment. Told his prognosis is good, ten weeks brings the added frustration of no noticeable improvement. Despite encouragement and support from his wife and friends, he reaches the point where he is ready to give up, just sit on the floor and cease any effort to overcome these challenges. Instead, he realizes it wouldn't be fair to his wife, that this has been just as hard on her, so he tells her this and they cry together. He explains that there have been only two people he could trust completely: her and himself. "Now I can't trust myself, so you are all I have left." They continue these discussions, especially when either feels frustrated*

or despondent. They let themselves be vulnerable with each other, which helps maintain their trust and feelings of love and being loved. After three years, he is functioning well, and their Spiral of Love, which was never in jeopardy, continues to grow.

10. *After suddenly losing his job, a man who used to think he could easily land another finds himself without offers despite his best efforts and many interviews. As his self-esteem drops, he loses the playful cheerfulness his wife always enjoyed, and he begins to notice her disappointment with each new failure. Feeling unloved and unsupported in this difficult time, he begins having outbursts of frustration and anger, which makes her feel like she must constantly walk on egg shells to avoid provoking him. Both are especially vulnerable, but not protecting each other. After another rejection, he drives around until late rather than come home to face her. Feeling belittled and hurt by his lack of consideration, she accosts him that night with suggestions he might be less of a man than she thought she'd married. Their respect for each other plummets. He begins refusing to answer her questions about his job search because it makes him more vulnerable to her verbal attacks. His loss of trust in her not to hurt him reduces the number and meaningfulness of their encounters, which leads to a decrease in feelings of love and being loved until it damages their sex life.* If he will keep telling her about every effort and every prospect, plus share his feelings so they are "in this together," they can work together on bolstering his self-esteem as she sends him messages of love. Feeling like he must protect himself by hiding all this from her is failing to protect their relationship and Spiral of Love.

Other Common Ways Outside Factors

Enter the Relationship Spiral

Realize that some negative outside factors are already both outside and inside the relationship from their beginning. For example: anything that one partner keeps secret from the other, such as an affair or involvement in criminal activity. The feelings of hurt will occur when the other partner finds out, but the violations of trust occurred back when the secret activity began.

The psychological barrier preventing any outside event from *directly* affecting one of the steps is lower for self-esteem than it is for the other steps, which are generally dependent on some encounter between the partners. The trust and respect you have for your partner are psychologically separated from trusting and respecting others like your co-workers or even other family members.

Likewise, your senses of vulnerability and protection, and of feeling loved and loving, are also centered on your partner more than others. Self-esteem is all-encompassing, more easily affected by outside factors such as problems on the job. A feeling of guilt about anything, whether realistic or not, often reduces self-esteem. (See Example 10 in this section) Once outside factors have begun to affect a partner's self-esteem, she/he might immediately become less assertive, more ponderous, and less spontaneous or outgoing socially; or to compensate she/he may become boisterous and extroverted, even to the point of being obnoxious.

Stress: Any event originating from outside the relationship can cause some change in a partner's or couple's customary modes of feeling, thinking, and activity. All change—even desired change like a job promotion—produces at least some stress. There is a Chinese curse: *May you live in interesting (changing) times.* Stress usually calls for some level of adaptation, which can have an impact on the spiral of a loving relationship. Initially, the result may affect only one partner at a particular point in the spiral before affecting the other. The spiral can move in either direction, or first in one direction and then the other. If the impact or adaptation to it creates a hurt or violates one of the principles in this book, and if it is not corrected, the spiral will turn downward.

The effects of stress: Mild stress results in extra attention to the source, along with varying degrees of preoccupation. Usually stress carries with it an unknown outcome and its attendant worry and anxiety. At a slightly higher level of stress, a person often becomes irritable and grumpy, and has a lower tolerance for frustration. These changes in disposition are manifest by the person becoming short or abrupt, or by having emotional outbursts, especially around the partner and/or children. Young children are apt to consider this "anger" to be the result of something they did unless the one having an outburst or the partner correctly explains the cause. The partner may be hurt by this behavior and take it as a put-down or rejection, even though the intent might have been to be helpful. An "Ouch" may result in momentary reflection and apology, yet it may be followed within a few minutes by another emotional outburst.

Stress and anxiety may be disruptive to sleep, which adds to irritability the following day. Anxiety also interferes with short-term or retentive memory. Hence, the individual may forget a request by the partner, which results in a hurt. Stress, anxiety, and depression often cause a reduction in sexual desire, which in turn may trigger the whole array of possible thoughts and feelings associated with the couple's sexual relationship. These are some of the common ways outside factors can affect the spiral.

Stress also affects the Spiral through depressive symptoms with or without anxiety symptoms. Perhaps the mildest depressive symptoms to expect are withdrawal and isolation. Others include difficulty concentrating, disinterest in the usual things, lack of energy, feeling ill or other physical complaints, difficulty sleeping, a reduced sex drive, and either a decrease in appetite or excessive eating.

Stress is cumulative. For example, as a period of unemployment stretches, there will be added stress from reduced income, which may lead to other stress-causing problems like loss of the family car. This loss of transportation affects other members of the family, and it adds difficulty to searching for another job.

Stress from outside factors may accumulate. For example, job loss followed by the death of a parent, then a child acting up in school. Stress can lead to the inability to function—a "nervous breakdown"—perhaps requiring hospitalization. At least the hospitalization stops calls from creditors, plus gives the patient a respite from the world and time to re-integrate his/her self-image. Maximum stress may result in a post-traumatic stress disorder (PTSD), symptoms that occur as the result of a seriously traumatizing event like combat or rape.

Coping

When problems caused by outside factors can't be solved, eliminated, or by-passed, how a couple copes will make a world of difference—perhaps the difference between losing the relationship and strengthening it through increased acceptance, support, and understanding.

Before we suggest steps for addressing the outside factors, we recommend three strategies for protecting yourselves, ways to strengthen your protective armor against outside events negatively affecting your spiral. These will help the two of you keep from being overwhelmed as you deal directly with the issues.

Turn toward each other: Realize that the sooner you turn toward each other, the better for the relationship, and in many cases the better the chances the two of you will have to ameliorate the issue(s) and potential complications. Use each other as your confidant. Talk over the new developments, including your new thinking, of the issue(s) as they emerge, and when appropriate weigh your depth and intensity and those of your partner. By "talk," we mean expressing your personal thoughts, your worries, any feelings of guilt or blame, and your hopes. This also means you must listen patiently, without assumptions or being quick to judge. Listen for views that are similar to yours as well as those that might be different. If an issue isn't out in the open, ask about it. If a major decision has to be made, discuss every aspect, and give yourselves as much time as possible to make it. Even if a decision falls primarily to one partner, such as choosing the best of several bad options for dealing with an infirm parent, the partner with the most responsibility should seek his/her partner's agreement. Through frank, open, and honest discussions, and by weighing depth and intensity, you give yourselves the best chance for both of you to support the final decision.

In an intimate relationship, nothing happens to only one person. This means you must devote time together to your relationship, not only to address your problems, but to continually find new ways to strengthen the relationship. In Chapter 8 we discussed different ways of using time; pay special attention to *Couple Time*. This is how to build relationship solidarity. It's by sticking together as a team that you will both stand stronger in the face of difficulties than any one partner can alone.

Protect your and your partner's self-esteem: Of all the steps in the spiral, self-esteem most readily crosses the boundary from outside the relationship to inside. Resist the common impulse to take misfortune personally. Bad things do happen to good people, and good people do make mistakes. You don't deserve all the hardships your relationship may face, nor do the hardships mean that fate is against you. When you and/or your partner are feeling down on yourselves, find ways to build confidence and bolster self-esteem. Do things you're good at, and make sure you recognize each other's accomplishments. Compliment each other. Even simple gestures like a smile can make a difference.

Perhaps most importantly, you and your partner should make every effort to separate your self-esteem related to outside factors from self-esteem related to yourselves as partners, lovers, parents, friends, neighbors, and from your personal interests. No outside issue, not even your job, determines the total you.

Pay attention to anything that might hurt your respect for each other. Don't let your personal appearance deteriorate; make the effort to look attractive for each other. Don't be idle, either, especially if you've lost the way either of you customarily filled your time due to factors like being laid off, retiring, suffering the death of your child, or simply facing an empty nest when the youngest moves away. Becoming idle can lead to self-pity and lower self-esteem. Find new ways to make a difference and continue to earn your partner's respect. Take advantage of any opportunities to contribute to the family. Take on some of your partner's responsibilities. Spruce up the house or yard, help a friend, or volunteer in the community. Feeling good about yourself, even in the face of adversity, is an important step toward feeling good about your relationship and each other.

Deal with stress, anxiety, and depression: If stress and its many challenges begins to strain your relationship, be sure you find ways to protect each other. Be understanding, ask for and offer patience and tolerance, and remember to consider the situation when evaluating what is said to you. (See the example under "The Target or Addressee," Chapter 15) Give yourselves a longer fuse to delay or blunt negative reactions, and be extra quick to apologize if there is any chance you've over-reacted.

You will do better, both in terms of progress on your problem and your mental health emotional balance, if you periodically take time out from even thinking about your problem. Try to have some enjoyment during those breaks. Shut out the worry by pampering yourselves physically and emotionally. Snuggle to feel close, accepted, and loved. You might intensify these feelings through sexual intercourse if you avoid the pressure of expectations. Don't always seek sky-rockets when "memorial day" sex can be just as satisfying and take you both back to easier times, if only for a while.

Consider getting away, not necessarily for an elaborate vacation, but rather for simple *Couple Time*, maybe shutting off the phone for a while as you listen to music, give each other massages, take long baths, or hold and play with your pets. Seeing a movie, taking a walk in the park, watching birds, gazing at the stars—there are lots of ways the two of you, maybe with some close friends, can put aside your worries.

In addition to working on the problem, take active steps to reduce or cope with the anxiety and depression that grows out of stress. Resist getting down on yourself. Avoid thoughts about what you "should" or "ought" to do unless there is a genuine moral issue. Don't dwell on what is past, but rather on how the future can be better. Identify and seek ways to accept what simply cannot be changed, even when that is difficult. Don't "catastrophize," letting yourselves get caught up in imagining the worst, especially when it may never come to pass.

Try some of the popular techniques for reducing the effects of stress. For some, that might be physical workouts, or exercises that integrate the mind and body and aid relaxation like meditation, yoga, or the martial art of Tai Chi. An effective way to reduce muscle tension is to lie in bed and practice tightening, then relaxing, each muscle group for twenty-second intervals. Once you have moved through your entire body, relax and let yourself "sink" into the bed. Another way is to lie still and focus your thoughts on something soothing and pleasant. Some find it effective to visualize a "happy place," a setting that is comfortable. Imagine all the senses: how this place looks, the sounds you hear, the aromas and flavors and physical sensations, and how it all makes you feel. This will help clear your mind, and might even help you sleep.

Watch for ways to reduce the physical effects of stress. Cut back on caffeine, even from chocolate and soft drinks. Let your mind lead your body into relaxation with techniques like focused breathing or repetition of a mantra, which can lower your blood pressure, help your immune system, and move you away from that state of tension where you're poised for fight or flight. Laughter can serve as an excellent release, so make time to enjoy whatever you find humorous, and encourage yourself to laugh out loud, even if you have to force it a bit at first to open the gates.

Stress, along with anxiety and depression, alerts you that something is wrong, but you don't always have to be trapped into dwelling on the symptoms. Seek balance between working on your problems and taking the time to let go of the worry. Then if the effects of stress continue to be a serious problem, consult your physician and consider treatment, including the possibility of medication.

Don't try to go it alone: The two of you should not try to cope with seriously difficult issues alone. Try to locate people who have lived through the same kinds of problems; then share your experiences with each other. You can generate ideas, learn what has succeeded for others, and possibly find some relief in spreading the emotional burden. People will almost always try to be helpful, even if it is just to reassure you that others have faced similar problems, and to offer hope that you, too, can get through this.

In most areas you can find organized support groups. Some are private while others can be found through county or parish agencies, churches, hospitals, treatment centers, and state or national organizations. Most communities have an emergency hotline offering information about various resources. You can also check the phone book and the internet to find support groups. Examples include networks for crime victims, relatives of Alzheimer's patients, parents of seriously ill children, cancer patients, and grief recovery groups. The human relations departments of many large employers are good sources for referral, as are physicians and clergy. Human beings are social creatures and members of a community, so don't the two of you try to go it alone.

Coping Steps

Now that you have strengthened your protective armor and prepared yourselves to face problems together, we recommend the following steps for addressing any outside factors that interfere with your upward spiral.

Identify the outside factors: The actual cause of the problems might not be as obvious as you assume, and the two of you might not see it the same way. Separately make lists of all the outside factors you think have changed and are causing difficulty. Then look for and identify any factors that are secondary to the first ones, such as too much overtime at work cutting into Couple Time, which might be creating the suspicion that one spouse is volunteering for extra hours in order to avoid responsibilities at home. Next, identify and list all the ways these outside factors impact your lives and the relationship, which might be one or two major ways or quite a long list of smaller ways. Make these lists separately from your partner's to ensure completeness. Now compare your lists with each other's. Discuss any differences and try to reach agreement on what you both feel is contributing to your current problems.

This step usually results in some surprises, either in how much you agree on something you've both avoided acknowledging, or in how differently you are both seeing the same problem. There is no limit to the ways outside factors can cause reactions that negatively affect an otherwise positive spiral.

Look for ways to change the outside factors: Are there any? Some will be obvious while others may require a lot of thought and discussion. Write down whatever occurs to each of you, even those thoughts that seem ridiculous. Then take it a step further by reflecting on them together. Do they contain the kernel of an idea that might be useful or lead to a new way to look at the problem?

Concentrate first on what you can change. That might mean taking control of a situation, or distancing yourselves from it as much as possible. Attempt to right any wrongs either of you are realistically responsible for, forgive yourself and each other for any aspects that remain, then move on.

You might benefit from more information, new ideas, suggestions from others, or outside advice from experts. Asking friends, family, or members of the community for referral doesn't mean you have to reveal your personal business to everyone. If the issue is financial, you can ask someone with similar experiences to recommend a credit counselor or investment advisor without you having to offer private details.

When you can't change an outside factor, look for ways to reduce their negative effects. You might need to develop a new perspective, learn to compensate for loss, or even undertake adapting to a new lifestyle. For example, those suffering from one spouse losing a job and having trouble finding another might find it less stressful and better for long-term happiness simply to cut expenses and maybe live somewhere else.

Giving the problem time can be one of the most important steps you take. No matter what you change, it may take time for the old negative feelings and thoughts to fade. Issues like grief over the death of a loved one can leave you feeling helpless, but even then time will give you the opportunity to adjust and remember all the good to count among your blessings. Outside factors can create problems that seem big at first, but given time and space you can discover very few are worth sacrificing your relationship.

Identify thoughts and feelings associated with those factors: Understanding and sometimes even adjusting how you feel and think about interfering factors can lessen their impact. Go through this process together so you can understand each other's viewpoint and arrive at a common understanding. Together, write down all the thoughts and feelings triggered by the outside factors you have identified. Do not hurry this step; let your thoughts flow.

There is a tendency to attach blame to everything negative that happens, whether it is rational or not. Self-blame is called guilt. Self-blame is often more destructive to the relationship than blaming your partner because blaming the partner is usually out in the open, whereas one person's struggle with guilt might not be known to the partner. Hence, the partner's support will not address the guilt. Usually, when guilt is brought into the open, the partner is surprised, and is able to reassure the other that his/her guilt is not deserved. Second-guessing yourselves and the resultant blame or guilt are apt to be especially strong in instances with higher stakes, i.e., injury or death rather than mild embarrassment or loss of small amounts of money.

Look for signs that you or your partner are experiencing guilt or assigning blame to the other for being vulnerable to outside factors, such as dwelling on unchangeable choices from the past. *If only I* is a statement of self-guilt, e.g., "If only I hadn't let our child cross the street," or, "If only I had moved my family to a safer neighborhood." *If only you* is a statement of blame, e.g., "If only you would stop rushing to help every time your relative calls," or, "If only you had sought medical attention sooner we might be able to conceive children." Since neither of you can change the past, drop all the "*If onlys*" and cut the irrational "crud" from the current problem(s). If either of you feels guilty, talk it over. Chances are, you both either made the best decisions you could at the time, or you've since learned from those mistakes. A good discussion might not only relieve the guilt, but could even show you how it was never rational in the first place.

If your partner doesn't think you are to blame for the problems, and if she/he still loves and respects you, then don't get down on yourself. Keep in mind that there are no outside factors that can change your capacity to love each other, your family, and your friends. It is not reasonable to think that their love for you might change strictly because of outside factors. Don't invite others to change their attitudes by expecting it. However, be aware that their attitudes might change based on how you *deal with* those outside factors. Have faith in the people who love you, search for solutions, and seek the support of each other as well as from people facing similar difficulties; then accept what you cannot change and take comfort and strength in facing your problems together.

Reinforce every step in the spiral: If you find that your relationship is still slipping under the stress created by outside factors, together you need to examine your interactions at each step in the spiral. If you can identify where your relationship is spiraling downward, focus your attention and efforts there to find creative ways to shift it back toward relationship growth. Like most relationships, yours at some point will likely face challenges outside your control; it is how you confront them that can lead to yours emerging stronger and more positive than ever before.□

√ *It is important that in times of stress— regardless of the cause—partners turn toward each other. In an intimate relationship, nothing impacts only one. Each partner is the other's source for comfort, support, solace, and validation.*

IN BRIEF

Love can grow or decline. A growth Spiral of Love results in an increase not only in love and a sense of lovability, but also in trust, self-esteem, respect, and willingness to be vulnerable with the realistic belief that vulnerability will be protected.

YET TO COME

Sometimes there are breakdowns in spite of maintenance. Section IV deals with understanding obscure and/or stubborn problems.

Section IV
Understanding Stubborn Problems

We develop habits for dealing with hurt feelings starting in childhood, then continuing through adolescence and into adult life. These techniques for dealing with hurts were probably conscious when first tried, but have become automatic responses, often below conscious awareness.

We may not have had good teachers to help us understand anger and its components any more than we had good teachers for understanding and responding to hurt feelings.

Hurts and our defenses may become compounded, which often obscures our understanding, even when we try to modify our responses.

Problems and potential problems of hurts can pile up, one superimposed on another; or several issues can be intertwined, especially when we try to balance protecting ourselves while maintaining vulnerability and closeness in a valued relationship.

We develop ways to minimize future potential hurts based on our experience of past hurts. These avoidance techniques also become automatic habits. Trying always to be in control and able to dominate others is a protective mechanism, though it often interferes with close relationships.

Not all intertwined issues are recognized. Some may be outside of conscious awareness. One obscure issue may underlie myriad other issues, giving the impression that the relationship has a large number of troublesome issues. The most common of these are our identity, autonomy, and addictions. There can be no real improvement in the relationship until we have recognized and dealt with these.

An addict's vicissitudes may be manifest in many different attitudes and behaviors—from helplessness to retaliation, anger, twisted logic, accusations, and control. Addictions are probably the most devastating issues that underlie other hurt-anger issues. Often an addiction is kept secret. In other instances, loved ones know of the addiction, but don't fully appreciate its detrimental effects.

CHAPTER 14
TRANSFORMATION OF HURTS

Feelings of hurt that are not resolved by clarification tend to undergo transformation to some other form, often to withdrawal, depression, anger, or domination-control. This chapter will survey the various types of transformations of these hurts.

Mild feelings of hurt may decay with time. However, most moderate and strong feelings of unresolved hurt from a loved one decay very slowly, if at all. They cannot be ignored. They hang on, especially those judged as undeserved and unfair. They are psychologically painful and, hence, unstable. They undergo transformations.

The transformation of feelings of hurt is seen most easily in children who feel hurt from a parent they judge as unfair. They tend to pout about these hurt feelings. A pouting child will fantasize a number of different scenarios like being kidnapped, injured, or dying—all to create feelings of remorse or guilt in the parents, and to make the parents realize how much they love the child. Children's fantasies may include running away, with the parents worried sick, and years later returning to save the family or as a famous hero. These fantasies may also include anger and retaliation, such as hurting the family pet or breaking a prized possession. The movie *A Christmas Story* portrays young Ralph as considering a number of these fantasies. Children may also fantasize explanations for the feeling of injustice: *"I was an unwanted child. Even after I was born, I was never wanted."* Or, *"I was adopted (or kidnapped). My real parents wouldn't treat me this way; they would love me."* The child may become sullen, withdrawn, and depressed.

These are all potential transformations of feelings of hurt. These responses are exaggerated when the child perceives that the parental hurt was delivered in anger, especially if accompanied by a character assassination statement such as: "You are no good and never will be."

> √ *It is OK while you are angry to stop or correct a child's negative behavior, but it is not OK to punish or to set punishment until your anger has passed.*

Because of these dynamics, child therapists advise parents never to punish in anger. Often the punishment is recognized as too harsh when the parent reconsiders the situation in a calmer mood. The parent then faces an awkward choice: (1) to let the unfair punishment stand, (2) not to enforce the punishment, or (3) to acknowledge to the child that the punishment was too severe, and then to modify it. Surprisingly, few parents make the third choice, even though to do so would reduce the child's sense of injustice and resentment and increase respect for the parent.

√   *The number of options a person has in his/her repertoire for dealing with feelings of hurt is one indication of her/his mental health and maturity.*

Adolescents and adults may at times brood about hurts and create fantasies both to explain and deal with them. As feelings of unjust hurts accumulate in an individual's mind over the years, a particular transformation becomes favored, and it predominates over other scenarios. In time, that scenario—with its explanation, including the character assassination statements—becomes habitual. Some authors refer to these thought-habit patterns as "life scripts" or "mental tapes."

Adult women tend to transform their feelings of hurt into emotional withdrawal and depression. Men are more likely to transform theirs into physical withdrawal and/or anger. Sometimes men move to anger so fast that they may not be emotionally aware that they feel hurt.[7] There may not even be a fleeting thought that the hurt might be a miscommunication. Their feeling of anger shuts out the feeling of hurt, even though the individuals recognize the slight and regard it as an intentional put-down.

In time, these same mechanisms of transformation are used more and more frequently in regard to anticipated hurts, as well as hurts that have already been experienced.

Emotional Denial

To avoid future hurts, some individuals turn their emotional sensitivity to *Off.* They live life by going through the motions without feeling, as if nothing of an emotional nature has happened or can happen. They have withdrawn from life in favor of existing like a zombie. In this way they hope to avoid unpredictable hurts.

Since these individuals don't register hurt feelings, they may need to equate a hurt with the intellectually recognized put-down, and to talk about that instead. Usually, as children, their egos and self-esteem were severely squelched by parents who used blame, severe reprimands, and character assassinations to correct them. Statements like "How dare you talk that way to me, you little snot!" might be accompanied by physical punishment or a restriction that is too long. When this scenario is repeated over and over again, children learn that they don't deserve the same respect as others do. This thought becomes habitual and chronic, resulting in a *life script.* Even as adults, they don't believe they have the right to express themselves, or that they are entitled to enjoy the good things of life—even those that are available for the taking.

---

[7]   If they withdraw, they must continue to be aware of the hurt because they need to reconnect with the other person, which requires deciding when and how.

The emotionally turned-off individual may wear a fixed smile all the time or may wear a blank expression. She/he has little or no personality. Perhaps the attention and affection of courtship lifted the person out of the fear of being hurt, but often only temporarily. The hurts that gave rise to this extensive withdrawal may have occurred in an earlier romantic relationship or from repeated experiences outside of the romantic or parental relationships. Regardless of the cause of the change, the partner may complain:

"You are just there in body, but not really there. I can't interact with you. Whatever I suggest is always fine. You rarely suggest anything."

Ironically, this trait of being willing to go along with whatever the other suggested was likely one of the personality traits the partner-to-be found attractive during courtship.

The emotional withdrawal from life may be partial or incomplete, or may be limited to certain areas. Some people withdraw into alcohol and drugs, and may eventually become addicted. Others escape into less severe forms of withdrawal as a way to transform or avoid feelings of hurt. They are more likely to drop out of school and have trouble keeping a job, or they may immerse themselves in school or work responsibilities to avoid having time to be aware of the hurt of an unsuccessful social life. They might avoid all social contact, preferring solo activities like reading or watching TV, or they might cultivate a large pool of "friends" to avoid the risk of closeness or commitment with one or two.

Because sexuality is the area in American culture that is least integrated with the rest of the personality, some individuals withdraw into blandness, except in the sexual area, where they may be very demanding and controlling.[8] One college coed said having intercourse was the only thing she had ever found that she was good at. Some women have described their significant others as: "Not much at parties or with people, but a different man in bed."[9]

Martyrs

Some people collect and savor their misfortune, both real and feigned hurts. They are the opposite of withdrawn; they put their hurts on display. They relish the attention

---

[8] This is the picture of one class of rapists. It also fits the description of Jeffery Dahlmer, who killed and dismembered a number of young men and stored their bodies' parts in his refrigerator and freezer. What produces a greater feeling of control over another person than killing him/her face to face?

[9] In medicine, this condition is called Munchausen's Syndrome after the first physician to describe it. Munchausen's By Proxy is the term used to describe a person (e.g., a parent) who hurts another (e.g., a child) in order to garner sympathy as the caregiver.

and sympathy they receive, but they realize they can't appear too happy or outgoing. They are, after all, suffering. Their suffering may have religious overtones. (See Chapter 12) They see themselves as deserving more from life. Their philosophy is apt to be, "It is better to deserve the good things of life than to have them." They are often self-righteous. Rather than eliminating the feeling of the hurt by transforming it, they have changed the significance that the hurt has for them. It has made them more deserving of sympathy and—maybe—extra compensation in heaven.

Some people can tolerate the feeling of hurt, but can't allow themselves to experience any anger. Chances are that during childhood any expression of anger was severely suppressed by adults. Religious teachings against anger may have reinforced that attitude and lifestyle. During therapy, these people become aware of their anger, but as they contemplate any thought of expressing it, they describe two contradictory sets of thoughts or fantasies:

1. Their anger would be impotent, ineffective, inconsequential. *"I picture myself hitting someone with all my strength, but he doesn't even notice, or he turns to me and asks, 'Did you want something?'"*

2. *"I am afraid that if I ever let my anger out, it would be so powerful it would devastate everything around me."* These are the people who may explode with anger one day.

Low Self-Esteem

With their transformation of hurts to anger blocked, some may hold on to the hurt and assume that somehow they deserve it. This dynamic is often true of adults who as children were repeatedly hurt physically or psychologically by a parent or caregiver. This may be true even when they don't have any idea how they came to deserve the hurt. They blame themselves, but don't have a clear picture of what could be done in the future to avoid similar hurts. As a result, they have feelings of worthlessness and hopelessness. They feel they don't deserve affection, success, or happiness, though they may have some joys in their lives at times.

The key to avoiding this self-degradation and low self-esteem is to focus on the future instead of the past. The difference is "next time" versus "if only" or "damn me." The *next time* leads to a recognition of learning, of knowing what to do next time, which in turn generates a sense of mastery and feelings of adequacy and hope.

Self-Righteousness

Children may recognize that the hurts are not justified. They conclude that the adults are wrong. Even without character assassination statements, they often use the psychological mechanism of reaction formation—substitution of a painful idea with the opposite idea—to deal with low self-esteem:

"I am good. My heart is in the right place. The adults are wrong about me! They are jerks! I am smarter and better than they are."

The "better" may become self-righteousness.

As teens they might adopt a religion or belief system different from their parents', or reject their family's values and lifestyle. This has within it an expression of hostility to the parents. These teens are especially vulnerable to peer pressure and risky behavior.

Depression

Some people who think they have repeatedly suffered unjust hurts are chronically depressed. Unhappy and frustrated, they give little joy to those around them. Often they feel helplessness at being unable to control their lives. They usually don't strive, and they may even sabotage themselves when good things are about to happen.

Clinical depression is deeper, more constant, and longer lasting than is depression in the social sense. Clinical depression can affect almost every body system. In addition to feelings of worthlessness and hopelessness, there may be a lower level of energy and a loss of sexual interest. These people may have difficulty concentrating and making decisions. Depression can affect sleep patterns, eating habits, and menstrual cycles. Thoughts of death, dying, and suicide may form a constant backdrop to other thoughts.

Like emotional withdrawal, depression can be used to avoid anticipated hurt, a way to show vulnerability and thereby stop an attack. (See Chapter 4) One message sent by these individuals is: "I am no threat to you or anyone; hence, there is no need to even consider me, let alone hurt me." Another message is: "I am already down and vulnerable; you wouldn't kick someone who is down, would you?"

Resentment and Defiance

With some justification, depression has been called anger turned on the self. Anger has been called depression turned outward. At adolescence, the child who has been withdrawn or depressed may become overtly resentful and defiant—especially if his/her hurts have been unpredictable, inconsistent, and capricious attitudes or acts on the part of the parents. Often this resentfulness, negativity, and defiance are generalized to everyone in a position of authority.

From the parents' viewpoint, the standard of appropriate parental control for adolescents tends to be the level of control they experienced from their own parents. However, the adolescent may see this as over-controlling. As judged by the adolescent, the standard of appropriate parental control is that degree she/he perceives is exercised by the parents of her/his friends.

When one's own parents are perceived as being uncommonly strict, it raises a number of issues in the teen's mind: respect, trust, autonomy, and whether the parents want him/her to have fun with friends. These issues affect the perceptions of the teen's peers, and often result in peer pressure for the teen to rebel. The teen's response to the pressure affects his/her popularity and sense of identity. Each of these issues has its own hurt and the feeling that is associated with it. These thoughts and feelings are exacerbated if the teen perceives the parental decisions are capricious or based on how the parent feels at the moment. The situation is even worse if the teen perceives the parent is motivated by a personal need to dominate. This often results in defiant behavior toward the parent.

On the other hand is the adolescent who sees her/his parents as not being involved with her/his activities, or too lenient, not caring enough to set limits. This adolescent may create tests of parental love by getting into difficulty with school authorities or police, or by acting out sexually. These acts are also expressions of hostility and autonomy, as well as tests of love.

Some parents are so frustrated about setting teenager limits that they alternate from trying to control—which the teen sees as over-control—to giving up all attempts to set limits, which is seen as not caring. The parents may be fairly consistent in their limit setting, but the teen may perceive an alternation of parental attitudes.

These two contradictory perceptions of parental attitudes don't cancel each other out in the teen's mind, but are additive to the hurt of feeling unloved. In response, the teen may become depressed with suicidal thoughts or may become resentful and hostile with thoughts of injuring someone else—even the parents.

√   *Adolescents are very astute at discerning which behaviors will bug (hurt) their parents most.*

The parents would do well to catch this situation in its verbal stage. Parents may try once or twice to deal with the situation by setting time aside to listen to their teen's grievances with patience and concern in spite of some hostility. The parents need to be willing to modify their own attitudes and behavior. Alternatively, the parents may need to seek professional help.

The teen may have a mixture of both depression and hostility. When this mix occurs, the parents are in a *no win* position with their teenager. The parents tend to feel confused, frustrated, and impotent. These feelings, in turn, often generate anger toward the teen. This parental anger tends to confirm the adolescent's view that she/he is not loved by the parents. A mixture of depression and hostility is usually an indication for professional help.

Adults may carry sensitivities from their teenage years into intimate relationships. Without the skills to communicate in intimate relationships the individual is apt to feel not adequately considered and is subject to re-experience many situations they suffered with their parents. They may again feel unloved, controlled, and dominated. Their responses are likely to be the same: depression and/or resentment manifest by passive-aggressive behavior including sarcasm, cutting remarks, sniping, foot dragging, and subterfuge.

Retaliation

Feelings of hurt that remain unresolved often lead to retaliation. Retaliation is really a subcategory of anger, but it is so common that it is dealt with separately here. The purpose of retaliation is to make the other person feel hurt. It can take many forms of hurt or put-down. Sometimes the need to retaliate is unconscious. At other times it can be deliberate, either in taking advantage of an opportunity or actually planning it. The retaliation may be subtle or obscure, or it may be open and easily recognized. Perpetrators may conceal their identity or may announce their authorship.

> ■   *One of our patients could not stand up to any other adult. He regained his feeling of mastery through retaliation, but carried it to an extreme. Listening to his statement of what he did when he got hurt was a most chilling experience. With a deadpan, matter-of-fact expression, he replied, "I don't get hurt, and I don't get angry. I just get even."*

Although intellectually he recognized his hurt and his anger, emotionally he did not let himself experience these feelings. Instead, he went straight to revenge. He never communicated his feeling of hurt. There was nothing others could "read" that would act as feedback.

√ *People seem to need to retaliate.*

Most acts of retaliation between a couple are obvious, first by the fact that you experience a hurt, and second by your evaluation of the other's intent, either conscious or unconscious. Beware of hurts masquerading as jokes. They are still hurts, and your partner did or should have foreseen it would hurt you. Sexual put-down jokes are often retaliation for hurts or unmet expectations in the sexual relationship. Therefore, sometimes the honest answer to "Did you mean to hurt me?" will be "I wasn't aware of it, but I guess I did."

Then the question becomes: "Where or when did you get hurt that led to the need to retaliate?" An individual may start the inquiry with: "That really hurts. Are you retaliating for something I said, or did that hurt you earlier?"

If one partner goes into a tirade because of a hurt or to ward off an anticipated hurt, a common reaction is for the other also to go into a tirade or to retaliate. Sometimes it is beneficial to let the tirade run its course before asking the question. However, partners who remain cool can move toward resolution by saying something such as: "Hey, I hear a lot of anger. Where did you get hurt? I haven't intended to hurt you or put you down."

√ *Curiosity and inquiry without an edge to the voice are better responses to tirades than aggression.*

Occasionally a couple gets caught up in a spiral of hurt-anger-retaliation with intentional hurt. The spiral can be broken by directing the discussion back to the first hurt either had since they were feeling OK about each other.

"How did this get started?" Or, "My first hurt occurred when _____. Did you have a hurt before that?" Or, "How did this get so out-of-hand? I've had enough; give me a moment to figure out where my first hurt was. I was feeling close to you until _____."

Frustration

Anger arises from some kind of hurt or many hurts—put-downs, rejection, being dumped on or ignored or not considered, etc. Some people feel that frustration is an exception to this statement.

We view frustration as a subcategory of hurt. The hurt of frustration is the hurt of an expectation that is chronically unfulfilled. If the expectation was of oneself, it results in a feeling of inadequacy. If the expectation was of someone else, it results in feeling unloved or insignificant.

Anger

Whenever anger arises, either in yourself or in your partner, the appropriate question is: "Where is the hurt?" In some cases the answer will come easily. At other times the question must be pursued:

"When did the hurt occur? What was hurtful in what I said? What expectation resulted in frustration?"

Perhaps you'll discover it was a miscommunication, or an expectation that was outside either your or your partner's conscious awareness. Once you name the expectation, it may be blatantly obvious that it is unrealistic. At other times, the expectation may seem very sound, a basic right. The hurt may be further complicated when you realize this expectation was often unfulfilled, resulting in chronic feelings of hurt and anger over these issues.

Feelings of hurt and anger occur in even the best of relationships. No one is perfect. Avoidance of hurt is only part of the answer; dealing adequately with the feeling of hurt or anger when it does occur is also essential.

Anger can be used in several additional ways to transform feelings of hurt:

- To avoid looking at yourself and having to recognize you made a mistake which resulted in feelings of self-blame or inadequacy.

- To interrupt any continuation of the hurt—either physical or psychological—conveying the hurt's depth and intensity.

The more mature and secure you are, the higher your threshold of hurt that immediately triggers anger. However, because so many people in our society short-circuit hurt directly to anger, anger must be taken to have one of the same functions as recognition of a hurt—namely, "the signal function."

Anger is emotional feedback to yourself and others that something negative has happened from the outside. This function is like the red indicator light on the instrument panel of a car: something is wrong. Whenever you hear expressions of anger from your partner, you have the option of responding as though she/he had said, "Ouch!" with significant intensity.

It is important to mentally review the recent interaction prior to the recognition of the anger to locate the hurt. Partners need to look at the hurt together and, if possible, to identify what each can do to avoid hurt the next time a similar situation arises.

As a transformation of hurt, expressions of anger are a means of self-assertion, thereby nullifying the feeling of being put down or being placed in a subordinate position. Anger can also be used to avoid anticipated hurts. The best defense is a good offense, and anger is that offense. Expressions of anger can be intimidating. Often the other person will drop the issue because of the intimidation, a desire not to put the relationship at greater risk, or because the issue is not worth it. In this sense, expressing anger is also a means of controlling and dominating the situation, if not the other person.

A supplemental discussion of components of anger and its vicissitudes, including displaced anger, is presented in Chapters 15, 16, & 17.

Domination-Control

Feelings of hurt—actual as well as anticipated—can be transformed to domination-control. "If I have power and am in control, then I can control my life and I will be much less likely to be hurt." This transformation of hurts may become a pervasive habit; nobody wants to mess with "the meanest S.O.B. in the valley."

This dynamic may be the major effect of anger. Sometimes partner **A** will break off a relationship preemptively when she/he senses that partner **B** is about to do the same thing. In that way, **A** feels in control.

■   *After six months of marriage, the husband awoke on Saturday and felt angry toward his wife, and told her so.*

"Why? What have I done or not done?"

"That's part of my problem; I can't think of anything. There is no hurt. I am just aware of the feeling."

"What do you want me to do?"

"Just give me some time and space to figure this out. During that time my reactions are apt to be screwball."

"OK, I can do that."

Two to three hours later he went to her and said, "I've got it figured out. This relationship is just too good to last. I feel it will blow up on me, so the anger was a way to take control by blowing it up myself. In a twisted way, I felt I would hurt less."

"Well, what are you going to do?"

"I'm going to be vulnerable and do all I can to maximize the relationship. I can pick myself up if it blows, but I'm not going to blow it."

That was over 40 years ago, and the couple is still happily married.

√   **The person who always needs to control is one who doesn't feel enough self-confidence to be vulnerable.**

Revenge, whether clandestine or overt, is intended to engender feelings of superiority, domination, and control while causing feelings of hurt or humiliation in the other, especially by making the other person feel the same hurt experienced by the one seeking revenge—turning the tables, so to speak.

Wife beating is an example of domination and control by making the wife feel physically hurt and humiliated, just as the husband felt psychologically hurt and humiliated.

This domination and control can be displaced to another person—as the school bully does, or to a representative of some group—as a racial, ethnic or gay assault.

√   **A hurt is often the trigger that releases behavior(s) that can be as damaging as a bullet.**

Displaced domination and control are component features of voyeurs, exhibitionists, and rapists. The triggers that release episodes of these behaviors are either hurts—usually humiliation—or the recognition of opportunities to engage in that particular behavior—to act out.   In the latter case, the behavior has become a habit that is reinforced by sexual feelings as well as feelings of domination-control. (See "Allergy" and "Neurotic Anger," Chapters 16 and 20)

Addictions as a Transformation of Hurts

Addictions, especially psychological addictions, have the transformation of feelings of hurt as one of their main causes, either directly or via low self-esteem or depression. For example, some people have a major compulsion to eat whenever they have experienced a hurt or frustration. Consider the following statement by an anonymous sex addict:

■ *"As a teenager I would deal with my feelings and my problems by masturbating whenever I was lonely, confused, anxious, sad, angry, scared, tired, or thought I deserved a reward. My preoccupation with sex continued into college. I dealt with feelings of confusion, frustration, or loneliness by being sexual with someone. As a result, I was having sex with five different women during the week, not a steady sexual relationship with any one of them. Then I'd spend the weekends with my fiancée."* [10]

Communication with the partner is distorted by most addicts' need to keep the fact of their addiction or its extent secret. Further, addicts will say or do almost anything to be able to engage in their addiction the next time. To this end they lie, deceive, act self-righteous, and manipulate their partners. The exception to these generalizations occurs when the partner is aiding and supporting the addiction. (See Chapter 20) □

√ **Human beings are by nature kind and loving, except as a result of unresolved hurts and their transformations.**

IN BRIEF

Hurts are unstable and tend to undergo transformations—immediately or delayed, consciously or out of the individual's awareness—most commonly to one type of the habit patterns: withdrawal, depression, anger, domination, control.

YET TO COME

The next chapter looks at the various components of both appropriate anger and anger gone awry.

---

[10] Anonymous: *What Everyone Needs to Know About Sex Addiction,* CompCare Publishers, Minneapolis, 1989, p7

CHAPTER 15
COMMUNICATION OF ANGER

The facets of anger: "Healthy, appropriate anger," and the anger gone awry.

The feeling of anger is a signal to yourself that something negative has happened from the outside, analogous to an alarm sounding. The expression of anger is a communication to the partner or another person of the same information.

An episode of anger may be viewed in component parts:

- The target, or the person who is causing the hurt;

- The issue or subject of the anger—what the anger is about;

- The depth and intensity of the anger;

- The appropriateness of the expression of anger;

- The effectiveness of its expression; and

- The price of the expression of anger.

The habitual unwillingness to express anger usually gives rise to fantasies of the effects it would have if it were expressed. (See "Martyrs," Chapter 14)

The Target or Addressee

The appropriate target of the anger is the person who caused the hurt. Anger can be misdirected. The classic cartoon example of mis-targeted anger is the individual who is angry at his boss, yet comes home and kicks the dog. Today's counterpart is the individual who, after a frustrating day at the office, comes home and takes the anger out on the spouse or children.

Also, anger that should be targeted to the self may be displaced to the spouse.

■ *While on vacation a couple finds a small glass chandelier in an antique shop. The husband is much more attracted to it than is the wife, but they both agree they like it and decide where it will be hung. Upon getting it home, the husband suspends it by a rope that he holds with one hand, then begins cleaning it with the other. About halfway through the job, the rope slips and the chandelier crashes to the floor, breaking into hundreds of pieces. The husband turns to his wife, who is working on something else nearby, and berates her for not recognizing that he needed help.*

The wife realizes her husband's disappointment and simply says, "I don't think I have that coming. If you feel the same way in half an hour, tell me again and I'll take it seriously." Almost immediately, the husband realizes that he was in the best position to recognize he needed help and could have asked for it. He realizes he has displaced his anger from himself to his wife, and he apologizes. The wife had made allowance for all this and didn't take it seriously, but was prepared to do so if he continued to feel the same way.

The Issue

The issue of the anger should be the same as the issue of the hurt. If the issue of the hurt is telling offensive jokes, then the anger and discussions should be on the jokes and subjects that are connected to the hurt. Don't make put-down remarks to your partner on any other issue(s) to get even just because your partner is vulnerable there.

Don't use sex as a weapon to strike at your partner about a non-sexual issue. It may or may not be true that your hurt is such that there is no way you wish to be close— have sex play— at this time. However, on other occasions you might feel the anger-resentment is superficial, and thus want to reach through the resentment to the person behind the issue. You may wish to use sex to help generate feelings of closeness, to reconnect, and to emphasize that the issue of the hurt is superficial— to put it in perspective.

√ *Keep all expression of anger on target and on the issue of your hurt.*

The response of the patient who stated he expressed anger only by getting even (See "Retaliation," Chapter 14) was unrelated to the issue that caused his hurt. His anger was on target, but off issue. For a discussion of neurotic anger, see "Neurotic Anger," Chapter 16.

Gunny Sacking

Anger can be carried over from one issue to another, even when one individual is the appropriate target for all the issues and the anger they cause. We call this gunny sacking— putting anger in a gunny sack until the sack can't hold any more, then dumping the entire sack load.

The belief that any expression of anger is intrinsically wrong— especially to a loved one— is probably the most common cause of gunny sacking. This belief may or may not have a religious foundation. She/he therefore tends to overlook minor hurts. Unexpressed resentments— anger— tend to fester as readily as they tend to fade. If the minor hurts are frequent, there won't be time for the first hurt and anger to fade before another incident adds to stored hurt-anger. In time, the individual's capacity to store more anger is exceeded, and an explosion occurs. The blast expresses not only the anger appropriate to the most recent incident, but also the dumping of all the stored-up anger. The partner is left confused and bewildered as to how this issue could hold such intensity for a characteristically easy-going spouse.

After a brief period, the individual who was angry realizes all that anger wasn't appropriate to that issue. The resultant feeling of guilt is reinforced by the belief that all anger is bad. Then she/he resolves not to express anger so easily, perhaps thinking, "I'll overlook the next hurt to compensate my partner for this outburst." Unfortunately, this sets up the process to repeat itself. To make matters worse, the targeted partner grows more confused because instances similar to the one that caused the big blow-up are now overlooked. The partner is most apt to try to find an explanation for the occasional blow-ups rather than for the overlooked instances. These guessed-at explanations might include indigestion, pressures at work, chronic worry, hormones, and just plain craziness. Gunny sacking has disrupted the communication feedback system of the issue, as well as its depth and intensity. As a result, the targeted partner is at a complete loss.

In our experience, the most efficient way to deal with gunny sacking is to express little slights and hurts when they occur. This can be balanced by expressing little enjoyments, too. In therapy we often ask if the partner wishes to be told each time something occurs that detracts from the feeling of closeness. Almost invariably, the answer is yes. With this statement, they can both recognize that they want to enhance their own and the partner's happiness. In order to do so each must provide the partner the kind of information she/he would wish to receive.

Depth & Intensity

Anger, in addition to being a signal to the partner, also functions to convey the depth and intensity of dislike and hurt. Just as simply saying "I love you" is rather skimpy for conveying the depth and intensity of a feeling of affection, saying "I don't like _____" often fails to fully express the depth and intensity of the hurt-anger.

√ *The larger the repertoire for expressing hurt-anger, the more mature and better adjusted the individual.*

Generally, small hurts give rise to smaller angry feelings than do larger hurts. If the anger is not proportional to the hurt, the communicative function of anger is impaired. The partner who wishes to enhance the other's happiness is apt to become confused or to misunderstand the other's depth and intensity about the issue, and to construe the other's priorities incorrectly. As couples improve their hurt-anger communication in therapy, it is not uncommon for one partner to say something like: "I know you have told me that before, but I didn't know you felt that strongly about it."

There are people who can't, or who have major difficulty, expressing any anger, and there are those who can only express anger at the **9–10** level. (See "Emotional Denial," "Martyrs," and "Low Self-Esteem," Chapter 14)

Clear Communication

In therapy, we ask people how they express hurt-anger to their partners. Most people have several ways of doing so. It is not uncommon for them to believe they are expressing hurt-anger in one manner, only to find that it is not recognized by their partners:

> *"I know you are angry when you say so, and when you are unusually silent, but I didn't realize you are angry when you go to the basement to work out on the punching bag."*
>
> *"Oh, not always. Not when I put on my sweats. But when I go down in my street clothes and punch the bag, it's usually because I'm mad."*
>
> *"I thought you were just stealing a moment to have fun."*

Usually more revealing about a couple's hurt-anger communication is the sequence that starts with the following questions:

1. "Of all the times you get hurt-angry, what percentage of the time do you think your partner is aware of it?"

2. "Of all the times you recognize your partner's hurt-anger, about what percentage of the time are you quite sure of the issue without having to guess?"

Often these are surprisingly low percentages. How can anyone expect to enhance the partner's happiness—by being empathic or supportive or taking some corrective action—if the disturbing issue is known only 50% of the time? The basic assumption is that your partner wants and needs that feedback, even though it is negative. And, in love, your partner is entitled to that feedback.

Appropriateness of Expressing Anger

The expression of anger needs to be adjusted to be appropriate to your relationship and situation. For example, the appropriate expression of anger will vary if:

- Your target is your 15-year-old son or daughter, your sibling, your friend, your boss, your elderly parent, your partner and lover, or the police officer who has just stopped you.

- The other's mental or physical state is poor, and whether that state is temporary or permanent.

- Where you are and who else is present; e.g., in the privacy of your own home, as a guest at a party, or in a public place such as a restaurant. Can you delay the expression of your anger?

Effectiveness of Expressing Anger

What is the best way to express anger to achieve the goal you want? Perhaps your goal is to redress the issue by motivating the other person to modify the past action that triggered your anger. Is your expression of anger apt to achieve this goal? Or your goal may be for the other person not to repeat the behavior that triggered your anger. Perhaps your goal is to establish simple dominance over the other person. Anger may be used to stop a conversation. If words were used instead of emotion, the message would be: "I really don't want to talk about that."

√ *Effectiveness of the expression of anger is to be judged by the success of obtaining the result you desire.*

Sometimes you will realize not expressing anger is the best path to obtaining the result you want.

The Price of Expressing Anger

The price to be paid for physically expressing anger may very well be police arrest on a charge of battery, or spousal or child abuse. Most of those arrested realize this too late. The message the police and judicial system hope to get across is: "The price is too high." Similarly, the price may be too high to vent your anger or frustration by breaking your own things or by hitting the wall with your fist. We know of men who have broken their hand in this manner.

Even when the expression of anger is confined to words, the long-term effects may exact a price you feel is too great. One irate father called his 15-year-old daughter a whore because she was out till 2:00 A.M., three hours after her curfew. We submit that no reflective person would think that these words will result in the daughter wanting to please her father by coming home prior to her curfew. Not only was the father's anger ineffective, but the long-term effect on their relationship—and maybe on his relationship with his wife—was too high a price to pay. Some punishment was probably in order, *after* listening to her account of the evening.

Never set punishment in anger. Rather, say something like: "You have a punishment coming, but right now I am too angry to trust my own judgment. I will set it tomorrow after I have calmed down." When a child's punishment is set with anger, the child will likely hear it as lack of love rather than your dislike of the behavior. The price of your child feeling chronically unloved-unlovable, with a tendency to withdraw, is probably a price you won't want to pay.

An excellent corrective message was delivered to a nine-year-old by the ward staff in the University of Michigan Children's Psychiatric Hospital. The boy had smeared finger paint on the tiled wall. The staff member said: "You are OK, but that paint has to go. Now go get a bucket of water and sponge and wash it off."

Trying to hurt your partner in anger, you may say things that will cause long-term loss of respect for you, or a decrease in love, or a partner who is much more reluctant to be spontaneous or tell you what she/he is feeling. She/he may withdraw. Once spoken, statements cannot be unsaid, but they may be forgiven—especially following a sincere apology.

Needing to retaliate by hurting someone else, some people also hurt themselves in the process, sometimes most severely. Often this type of retaliation is thought out ahead of time. The result was foreseeable, though perhaps not foreseen. Sometimes it seems the retaliator realized she/he would hurt the self along with the partner. Some of these individuals are so guilty about expressing hurt-anger by retaliation that they have to build in their own punishment or penance.

When your communication of a hurt(s) is ignored or minimized, or when you believe your partner hasn't gotten the depth and intensity of your other messages, the expression of anger can be quite healthy. Get your message through!

In short, keep your anger on target and on issue. Keep your anger proportional to your hurt. Keep your anger appropriate to your relationship with that person. These elements are controlled much more easily if you can choose the time and place to express your anger, as opposed to anger that arises spontaneously from an ongoing discussion. Remember there is always a price to pay for expressing: usually a few moments of unpleasantness and stress in the relationship, but the price can be greater. You can keep your price low by remembering your goal is not to hurt your partner—as you have been hurt—but to correct the issue. Try to stay with "I sentences." Not:

> *"Damn you. Why won't you ever listen to me? You are nothing but an inconsiderate, arrogant, self-centered son of a bitch!"*

We consider the last sentence psychological abuse. It is better to say:

> *"Damn it. I can't seem to get through to you. What do I have to do to get your attention about this?"*

After an episode of anger, mentally evaluate each component as described earlier. What might you have done differently to increase the effectiveness of expressing your anger? □

√   *The larger your repertoire for expressing anger, the greater the likelihood of choosing the most appropriate and effective method of expression.*

IN BRIEF

For the communication of anger to be useful and not have unwanted side effects, its expression needs to be controlled and modulated. Abandoning control in the expression of anger is as immature as a temper tantrum. Such expressions of anger can be dangerous and destructive to your surroundings, to the target of your anger, and to your long-term happiness.

YET TO COME

Many relationships can benefit from both partners examining and discussing how each communicates issues of hurt-anger. The following "Hurt-Anger Assessment" provides simple questions the two of you can answer separately before comparing and evaluating what you have learned. Many couples are surprised by the results, and they discover areas where they can improve their effectiveness in communicating these issues.

Sometimes the issue(s) that generate the frustration and anger are not clear to you or your partner. Sometimes the two of you don't agree on them. Sometimes the apparent issue(s) are intertwined with obscure or more fundamental ones. Chapters 16–20 deal with these aspects of troublesome issues to help you and your partner identify what you two are struggling with.

HURT-ANGER ASSESSMENT

This is to help you and your partner evaluate your communication of hurt-anger, and to identify specific areas that need clearer communication. Each of you should answer the questions separately, on your own sheets of paper, without seeing each other's responses. If both of you are looking at the questions at the same time, be careful not to make remarks or otherwise prompt each other's answers.

Many of the questions call for quantitative responses. To derive the most benefit from this exercise, you and your partner need to agree in advance what kind of scale you will both use. You may adopt a scale from 1 to 5 or from 1 to 10, or you may estimate percentages, or use common fractions, e.g., one-third. However, avoid phrases such as "seldom," "a lot," or "some" unless the two of you assign these labels to your scale just for convenience.

After each of you has completed the assessment, both of you together should compare your answers using "Evaluating Hurt-Anger Assessment" that follows.

1.   Forms of hurt-anger messages:

1—S1:   **Your sending:** List all the different ways you send messages to your partner that you feel hurt or anger toward your partner.

1—R1:   **Your receiving:** List all the different ways you receive messages of hurt or anger from your partner.

2.   Do you fail to send messages?

2—S1:   **Your sending:** Of all the times you are hurt by your partner, how often do you communicate that fact to your partner?

2—S2:   **Your not sending:** What are your reasons for not communicating a feeling of hurt or anger? Please list all your reasons.

3.   Intimidation:

3—S1:   **Your hesitation about sending:** Of all the times you feel hurt-angry at your partner, how often are you afraid of having a serious disagreement with your partner because of his/her likely response(s)?

3—S2:   **Your sending:** Do you use anger or other responses to intimidate your partner's communication of his/her hurt-anger?

3–R1:   **Your receiving:** Do you believe your partner uses intimidation to stifle your communication of hurt or anger?

4.   The target:

4–S1:   **Your sending:** Of all the times you *send* a hurt-anger message, how often do you think you are clear as to who the target is?

4–S2:   **Your sending:** How often does your partner ask who your target is?

4–S3:   **Your sending:** How often do you "blow off steam" out of frustration that is not directed at a specific person?

4–S4:   **Your sending:** Do you think this (4–S3) confuses your partner?

4–R1:   **Your receiving:** Of all the times you *receive* a hurt-anger message from your partner, how often does the message clearly indicate who the target is intended to be?

4–R2:   **Your receiving:** When the intended target of your partner's message is not clear, how often do you ask?

4–R3:   **Your clarifying upon receiving:** How often does your partner "blow off steam" without a specific person in mind?

4–R4:   **Your reaction upon receiving:** When your partner blows off steam (4–R3), how often do you tend to take this anger personally?

4–R5:   **Your coping upon receiving:** What are the ways you cope with this (4–R4)?

5.   The issue:

5–S1:   **Your sending:** Of all the hurt-anger messages you *send* your partner, how often do you think you are *not clear* about the cause of your hurt or anger?

5–S2:   **Your sending:** How often does your partner ask you to be specific about your issue?

5–R1:   **Your receiving:** Of all the times you *receive* a hurt-anger message from your partner, how often do you find yourself doing some guessing about the issue that caused the hurt?

5–R2:   **Your receiving:** When you are not clear about the issues that cause your partner's hurt, how often do you:

- Ask for clarification?

- Just guess at the cause?

- Try to ignore the communication?

- Other; please specify.

6.   Depth and intensity:

6–S1:   **Your sending:** How often do you *send* messages *without* what you believe to be clear indications of your depth and intensity?

6–R1:   **Your receiving:** How often do you *receive* messages from your partner *without* clear indications of depth and intensity?

6–R2:   **Your receiving:** Of all these times (6–R1), how often do you ask for and receive a clear indication of your partner's depth and intensity?

7.   Taking the hurt-anger message seriously:

7–S1:   **Your partner's response to your sent message:** Of all the times you *express* hurt-anger to your partner, how often does your partner take your message as seriously as you would like?

7–S2:   **Partner's response:** On all the issues of significant depth and intensity, how often does your partner continue the discussion until the issues are resolved?

7–R1:   **Your receiving:** Of all the times you *receive* a message of hurt-anger from your partner, how often do you take it proportionally to the depth and intensity you received—as seriously as your partner intended?

7–R2:   **Your response upon receiving:** On issues of significant depth and intensity for you, how often are you willing to continue the discussion until the issue is resolved?

8.   Effectiveness:

8–S1:   **Your sending:** Of all the times you *send* a hurt-anger message, how often do you feel your message is effective—that you achieve your desired goal(s)?

8–R1:   **Your receiving:** Of all the times you *receive* a hurt-anger message, how often do you feel your partner's message is effective—that your partner's goals are achieved?

End of Assessment

Now compare and discuss your answers using the following evaluation:

Evaluating Hurt-Anger Assessment

After both of you have answered all the questions, compare and discuss your responses, paying particular attention to the areas highlighted below:

1.   Forms of hurt-anger messages:

Compare your answers about **Sending**, your 1–S1, with your partner's answers about **Receiving**, 1–R1, and vice versa.

Is there a form of sending that is not being received? If the receiver's list contains a form of hurt-anger message that is not on the sender's list, it means either: 1) the sender overlooked that form of message and now can acknowledge it, or 2) the receiver is getting a hurt-anger message when none was intended. Either the sender should modify the behavior that is being misinterpreted so its intent is clear to the receiver, or the receiver should discount that form of message or re-interpret it the way the sender says she/he intends.

If the sender's list contains a form of message that is not on the receiver's list, the receiver may: 1) acknowledge it when it is called to his/her attention, or 2) recognize that the sender is hurt-angry more often than the receiver was aware. Again, either party can adapt. Perhaps the sender can use a different mode, or perhaps the receiver can interpret that behavior as a hurt-anger message.

2 & 3. Failure to send hurt-anger messages; Intimidation:

If one or both partners are not sending messages because the hurt-anger is of a low level, especially if both of you are busy, that is understandable. Try to determine the cut-off point based on the scale you both agree to, e.g., hurts or anger at or below **3** on a scale of **1–10**. Seek agreement with each other on whether or not you want to know of any below that level. We recommend you begin by communicating those that are just below the cut-off point that either of you has been using.

If the cut-off point is in the medium or high range, e.g., anything **5** or above, this is a danger sign. We have seen several cases where one partner put off exposing hurt until the youngest child graduated from high school, only to find out that the partner was unaware of the hurt and was quite willing to change. Don't let this happen in your relationship.

If you don't send hurt-anger messages out of fear of intimidation, either because your partner gets angry at you or just "blows off steam," inform your partner. Ask if she/he would like to change this interaction pattern; again, it is dangerous for the relationship.

4.   The target:

Compare your **Sending** answers, 4-S1, to your partner's **Receiving** answers, 4-R1, and vice versa.

It is unpleasant, if not stressful, to be around someone who is angry and blowing off steam. If there is any ambiguity about the intended target, it is natural for your partner to take the anger personally. If you do tend to take it personally, your partner needs to be aware of this fact. The way to avoid this is to ask who the intended target is.

5.   The issue:

Compare your answers in **Sending**, 5−S1, with your partner's answers to **Receiving**, 5−R1.

Recognize that without the issue being clear, the hurt-anger message is very apt to be taken personally. Anger is not likely to be effective if the issue is not clear. Ask.

6 & 7. Depth and intensity; Taking messages seriously:

Compare your answers for 6−S1 to your partner's for 6−R1, and vice versa.

If there is the slightest doubt in your mind about your partner's depth and intensity for a given message, ask, "How seriously do your want/need me to take this?" Don't discount each other's depth and intensity. Habitually belittling or making jokes of things that are serious to the other courts relationship disaster in the long-term. Sometimes the original issue may be compounded by messages not being taken seriously, which may be a deeper hurt. (See Chapters 16 & 17)

8.   Effectiveness:

Serious hurt-anger messages that are not resolved as miscommunication should result in future behavior modification by at least one, if not both, of you. □

CHAPTER 16
PERSISTENT TROUBLESOME ISSUES

Some old issues never die because of ambivalent communication, depth and intensity not clearly communicated, affixing blame, neurotic reactions, or another underlying issue.

When the same hurt-anger issue recurs over and over again, it has probably never been clearly identified, discussed, and resolved.

Ambivalence

An issue may remain chronic because you and/or your partner have not recognized your own ambivalence about it. As a result, conflicting messages are sent. One might convey the attitude: "It's the hours you (or I) work," but conflict it with: "I am unwilling to give up any of the money we make." It is an immature reaction of wanting to have your cake and eat it, too. The fact can't be accepted that giving up one is the price of keeping the other.

The solution begins with recognizing the contradiction. The partner who first recognizes the ambiguity may say, "I'm getting double messages from you. I hear you say X and then I hear Y. They seem to be contradictory."

You can have ongoing ambivalent feelings about an issue, but you cannot expect to be taken seriously by your partner if you consistently express a desire to live in two different conditions. A conscious choice needs to be made, and you need to strive to accept its price without complaining. The most common problem is that the depth and intensity have not been adequately weighed. Sometimes the difficulty of a recurrent hurt-anger issue is a falsely held philosophical or religious view: "If you really love me, you will know what I want," or, "All anger is wrong and sinful." Hence, even experiencing the feeling of anger produces guilt. Even the hurt-anger that was appropriate to your partner is turned back on you. This often leads to depression and, in the process, fails to accurately and clearly communicate your depth and intensity about the issue.

In our practice we saw cases of single-issue hurt-resentment in twenty- and thirty-year marriages where the wife had seldom clearly represented herself. She had tolerated the relationship, usually until the youngest child left home. Characteristically, for these marriages, the husband rated the marriage "satisfactory," if not "good."

■   *One woman who held both of the above philosophical concepts filed for divorce shortly after their youngest child entered college. She complained that her husband had never helped her the first hour or two after coming home from work, that in fact he expected her to wait on him. She had resented him and his attitude for 23 years. He was surprised that she wanted a divorce. Thinking they had a good marriage, he was astonished at the reason for her resentment, and more specifically, that she had never said anything. The wife felt he should have known that she was fatigued at those times and therefore should not have added to her burden by making requests of her.*

The examples she offered were requests to bring him the paper, fix a drink for him, etc. He said he had not given those a second thought, and could have done them himself. He pointed out a number of things he did for her and them later in the evening, mentioning their enjoyable social life, vacations, gifts he had given her, and their sex life. She acknowledged those were gratifying, but that they didn't compensate for the other. She felt it was wrong to get angry, and she was apprehensive about verbalizing her needs to him.

As the wife begins to express herself, she finds that her husband is considerate, and he makes a number of changes. Paradoxically, the more willing he is to change, the more clearly she realizes she could have changed the relationship years ago, had she been willing to risk verbalizing her hurts and her needs.

√ **Anger that is diffuse rather than focused contaminates everything around it.**

Some people in similar situations let go of the past and move full force to maximize present enjoyment. Others become resentful, realizing the enormity of their loss of enjoyment, satisfaction, and happiness over the years. They may aim their resentment and anger at society, at themselves, and/or at their partners. Rather than putting their energies into the present and the future, they may become obsessed with the past. These people seem to need to dig up each hurt, express it to their partner, have them acknowledge it, and say what they will do differently in the future. Expressed in another way: Their anger is diffuse rather than focused, and it contaminates everything around them.

Blame

Some people want to affix blame and look for some kind of compensation from their partners. These old "bad debts" either must be:

- Consolidated, then settled through an agreement involving very specific actions,

- Written off as uncollectible so the relationship can be restarted with a clean slate and the commitment to communicate hurts precisely and promptly (the emotional equivalent of a "cash and carry" basis), or

- Acknowledged as unresolvable so the relationship can be ended.

Some individuals seem more concerned about working to produce a feeling that they deserve to be happy than about actually working to create happiness. If you attempt to affix most or all of the blame on your partner, your partner will likely sense this and become defensive by taking the offense in trying to affix the blame back on you. All attempts to affix blame sabotage the resolution of the issues. What each of you needs to focus on is how you can change the relationship in the mutually desired direction for the present and the future. Sometimes this may be direct change or changing something that makes it easier for the partner to change. The important question is: "Am I doing everything I reasonably can to effect the changes I/we want?"—not how fast the partner is changing.

√ *Do everything you reasonably can to effect the change you want. Blame only enters the picture with separation or divorce.*

Trying to assign blame is a waste of time in an ongoing and committed relationship for two reasons:

- In any successful intimate relationship, over time there are two winners or losers: there is no such thing as one winner and one loser.

- Where blame is appropriately assigned, there is invariably a "sandwich effect" of alternating layers of blame.

Sandwiched Layers of Blame &

Opportunities to Alter the Outcome

It is imperative that feelings of anger be acknowledged to yourself and your partner, and that the triggering hurt be clearly identified and communicated. The deeper the hurt, the more intense is the anger. Each person is the world authority on his/her own hurt, so the feelings need to be accepted non-judgmentally. Then steps can be taken to resolve the current hurt and to change this recurrent scenario.

■ *A couple had recurrent problems in social situations. The man would become engrossed in conversation, and the wife would feel ignored by him. She would leave his side and begin talking with others. He perceived this as flirting with other men, and thus would become jealous. At home afterward they would argue that each was ignoring the other, and as the accusations flew back and forth, each felt resentful that their hurts were being ignored. She would vent her hurt and anger by calling him names. Unbeknown to her, the names she used were similar to those the man's father and older sister had called him in situations where he felt completely defenseless. Anger escalated to physical abuse.*

Now let us look at the sandwiched layers and consider what each could do at various points.

- When she feels ignored because he becomes engrossed in conversation, she could join in, touch her husband's arm to draw his attention to her, move partially to stand in front of him, or say *Ouch!* and take the other steps previously described.

- When he sees his wife talking to other men—flirting, in his mind—he can recall her stated feelings and invite her into his conversation. Or he can touch her and in some way turn his attention to her. If he squeezes her hand, he acknowledges his jealousy; and when she squeezes back, she acknowledges his message and the jealousy will fade.

- The next opportunity to change the scenario is when they get home. The use of **I** sentences prevents name-calling. The couple needs to back up their discussion to the first hurt either of them had that evening, describe their feelings, and state their intents. Recognizing and protecting the other's sensitivities and vulnerabilities, they can review the scenario of the evening, reinforce the understanding, and develop code words for future use. She can avoid calling him names. If she doesn't, he can bring it to her attention. He can shout *Stop!* or leave the house before the situation becomes physical.

Allergy

His reaction to being called "those names" resembles an allergy. In this case, it is an idiosyncratic response to what is normally just an irritant. It originates in past sensitivity. The individual is aware of the similarities of these situations and of his/her responses. Like other allergies, it represents a vulnerability. Hence, like with other vulnerabilities, it behooves the partner to protect the individual, the same as if the antigen (the substance that triggers the allergic response) were house dust or cat hair. Therapy can partially desensitize the individual to the antigen so the names don't trigger the vehement anger that was associated with his childhood feelings of impotence. In so doing, the old script of intense anger can be changed.

Neurotic Reactions

Anger may occur as a neurotic reaction, which is a set of thoughts and feelings that arise from someone's unconscious past experience(s) but that is triggered (or re-experienced) inappropriately in the current situation. One or more aspects of the current situation are unconsciously identified with aspects of a past traumatic experience, and the individual reacts as though she/he was actually reliving the past original situation.

The hallmarks of neurotic reactions are:

- Arguments arising from neurotic hurts are usually fairly frequent and occur at quasi-regular intervals.

- They are intense, regardless of the subject of the argument, which may be trivial.

- The words you and your partner use in the argument are fairly consistent, and not quite appropriate to the current situation. There may be a change in the sound of the individual's voice.

- The emotions generated are the same from one argument to the next, regardless of the content.

- The psychological connection with the original traumatic situation is unconscious.

Actually, the individual may unconsciously set up a current situation out of a desire to relive the original traumatic situation and have it come out differently—a way for that individual to triumph instead of being hurt. This is called repetition compulsion, and it accounts for the periodic need to relive the situation at intervals. It also accounts for the similarity in the words used and any change in voice. These original traumatic events usually occurred in childhood or adolescence and were repressed—pushed out of one's recallable memory for some compelling reason. An example is the child who is sexually abused by a parent. The memory may be repressed in order to preserve the dependent relationship with the parent, or to keep the parents from fighting or divorcing. Sex play as an adult with a partner may trigger the same emotional response.

Often in repeating the original trauma, the individual inadvertently sets up the situation in a way that results in it still being traumatic rather than triumphant. In the following example, the gender roles could be reversed:

■ *Pat was verbally abused by her father. She tried repeatedly to win his love, to no avail. She chooses a mate who is somewhat distant or standoffish. As a result of being neglected as a child, he carries a fear that those he loves may neglect or leave him. This anticipation prevents him from getting too close so he won't hurt too much when the one he loves ignores or leaves him. While courting, the fact that they separated by going to their own homes at night created the distance he needed. Now he creates the distance by withdrawing or by making verbal put-downs. Either of these actions triggers his wife's feelings of losing his love; she tries harder to create closeness, which drives him further away.*

The relationship has spiraled downward and may continue the downward spiral. He needs to tell her when he needs distance, but first he must recognize the need. She needs to grant him *Alone Time* or distance as described in "Couple Time—Alone Time," Chapter 8, and the vacation vignettes in "Feeling Controlled," Chapter 19. This is her protecting his vulnerability. He needs to be mindful of her vulnerability to being called names or otherwise belittled, and to protect her vulnerability. Further, he needs to select the times he can freely be close to her and to give. He needs to initiate this interaction, giving her his undivided attention and love in ways that are most meaningful to her.

Otherwise, as these dynamics are repeated in future encounters, each individual will examine their interaction and generalize the partner's responses and motivations. He is apt to see her as demanding and controlling, the one who insists he show affection whenever she chooses, in the manner she desires, for as long as she wants. She will tend to see him as unappreciative, one who rejects all the love and affection she has to give. These are the dynamics of rejection-control, which are elaborated in Chapter 19.

Neurotic reactions may also arise from trauma in a prior romantic relationship. In these circumstances, at least part of the traumas may be available to recall, but some aspect of the original trauma or its connection to the present are unconscious. Therefore, just knowing the prior trauma(s), plus having good intentions and will-power, are not necessarily sufficient to eliminate neurotic, unwarranted reactions.

Inappropriate suspicion or jealousies can be very troublesome to a relationship. The root of the problem is often fear of abandonment, which can have its origin in the loss of a parent for an extended period of time, sibling rivalry for a parent's love, or the unexpected abandonment by a prior lover. Therapy may be essential.

Jamie Turndorf in her book[11] lists a number of scars from childhood and adolescence that might resurface in an intimate relationship. She describes many examples of neurotic problems that can produce arguments and hurts. She also describes strategies that a couple can employ that may result in continuing corrective emotional experiences, thereby triumphing over old traumas.

Therapy

There are many different types or forms of therapy. Sometimes therapies with different names are only slightly different, perhaps only in emphasis. However, therapies that are appropriate for the allergic problems will be different from therapies in which a sub-goal is to recover unconscious memories.

Therapy is often necessary to deal with neurotic problems. The first goal of therapy is to identify the triggers that begin the detrimental feelings and thoughts that in turn

---

[11] Turndorf, Jamie: *Till Death Do Us Part (Unless I Kill You First)* , Henry Holt and Co, New York, 1999

lead to inappropriate actions or interactions. Therapy will then try to find ways to prevent the harmful responses. The next goal is to identify the traumatic experiences that sensitized the individual. The therapist will have a variety of techniques to assist you. One is to ask you to describe your feeling as minutely as possible in the current situation, then ask you when you experienced that combination of feelings previously.

To this point we have been using the words "hurt" and "anger" (with their transformations) as though they were pure emotions, and were experienced the same on each occasion. That usage has been adequate for our prior discussions. However, it is not adequate in discussing therapy for neurotic problems. Anger, for example, is seldom "pure;" it has added mixtures of other thoughts and feelings. Just as the source of an oil spill can be traced by identifying the presence of other chemicals and their proportions in the oil, so hurt and anger can be traced back in time by identifying the presence of other feelings that are mixed with the anger, e.g., feelings of inadequacy, a craving for affection, and feeling sorry for yourself. This is one way a patient and therapist can examine past instances and be reasonably sure they are on the trail of the same problem.

Usually there are three to six prior meaningful episodes. Each is explored for its circumstances and the conclusions the individual drew from the experience at the time. Those situations and conclusions need to be re-evaluated and reinterpreted, often in the light of adult understanding, as opposed to the original childhood understanding. The distinctions between the past and the current situation should be recognized, emphasized, and kept in focus. Often a patient needs a sentence—a sort of mantra—to repeat whenever those fears surface from the past. The mantra reinforces the distinction between the past and the present.

Both individuals will need to tolerate the anxiety that has not yet been eliminated in order to avoid the neurotic friction in the relationship. This depends, of course, on recognizing it as neurotic fear.

In seeking reassurance from your partner, try to keep your sentence brief. One might say, "I am having some of that neurotic anxiety. I just need you to let me know that you are still there for me (or still love me), and I'll deal with the rest of it for now."

When that reassurance is received, drop the subject. If you two are physically together, you don't necessarily need to talk about it at this time—just hold each other. If the strength of the feelings doesn't decrease, seek professional help. □

IN BRIEF

The opportunity, and hence the responsibility, for preventing a recurrence alternates from one partner to the other at each level. The appropriate emphasis for each individual is what the self can do to change the relationship in the desired direction. Sometimes this may be direct change or changing something that makes it easier for the partner to change. The question is not how fast the change occurs—or even if the partner does change, but rather, Is the individual doing her/his best to effect the change?

YET TO COME

Sometimes there is a more important but obscure anger issue underlying the obvious surface issue. That obscure issue must be identified and dealt with to establish any reasonable harmony.

CHAPTER 17
COMPOUND ANGER

Lurking behind various episodes of hurt-anger, often there are secondary or even tertiary issues. These have a greater emotional importance to at least one partner than does the surface issue, and they often spawn multiple surface issues.

The previously described techniques for dealing with anger are not sufficient when a second hurt-anger issue becomes interwoven with the original. We call this compound anger.

"You" messages, as opposed to "I" messages, are open to being compounded by the receiver, who may become defensive toward the accusation and the way it is delivered. Using an example from Chapter 2: "Your touch is too rough" may be received as "Don't tell me how to touch. I'm not your puppet. I've had lots of other lovers and none of them ever complained."

The original issue of degree of the quality of touch, level 1, is compounded by the issues of being told how to touch and by feeling like a student with a teacher or a child with a parent, level 2.

In this example, the compounding effect is obvious to both people. With other instances, your partner's thoughts and feelings may not be communicated directly; they might be expressed subtly without your having a clear idea of their source, especially if there is a time lag. Even if you guess the source, you may be reluctant to express a preference in the future, fearing that anything said may further compound the hurts. Then you psychologically retreat to brooding: "You don't care about my sexual enjoyment or my feelings."

Frustrated and sensing your partner's resentment and withdrawal, you may say, "Can't we talk without your taking offence? You are too sensitive," or, "You never want to hear anything I say."

This is level 3 of compounding the issues; both individuals are hurt and frustrated. At this point, you both are very close to using sweeping generalizations, making assumptions about the other's motives and personality. Either or both may resort to deliberately saying hurtful things and engaging in character assassinations.

√ *Using derogatory names is one type of psychological abuse.*

Calling someone derogatory names or using derogatory adjectives is psychological abuse. Name calling usually takes the form of "*You are...*" sentences. It is also a

superiority statement: "I can/will be the authority and tell you who and what you are."
Being called a derogatory name doesn't engender a desire to change behavior; rather, it
provokes an urge to strike back. One way to strike back is to repeat the behavior, since
it bugs the other person so.

The expression of an emotion—including anger expressed by name-calling—tends
to become habitual. Sometimes this encounter ends by one person storming out of the
house to defuse the situation and create personal space. The negative aspect of storming out is that frequently there is nowhere to go, and people are apt to end up in a place
or engage in behavior that is not good for the individual or the relationship. It is almost
never in anyone's best interest to go to a bar when feeling rejected and angry. Alcohol
impairs judgment. Often, opportunities abound for a pick-up.

> √ *It is almost never in anyone's best interest to go to a bar when
> feeling rejected and angry.*

Both partners may recognize the deterioration of their discussion to a critical level.
Both might realize it threatens their relationship. Both are fearful of and on guard
against a recurrence, but they don't know how to avoid it. Perhaps it is better to put up
with an irritating sexual touch. In time, this strategy may lead to the thought: "What
would sex be like with someone who could or would touch me in the manner that
would be most arousing for me?"

Professional Help

At this point the couple often can't untangle the issues; they are afraid to try to talk
with each other for fear of creating additional issues, and both fear they might become
so frustrated and angry that they will say something to deliberately hurt the other.
These are all indications this couple needs to seriously consider seeking professional
therapeutic help. When both partners agree to get such help, some of the tension
between them usually dissipates. It's clear that both value the relationship enough to
spend the time, energy, effort, and money. With the heat off and with the realization
that help is around the corner, sometimes there is a dramatic improvement between
them.

What a Couple With this Problem Can Expect From a Therapist

A good therapist will listen to and validate each partner's hurts, thereby reducing
any guilt. The therapist needs to be sure each patient hears the other's hurt, either by
being present during the original descriptions of the hurts or when summarized by the
therapist and confirmed by the individual's partner.

Next the therapist tries to elicit a statement from each proclaiming underlying love for the other, followed by statements that she doesn't want to reject him or even for him to feel rejected. Similarly, he is able to say he doesn't want to control her. Anything that interferes with the listener believing either of these statements must be identified and dealt with. As the two of you discuss your issue(s) in therapy, the therapist can point out how you fail to communicate and how you get back on track. Also, the therapist will probably suggest ways the two of you can deal with the issue(s).

Another Example

Let's take another common example, where the level 1 issue is the relative need for *Alone Time* versus partner interactive time, but the need for *Alone Time* is not thought to be legitimate, even by the partner needing it. The needs are not intrinsically in conflict; only the timing of attempts to satisfy them is. Often this conflict is most acute as one or both partners arrive home after a day's work. The amount of time and the timing of these needs are somewhat dependent on the intensity of interaction with other adults during time away from home. (See Chapter 8)

It is the person who has minimal interaction at work—perhaps working as a farmer, computer programmer, artistic painter, or night watchman—who will usually need togetherness. She/he also has a high expectation that the partner will or should desire closeness at that time, too. After all, they have been apart eight to ten hours. The one who desires the interaction is most likely the one who will feel rejected. "You care more about TV or that wood-working than about me." Or, "You even throw me out of the kitchen, rejecting my offers to help cook."

In some families with children, this confrontation occurs after completion of the supper chores. Interaction by one parent with young children all day may result in the need for *Alone Time*. The other parent can take the children for an hour or so while the first parent does his/her thing or finishes preparing supper. Being with young children all day may increase the need for meaningful adult-to-adult conversation. Individual **A**, seeking *Alone Time*, senses **B**'s hurt. In spite of feelings of affection, **A** resents having to meet **B**'s needs while not feeling up to it. **A** may eventually feel controlled.

■   *An auto mechanic whose significant other is a nurse feels he is second fiddle to television and to her needlepoint. She gets some quiet time alone while cooking. Occasionally he will come to help—and actually does help—but she finds his presence intrusive, so they agree he will cook sometimes. When he does prepare the meal, he still wants her around to talk to. "She doesn't have to help or do anything. Just be there to talk to." She feels guilty; she doesn't want to meet this need, and she feels inadequate to meet it when she tries. He senses her irritation, feels the relationship is threatened, and tries to do more things together. She experiences this as more control and pulls further away.*

To get away from his constant pressure, she spends more and more time with female friends. He feels further rejection, and says so. Now he feels he is second fiddle to most of her friends. He begins to see all her activities in terms of time together or time apart, and he looks at every interaction as an indication of affection or rejection. She feels like a bug being observed under a microscope, not able to take a breath without his reading something into her behavior.

The simplest issues remain unresolved because of the compounding issue's blocking effect. The couple doesn't recognize this single underlying issue; they only recognize its varied manifestations of level 2, 3, or 4. Hence, they spend enormous amounts of energy on what they perceive as an endless number of issues.

What the Two of You Can Do

Each of you needs to recognize and respect the needs of the other. Together you need to figure out a way to give the wife time alone at the beginning of an evening. The husband can stay in a different room for half an hour or so after she returns from work. If she is ready to interact sooner, she will initiate it. If she is not ready after half an hour, she will say so when he initiates interaction. He can hear her statements as a reflection of the kind of day she has had and not as a basic feeling of wanting to reject him.

She examines how she would like to give to him in a way that is meaningful to her. He had been so busy taking (controlling) that she hasn't felt free to give. As soon as she started to give, he took—like the starving man who was so hungry and impatient that he knocked over the soup kettle before he could be served. She initiates scheduling time together, which he takes as an indication that she wants it. This must be quality time, just being together, with no one else. One partner reading the paper to the other doesn't qualify. (See "Couple Time—Alone Time," Chapter 8)

As a result, he creates room for her to give to him without his taking. She gives, in her own way, and he finds much of it to be more meaningful than his trying to direct. His fear is reduced by what he recognizes as her free giving. The feelings of being chronically rejected dissipate. As he relaxes, he is less concerned about her 45 minutes on the phone with a woman friend.

They also arrange signals they can use in a group to let the other know that "I need more of you now," and to signal "I need more choices now." But they accepted each other's statement(s) of current needs without implications for the foundations of their relationship. □

IN BRIEF

Often the compounding issues are not recognized and the couple thinks they have a myriad of issues. These surface issues cannot be resolved until the underlying compounding issue is recognized and dealt with. Sometimes the resolution of the compounding issue is simple; sometimes its resolution is stubborn. When the underlying issue is resolved, the surface issues and accompanying animosity evaporate.

YET TO COME

The next chapters deal with the most common and detrimental compounding issues: autonomy, one partner feeling rejected while the other feels controlled, and addictions.

CHAPTER 18
AUTONOMY

The feeling or perception of having one's autonomy restricted or infringed upon can be a major compounding issue.

Autonomy is the right to freely express one's identity. Each person needs autonomy in life and in relationships. By autonomy, we mean some areas for which each individual is responsible and is able to do things her/his way. No relationship can survive without mutual respect for both self and partner.

√ *In the division of tasks, who is responsible for what? Don't usurp your partner's responsibilities or prerogatives.*

Implicitly or explicitly, every couple divides the responsibilities for the tasks of their relationship, with a foreperson for each task. We call this position "the Captain" in that task or area. The role of the Captain may be changed by joint decision, but it needs to be clear which partner has the leadership role at any given time or for any given task.

The partner of the Captain is "the Assistant." The Assistant may ask questions and make suggestions, but does not take responsibility for the job unless asked to do so, or unless the couple agrees to a change of roles.

Difficulty over the autonomy issue has resulted in a number of couples seeking therapy.

■ *For eight years of marriage a couple has had a good relationship, despite some friction. The wife has always been responsible for meals. One weekend she and the children go out-of-state to visit her sister. The husband, an efficiency engineer, rearranges everything in the kitchen, putting things "in their proper place" to improve efficiency. His intent is to save his wife time and steps. He fully expects his wife to be grateful; instead, she is incensed. She feels that her authority has been usurped and her autonomy violated. His surprise, prepared in loving consideration, is rejected—and he feels rejected.*

Instead of talking about their intent and their feelings, they both focus on the action. He maintains he arranged things the way they always should have been, pointing to his status as an efficiency expert. She doesn't give a damn about his efficiency of layouts: "It is my kitchen; I'll arrange it as I want!"

At this point she feels controlled, belittled, betrayed, and stripped of her prerogatives and autonomy. She feels she is not respected for her work, her ideas, or her feelings. She refuses to do any work in the kitchen until he apologizes and takes everything out of the cupboards so she can put things away—her way!

He feels that his wife lacks respect for his professional identity as an efficiency engineer, and he refuses to apologize.

For either of them to give in is to lose self-respect.

Examples of other issues with the same dynamics include:

■ *A man who owns a poodle gets married. The bride of four months takes the poodle for a fancy but very different style of hair clip, thinking her husband will appreciate it.*

■ *A wife puts away all her husband's tools and cleans his work area.*

■ *A wife who spends hours each week working in her rock garden asks her husband's help in trimming the largest shrubs to a height of about three feet. He decides that 18 inches would look better, so he prunes them his way.*

In the first one or two instances, intrusion on the partner's autonomy *may* be motivated by attempts to be helpful and considerate. However, when the partner expresses vehement hurt-anger, the individual should learn and avoid future intrusions. In cases that sought therapy with us, the intrusions had continued in spite of the partner's adequate communication of hurt and anger. The intrusions were usually coupled with an attitude of superiority, either: "I know better than my partner the best way to do this!" or, "I have higher standards than my partner." Doing the task the best way and being in control were clearly more important to the intruder than the partner's hurts. The partner clearly recognized hostility in these repeated instances, while the intruder seemed to be either deluded by the rationalization of helpful consideration and superiority, unaware of the hostility in his/her acts, or using the rationalization as a guise to cover conscious hostility. The intruder's actions may be habit that began in childhood as with domination-control, or the intruder had some deep feelings of inferiority and had his/her identity as an adequate person tied up in being "right," always needing to prevail in these situations. The partner also had issues of identity, personhood, and individuality: "I can't just be swallowed up; there has to be some reason for me to be in this relationship."

These examples of violation of another's autonomy clearly show a perverse application of the Golden Rule, *Do unto others as you would have them do unto you.* The intruder may use the rule to further justify his/her attitude and actions.

√ **It is the feeling of self-righteousness with its accompanying attitude of superiority that allows one individual to disregard the vulnerability of another.**

The persistence of such an entrenched attitude of superiority under these circumstances extends to self-righteousness. These two attitudes are the dynamics that are operant in some instances of spousal abuse, and in the atrocities of torture and beating deaths of individuals who are members of a group that is regarded as inferior; e.g., a different race, sexual orientation, or an opposing army.

√ *Without mutual respect for both self and partner, no relationship can survive.*

Some couples find that traditionally the wife is the one who notices things need to be repaired or improved. She may tell her husband as these needs arise. On his day off, she reminds him of the job or asks him to fix something she hasn't mentioned before, which may meet with some resistance. He feels like a kid with his mother. He doesn't mind doing the job, and in general has no trouble with her request—except when he had planned to spend his day off doing other things. He may even feel bugged by her, especially if the job is of long standing. She is frustrated and reminds him of his agreeing to do the job.

In some traditional households, friction over the issue of the man's autonomy for his time off gives rise to the "job jar." Both partners write on slips of paper the jobs that need to be done. He plans the time he will do a job, then takes a slip from the jar and does that job. Jobs that carry a high depth and intensity are best dealt with outside the job jar. The system is not foolproof, however; one wife took all of the various job slips out of the jar and refilled it with approximately the same number of slips, each with the same job noted!

All instances of infringing on another's autonomy are also instances of controlling. However, not all controlling issues are autonomy issues.

Autonomy was the issue underlying the surface issues in all the above examples. Any area in which one partner has exercised choices over some period of time may well be regarded as that partner's autonomous area. These can include household responsibility, hobbies, pets, work places, and interests initiated by either partner. If you wish to make changes in any of these areas, ask your partner how she/he would feel if that change was made. If you inadvertently intrude in an area your partner regards as his/her own, back out as quickly as possible, perhaps with an apology.

In any heated discussion, be alert for cues that your partner regards a given area as being within his/her area of autonomy. One of the key words is *"mine."*

■ *"That rock garden was mine. I thought of it. I planned it. I developed it. I asked your help for one specific thing, and you took it over. You didn't do it the way I asked. You did it your way like it was your garden. It was mine. It will take a year for it to look decent again."*

In essence, the same general statements could be made about the kitchen, poodle, or the work area. "That was my work area. I know where things are. Don't arrange it your way. Don't move my stuff."

The price for continuing to be an intruder in your partner's area of autonomy is very high. It involves one's sense of self, perhaps one's sense of adequacy, or one's sense of ownership—even a part of one's identity. To remain as an intruder or to repeatedly intrude is to strip the partner of some rights to be an autonomous person. Be aware! □

IN BRIEF

Make room for your partner's autonomy. Areas of authority and autonomy are essential for one's identity, integrity, and self-respect.

YET TO COME

Issues of control-rejection.

CHAPTER 19
FEELINGS OF REJECTION-CONTROL

One partner feels repeatedly rejected while the other feels almost constantly controlled. This dynamic and the issue of autonomy are two of the three leading causes of separation and divorce. The third is having a sexual affair. Sometimes the autonomy issue or the rejection-control dynamic underlies the affair.

The most common marital problem we see in our therapeutic work is where one partner feels rejected and the other feels controlled. This dynamic may begin with either feeling. The roles are not determined by gender.

Feeling Controlled

Any request by partner **A** that is turned down by partner **B** may result in partner **A** feeling rejected, neglected, or unloved. Partner **A** may nurse her/his wounds by becoming depressed or by withdrawing psychologically and/or physically. This feeling and behavior may be limited to interaction with the partner or may extend to other household members and to other relationships.

Trying to avoid a recurrence of this response, **B** may feel she/he has little if any choice in regard to the next request, thinking or telling the partner, "I feel the only way I can maintain peace in the relationship is to comply with most everything you ask."

√ *If a feeling of being controlled or rejected becomes chronic and is accompanied by a loss of hope for any improvement, the likelihood of infidelity, separation, or divorce increases with the passage of time.*

Several case histories are given below:

■ *Over a period of months, one person has initiated sexual play, and the partner has declined. The initiator feels rejected and shows it. The partner feels controlled by the other's feeling of rejection and subsequent cold shoulder. The chronic feelings may be verbalized: "I have to pay a big price every time I turn down your advances." Over time, just the thought of sex takes on an unsettling overtone. Typically this couple will have a wide variation in their estimates of the percentages of invitations that are rejected. (See "Rejecting an Invitation," Chapter 27)*

■   *A man in military service spends 22 months overseas. He is faithful to his wife, and spends a lot of time thinking about her. While he is gone, women's fashions change in the U.S. On his return, he requests his wife to "dress-up" in her old clothes when they go out, to wear one of the outfits he used to like. She feels that would make her look way out of style, and that she would feel very uncomfortable. He feels rejected. She feels he is trying to control her, and feels her autonomy threatened. The argument with its attendant hurts recurs every time they go out.*

■   *For a year or more a couple has had a minimum of time together, so they plan and take a two-week vacation. About the third day, one partner recognizes the need for some distance, and suggests some separate activities. The other feels rejected: "We planned this vacation just to be together. And after just three days you are going to take off. How do you think that makes me feel?" Now the one who needed some distance feels controlled by the partner's rejection.*

These dynamics are just as likely to begin when one individual asserts her/his independence and autonomy by saying "No" just to avoid feeling controlled. Often this is said with such emphasis and vehemence that the partner hears personal rejection. If the first individual is concerned about her/his autonomy, personal rejection probably was intended.

■   *One husband feels controlled by his wife scheduling multiple activities for each of their three children. He feels that this leaves little or no Couple Time, and he feels controlled by her continuing requests for him to transport the children. She feels rejected by his resentment to her requests.*

■   *The man who trimmed the shrubs in his wife's rock garden to a height half of what she had requested (See Chapter 18) said he felt like a hired man, so he was going to do things his way. He was proving to himself and to her that he was not taking orders. He was also expressing his resentment at being asked to do the job. He is seeing to it that she does not make that request of him next year. She feels a loss of her autonomy; her wishes are disregarded, and she feels rejected.*

■   *A couple has dated for two years. He has volunteered his labor for a number of projects around her family's home. One night he is watching a game on TV at a friend's house when heavy rain floods her family's barn. Her horses are standing in three inches of water, so she calls him and says she needs him to come help her do something about the water. He refuses: "I'm not going to be on call for you. I'm not going to be controlled by you." She feels crushed. Subsequent events show he can give freely when it is his idea and when he has no obligation. He can give, but he cannot meet a request from her.*

■   *A wife of 20 years tells her husband she feels embarrassed by the jokes he tells at parties. He is surprised, and points out that others laugh, and that he has been telling the same jokes for years. She says, "Yes, but humor has changed. I have changed. I'm embarrassed by many of them now." He experiences her request as an attempt to control him. He accuses her of being too sensitive: "You are going to tell me which jokes I can and cannot tell at a party?" She feels rejected twice over.*

All too often the rejection-control issue continues in a relationship, becoming a chronic problem that underlies many other issues. Feelings are facts; feelings are the essence of intimate relationships. For one partner to say "You are too sensitive" is not only ineffective, it may well compound the situation. The statement in itself is controlling! It is not an **I** sentence. The speaker is placing all the responsibility for change on the partner, putting the partner on the defensive. (See Chapter 2)

√   **In any disputed issue in an intimate relationship there is no such outcome as one winner and one loser after the argument is over. Rather, there are two winners or two losers.**

A person can always ask for clarification, provided the need for it is genuine and the tone of the question is curiosity or puzzlement rather than anger or sarcasm. "I don't understand. What embarrassed you in what I said?"

It may well be true that the partner hears control or rejection in a verbal interchange in which a panel of experts would not. So what? Some people have allergies to dust or pollen or cats; some people have allergies to feelings of rejection or being controlled. This couple is living together. Living with a panel of experts is not an option.

It behooves each partner to focus on what the self can do to maximize harmony rather than placing an expectation on the partner to change. In time, the partner will change, secondarily to the changes the first partner made. Recognizing these dynamics in your relationship is the first step to eliminating the problem. Several different interventions are possible:

"I hear that as rejection (or an attempt to control). Is that what you intended?"

Ask this with curiosity, not as a put-down. Each person is the world's authority on her/his intent. If your partner re-explains, go with the revised statement.

Make an effort not to sound controlling or rejecting. Sometimes just changing one word or phrase can make a big difference:

■   *One evening after many years of marriage a man asks his wife, "How long before supper?" This question had been asked many times over the years. This time she says, "I feel you are impatient and are criticizing me for not having supper ready earlier." The man is genuinely surprised. "Oh my goodness! I meant nothing of the kind. It is just that I don't want to start a 20-minute task if you will have supper in five minutes. I feel it would be a put-down to you not to be here when you are ready. In the future I will ask, How much time do I have before supper?"*

Accept your partner's statement of the way your message was received. If your partner is apt to hear rejection when you didn't intend it, you can reduce this sensitivity to a particular episode by changing the overall background of the relationship over time. For example: send many more spontaneous and genuine messages of affection and appreciation. By doing so, the impact of the message heard as rejection is one among a background of numerous positive messages, instead of one against a sparse background of few positive messages.

If your partner is apt to hear "control" when you speak, you might respond with the most meaningful points in the paragraph below. Generally speaking, a paragraph half as long as the one below is more effective. The balance of the statement could be added after the partner's response.

"I don't want to control you. I don't want you to feel controlled. How can I tell you what I want without your feeling controlled? I know you are not a mind reader. (Although you are good at reading my moods, you don't know my thoughts behind the moods.) How can I get my romantic and sexual needs met, as well as my needs of daily living, if I can't make a request of you? Do you want me to manipulate or use some kind of subterfuge? I don't want to do that. To me that would be more controlling than a simple request. By informing you of what I want (need), my intent is to increase your choices, not to order you around."

Any edge in your voice will be heard as control, even when the words are devoid of control. On subsequent occasions, a sentence or perhaps a phrase can remind your partner of the whole argument.

Once the feelings of being rejected/controlled in one area are frequent, the same feelings often spread to other areas, which leads both partners to perceive that the relationship is beset with multiple problems. □

IN BRIEF

1. *Any feelings of being controlled/rejected need to be acknowledged.*

2. *Both you and your partner need to give adequate reassurance of your intents not to be controlling or rejecting.*

3. *By paying attention to your partner's statements of what generates*

these unwanted feelings, changes can be made that dissipate—re-solve—the issue.

YET TO COME

Addictions.

CHAPTER 20
ADDICTIONS

A person's vulnerability to becoming addicted to a drug or alcohol is a combination of genetic, social, and psychological factors. Probably the most common dynamic of psychological addictions is the addict depending more on the object of her/his addiction for solace than on human relationships.

If you have a persistent problem in your relationships or myriad small problems that you cannot account for, and if you have not "seen yourself" in any of our previous discussions, then the cause of your difficulty may well be one of the addictions. You may not recognize that you or your partner are becoming addicted, or even that one of you has an addiction. Most addictive behaviors—not all—are normal in and of themselves. A person may slip into an addiction. Even when the addiction becomes troublesome and interferes with life and relationships, there is a tendency to deny the seriousness of the behavior. This is called emotional denial. At some level there is an awareness that the behavior is causing difficulty, but you may deny the extent of the damage. *If you are hiding a particular form of behavior from others, especially from your partner, then the chances are great that it is addictive behavior.*

As a partner of someone suffering from addiction, you may not recognize the addiction. Your partner might be successful in concealing it, or you may recognize some of the behavior, but not its extent or its consequences. It may be these consequences that create the impression that the relationship suffers from a seemingly endless number of unrelated problems. An addiction can cause slight to severe problem(s) in a relationship. Addictive behavior tends to become ritualized, and when the rituals are interrupted, the addict usually becomes anxious and/or irritable. In this state of mind, she/he may say hurtful things or become physically violent.

√ *Addictive behavior tends to become ritualized.*

There are many different types of addictions, including psychological addictions. Also, two or more addictions may occur together or be intertwined. Addictions also vary in degree of severity and in the frequency of the addictive behavior.

■ *Mr. X believes masturbation and intercourse outside or marriage are morally wrong and sinful. Usually he lives within his value system, but every six to eight weeks he deliberately gets drunk and goes on a sexual binge with prostitutes over a long weekend. He does not drink enough for the alcohol to interfere with his erec-*

tions, a possibility of which he is acutely aware, yet afterwards he claims he has on-ly a dim recollection of his activities. "I could never do those things if I were sober." Confession with absolution always follows. His alcohol addiction was evident to his boss, associates, and extended family, but not his sexual addiction.

Addiction to Alcohol

Alcohol acts to reduce inhibitions. A person's conscience can be diluted or dissolved by alcohol. Critical judgment is impaired, as is the awareness of the probable consequences of a contemplated action. With these functions significantly compromised, impulse control is weakened. Some individuals drink with the aim of grossly weakening these functions, which allows them to cast aside the judgment and impulse control that remains. It is not surprising that the most common location for sexual pickups is a bar. Alcohol also flows freely in casinos and some public auctions with expensive items. Of course, some people use alcohol only as a cover excuse with others. Alcohol interferes with the ability to think clearly. Never try to have a serious conversation with anyone who is drunk. Many people who drink excessively become irritable. Hence, the inebriated person may say hurtful things or become physically violent. Things are said or done that never would occur when sober. Alcohol can be a major contributing cause of a host of secondary problems. For the true alcoholic, everything else is secondary to the next drink—relationships, family life, friends, work, community standing, and financial security are all expendable for the sake of the bottle.

A person's drinking pattern can take many different forms. Some alcoholics believe they need "just a little stiffener" to get through the day. Others drink themselves into oblivion every night. The partner may drink to varying degrees. Some drink only on weekends. Still others go on drinking binges at quasi-regular intervals—every one to six months, as in the above case history.

> ■   *A wife calls emergency medics for her husband one morning. They find him on the floor dead. His body is cold. They ask, "How long has he been there?" She replies, "Since around eight last night. I thought he had just passed out, as he does most nights."*

This man had gone to great lengths to hide his drinking from his extended family and all others except two couples who drank with him. The only time he spent with relatives was at noon and early afternoon. He would drink then, but the relatives did not detect the existence of a drinking problem.

Some drinkers are very good at concealing the extent of their drinking—even from their partners. Breath fresheners, separate evening activities, and different times of going to bed help to maintain the secret. More commonly, the partner chooses to ignore or disregard the role of alcohol in their difficulties. Some partners actively encourage the other's drinking by always keeping a supply of alcohol available, by not questioning, and by covering for her/him when alcohol interferes with work, family, or social life. Some partners have their own difficulties when the other reduces her/his alcohol consumption or goes on the wagon. This situation is called co-dependency. (See "Co-Dependency," this chapter)

Tolerance and Dependency

Alcohol, nicotine, and some other drugs—substances—are addictive in both the physical and psychological realms. Physical addiction is manifest by increasing tolerance for the drug—i.e., more and more of the substance is necessary to produce the same effect. Physical symptoms occur if the substance is abruptly withdrawn and no longer available in the body. In extreme cases of withdrawal from alcohol, there is Delirium Tremens, DTs. As the term states, there are delusions, illusions and hallucinations, mental confusion, and disorientation, all of which tend to be terrifying. These symptoms are accompanied by poor motor co-ordination, muscle tremors, and perhaps seizures. Death may occur in extreme cases.

Definitions of Dependency & Addiction

The concept and definition of addiction has been expanded beyond alcohol (drinking) and other substances with a physical dependency to include things and activities that have only a psychological dimension, e.g., gambling or sexual addiction.

When someone seeks out and uses something (e.g., drug, behavior, another person) to fill a void within the self, that substitute can become the object of the addiction. A dependency is present when this seeking and use become a habit and a constant indulgence that the individual believes is necessary in order to get through the day and to make life bearable. Dependency becomes an addiction when the individual develops obsessive thinking and she/he becomes compulsive in seeking and having that substance, activity, or other person. This thinking and behavior become the most important aspects of the addict's day. If there is a threat to the fulfillment of that need, then everything else—family, friends, careers, education, hobbies, financial security—is relegated to a second place, regardless of harm flowing from the neglect. Unfortunately, the "fix," once achieved, is never enough. There is the ever-present danger and worry of the withdrawal or loss of the object. The result is an ever-present craving. The addict focuses on the next addictive act, its details, and the expected emotional benefit.[12]

Not everyone who drinks excessively is an addict. Some people are able to stop or limit their drinking when they fully recognize the impact of their behavior. This recognition is often precipitated by a crisis such as a traffic accident, or a confrontation

---

[12] Anonymous (op cit), pp7 & 9

with their partner, boss, or extended family. If this type of crisis is sufficient to elimi-nate the problem, well and good. If not, some form of therapy is indicated.

Causes of Addiction—Alcohol

It is now generally recognized that the vulnerability of a person becoming an alco-holic is a combination of environmental and multiple genetic factors. A number of studies have been conducted comparing the incidence of alcoholism in identical twins with alcoholism of fraternal twins. After sophisticated analysis of the data, the investi-gators concluded that 40-60 percent of the vulnerability to alcohol addiction has a genetic cause.[13] Many adult addicts began drinking as adolescents. Environmental factors that influence alcohol addiction include the subculture, peer pressure, plus the increase in self-esteem from acting like grown-ups and of doing something illegal. The amount of alcohol consumed can add to adolescent prestige and machismo.

Psychological Factors

Other psychological factors that contribute to addictions are needs to feel empo-wered, to feel safe, to control, to act with autonomy and non-conformity, and to enjoy a respite from having to be perfect around others.

Some addicts often have a fear of abandonment, which may have originated in childhood or adolescence, but which has been significantly augmented by some recent precipitating event(s). This childhood experience can take many forms—from death of a parent, to psychological abuse, to parents ignoring the child. Regardless of the details, the individual concludes: "My parent(s) didn't want me," or, "No one wants me." From this conclusion the addict develops four other life scripts: (1) *I am an unworthy person*, which extends to (2) *No one could love me as I am*. Therefore (3) *My needs will never be met if I have to rely on other people*, and (4) *The object of my addiction is my greatest need or my greatest solace*.

The addict has substituted—at least in part—the addiction in place of normal, healthy interpersonal relationships. These self-concepts are painful. Some life event that a healthy person would take in stride is interpreted by the future addict as confirmation of a doomed life script. Feelings of unworthiness and their associated pain is intensi-fied. The pre-addict learns it is possible to block out the pain by what will become the object of addiction. She/he finds that object or activity to be more available and more dependable than normal human relationships.

Some addicts are fully aware of their addiction; however, they cannot stop their addictive behavior for very long. Without the addiction, they experience their pain. They violate their vows, which reinforces their life script of being unworthy. These

---

[13] *Alcohol Alert*, National Institute on Alcohol Abuse and Alcoholism NO 48, 2000, www.niaaa.nih.gov

addicts judge themselves by society's standards, which causes increases in severe self-loathing. They struggle with themselves to control the urges and the behaviors. They make numerous solemn, believable promises to themselves, their spouses, employers, judges, clergy, and to God. But regardless of their sincerity, in a short time the sworn promises will be discounted or cast aside. Their awareness of the shame that would befall them and their families in the event of public awareness of their addictive actions—particularly sexual addiction—further reinforces the *I'm no good and completely unlovable* life script.

In the pre-addictive stages, addictive behavior is triggered by a hurt or slight to the individual's self-esteem. Later the behavior is also triggered by habit and the anticipated excitement and the hoped-for better feeling. Addictive behavior may also be triggered by the feeling and belief that a reward has been earned.

Addicts live in constant fear of the future absence of that all-important something that helps them through the day. As a result of this desperate need, they tend to believe that whatever they do to cover up and maintain their addictive behavior is justified. Hence, they are usually very self-righteous and judgmental. They are adept at twisting situations so that blame falls on someone else, often on family members.

Patrick Cranes gives the following example of a sex addict [14] The gender roles given here could just as easily be reversed.

■   *A man's wife becomes suspicious of her husband's activities and asks him about them. He lies. It is evident to him that she doubts him. He verbally berates her for not believing him. He assumes she would doubt him even if he had been truthful. This assumption gives his words and demeanor a sincerity and self-righteousness that causes the wife to doubt herself.*

It is for such reasons that support groups for family members of addicts are common and helpful: Al-Anon for partners, Alateen for teenage children, and groups called Adult Children of Alcoholic Parents for adults who carry scars from their childhood and teen years. The most effective treatment programs for addictions are the 12-step programs similar to Alcoholics Anonymous, AA. Some addicts also find simultaneous therapy helpful. 12-step programs are available in most major cities for each of these conditions. To find one of these in your area, check the telephone directory (including the index). You also might get the phone number of a program from the county health department or a crisis hot line.

Addicts often have two or more addictions that augment each other. Alcohol and sex addiction is a common pair, as the case history early in this chapter illustrates. These two—or others like sex and overeating—may interact, one being the trigger for the other, and the cycle perpetuates itself. For these people, sex by itself never meets

---

[14] Cranes, Patrick: *The Sexual Addiction*, CompCare Publications, Minneapolis, 1983, p8

the expected needs for a caring relationship; hence, the sex addict feels somewhat depressed after intercourse. She/he may overeat as a way to feel nurtured, minimizing the pain of depression. Similarly, the overeating itself does not provide the sought-for solace. "So I'll try my other tonic again: intercourse." Overeaters also put on weight, which makes them feel less attractive, and reinforces the belief that no one will love them as they are. To counter this feeling, they have intercourse again. And around and around the cycles go.[15]

√ **When a person has two or more addictions, they often augment each other.**

As we describe the various forms of addiction, please remember that these behaviors by themselves are not an indication of addiction. Some of these behaviors may be enjoyed for amusement and variety. Exceptions to this statement are exhibitionism, voyeurism, and surreptitious sexual touching.

Sexual Addiction & Love Addictions

Conforming to the definitions of addiction, some people substitute compulsively sexual behavior for caring relationships. An example of the compulsion of a sex addict appeared earlier. It is repeated here for your convenience.

■ *As a teenager I would deal with my feelings and my problems by masturbating whenever I was lonely, confused, anxious, sad, angry, scared, tired, or thought I deserved a reward. My preoccupation with sex continued into college. I dealt with feelings of confusion, frustration, or loneliness by being sexual with someone. As a result, I was having sex with five different women during the week, not a steady sexual relationship with any one of them. Then I'd spend the weekends with my fiancée.[16]*

Sexual addictions are found to run in families, from generation to generation. Often, members of the younger generation are not consciously aware of a parent's sexual addiction until after they have become sexual addicts themselves.

Sexual addiction is not limited to sexual intercourse. Some are momentarily satisfied simply by the willingness of someone to have intercourse with them, but in spite of this temporary satisfaction, the individual almost always follows through with intercourse. In men this is called the Don Juan Syndrome.

---

[15] Cranes, Patrick: (op cit), pp69-74

[16] Anonymous: (op cit), pp7 & 9

Although the overt behavior of men and women with sexual addiction may be the same, women addicts often realize they are looking for a caring relationship and are engaging in intercourse primarily to obtain at least a semblance of love. As a result, they may accept a statement of love from a man even when they know that it is temporary at best, or is completely false. In treatment groups such women refer to themselves as "love addicts" or "sex and love addicts." However, when the pre-addict or addict finds someone who is passionate with her/him, the experience tends to be discounted and additional assurance of lovability is sought by having another affair with someone else. In this way the cycle is repeated again and again with numerous partners.

Both men and women may try to prove their sexual desirability by getting the lover to violate her/his moral value system.

The sexual addiction label also applies to some men who subordinate a real relationship to sexual visual images such as pornography, pornographic movies, peep shows, or exotic dancing. The physical contact of stuffing bills into a woman's g-string or of lap-dancing may also be substitutes for a relationship. (For a discussion of pornography, see Appendix B.)

Addiction to One of the Paraphillias

Exhibitionism (exposing the genitals), voyeurism (as a Peeping Tom), transvestism (cross-dressing for sexual arousal) and frotteurism (surreptitious sexual touching or rubbing against someone) are also sexual addictions. The exhibitionist sometimes spends hours and hours driving around just to find a woman to whom he may expose himself. The voyeur has a similar compulsion to catch a glimpse of female nudity that the woman would not consciously have been willing for him to see. He too may wait for hours to momentarily satisfy his addiction. In these activities there is an element representing the earlier—usually from childhood or adolescence—sexual trauma. The behavior is in part a recreation of that trauma, which the man now expects to master. There is the risk that he won't be in control of this re-enactment, which adds to his excitement. There is also the excitement of victimizing the woman and doing something illegal, with the accompanying excitement of the risk of getting caught. For the addict, both of these forms of excitement are also expressions of anger—anger that is rooted in emotional abuse, perhaps sexual abuse—the fear of abandonment, and for him the lack of dependability of adult relationships.[17]

The triggers for these behaviors are hurts that in some unconscious way remind the addict of the original trauma. This triggering hurt may be from interaction at work, a social setting, or with the partner. Typically, these people state that the relationship with their partner is good, and the partner confirms that assessment. However, in many

---

[17] A checklist for self-administration for sexual addiction may be found in Anonymous (prev cited), p23.

cases the addict is psychologically unable to stand up to the partner and represent his/her full depth and intensity about an issue.

> ■   *One man wanted more time with his wife and to live a less scheduled and hectic life. At the wife's initiative there were numerous lessons for each child, as well as community activities. Whenever this disagreement arose again, he would always concede to her wishes with no more than a mild statement of preference. Yet this would trigger his going out and exposing himself.*

Once an addiction is well established, opportunity to engage in that behavior may also act as a trigger.

Addiction to Gambling

Emotional and financial damage generated by gamblers may extend to their families as well:

> ■   *A woman divorces her husband when she learns he has depleted their joint savings account by sustaining major losses from large bets at various casinos over a period of two years. He says it takes larger bets to give him the excitement of the adrenalin rush. He tells her he has dipped into the children's college funds, too, that he knows it was wrong, and that he has tried to stop and has repeatedly promised himself that he wouldn't gamble anymore. But he keeps going back.*

This woman's motivation for divorce is strengthened by the potential risk of losing their home and the children's college funds.

Addiction to Excitement

Risk always increases excitement. Risk and excitement are central features of extramarital sex, sexual activity in unusual locations, exhibitionism, voyeurism, and shoplifting, as well as gambling. The greater the accumulation of hurts and pain, the greater the need for excitement to keep the individual from experiencing the pain. This ploy is so effective that many addicts are not fully aware of the accumulated hurt and pain they carry.

Addiction to a Person

Sometimes an individual is addicted not to the activity, but to another person, a person who gives her/him more than she/he has previously received. Or perhaps the individual only dreams that this particular relationship will grow to fulfill unmet desires.

The individual regards this hoped-for possibility as rare. This relationship is the closest she/he has attained, and is the foundation of a precious dream. The result is a determination to hold on to the other individual and to the dream at all costs.

These people erroneously believe that the relationship can make them feel worthy, acceptable, and loved. These assumptions result in constant obsessive thinking and compulsive behavior in regard to the other person. Negative attention from their partners doesn't alter their own behavior. These dynamics often create the clinical picture of harassment, unwanted phone calls, "chance meetings," and other unwanted attention, even to the point of stalking. The movie *Her Married Lover* depicts a woman who has a personal addiction to a man.

Co-Dependency

Co-dependency is a subcategory of an addiction between two people who live together or have a close, ongoing relationship. This may involve an individual with a need to give or to take care of others and who considers either of these to be both loving and being loved. A co-dependent's life is intertwined with and focused on an addict and the relationship to such an extent that she/he takes inappropriate responsibility for the addict. The Co-dependents' actions often aid and abet the addiction, even when they claim to hate it, at the expense of their own free choices and a fulfilling relationship.

√ *12-step programs address core issues, enabling addicts to experience the pain while supported by acceptance and understanding of their sponsors and the group, thereby reversing the substitution of addiction for relationships.*

Co-dependents generally have a need to be helpful, emulating perhaps one of their parents who took responsibility for the other parent or for someone else. When co-dependents change relationships, it is frequently for someone with the same or similar addiction: "I finally left two alcoholics and end up marrying a third one!"

Generally speaking, co-dependents tend to fear abandonment. They tend to fear isolation and loneliness from possibly losing that relationship with the addict. A co-dependent often believes that the addict's acting out and the poor relationship is somehow her/his fault: "If only I were a better lover or more loving, or could buy the things she/he wants and deserves..."

Such thinking reflects a deep sense of inadequacy. Further, co-addicts believe they can potentially control the other person in such a way to stop her/his acting out. Such control of another person is an impossible task. They ignore the direct expression of their own needs. Like addicts, co-addicts feel that the object of their addiction—the addict they live with—can and will meet their needs: "If only I can change myself enough to be able to control his/her behavior, she/he wouldn't drink so much or act out sexually."

The co-dependent becomes just as obsessed with, and compulsive in dealing with, the addict as the addict is in her/his addiction. In short, severe co-dependency has become a subcategory of addiction to a person. When something interferes with this relationship, there is a sense of despair, isolation, and powerlessness.[18] Melody Beattie has written a guide to help co-dependents break this pattern and begin to take care of themselves.[19]

√ *If your relationship has a persistent problem(s) that doesn't have a logical, discernable cause, then addiction—especially alcohol addiction—may be the cause.*

Steps You Can Take

Talk seriously to your partner about problems in the relationship. Discuss what each of you think is the cause or likely cause. Discuss the damage the behavior is causing to the relationship. This is your statement of depth and intensity.

If the two of you agree on the cause(s), then together try to look at what pain the behavior is covering, and what occurs just before the behavior begins. Often these triggers are a feeling of inadequacy—being put down—or some threat to self-esteem. Perhaps this feeling arises within the relationship, perhaps elsewhere.

What can you as an individual or the two of you together do to relieve the pain the behavior is covering? If it is well established and/or ritualized, can the two of you create a substitute behavior? Can whoever is doing the behavior stop? If you resolve to stop, then together set a date to re-evaluate progress. If you try to stop and are unable to do so, then get help, either with a 12-step program, a therapist, or both. Realize that the triggers may be outside the conscious awareness of both of you. If so, the one with the behavior needs to find a psychoanalytic-oriented therapist.

If your problem is alcohol or other drugs that may produce withdrawal symptoms when discontinued, you should start your improvement with a detoxification program.

If your partner refuses to discuss the difficulties in the relationship, or if she/he turns off the discussion with anger, or if she/he denies a problem exists, then you need to consider an "intervention." We suggest you get some expert guidance on doing so. An intervention is a surprise gathering, as with a surprise party, of "all" the people who are important in the addict's life. It is critical that everyone who has supported the

---

[18] A checklist for self-administration for sexual co-dependency may be found in Anonymous (prev cited), p39.

[19] Beattie, Melody: *Co-dependent No More: How to stop controlling others and start controlling yourself*, Hazelton Foundation, Harper & Row, New York, 1987

addictive behavior—the co-dependents—be present. Then the whole group expresses their love for the person, as well as their concern about the addictive behavior. The combination of caring and concern with this type of confrontation usually breaks down the individual's emotional denial. The goal of an intervention is for the addict to proceed directly from the intervention to a structured treatment program, usually in-patient. One more promise is not an acceptable response. □

IN BRIEF

Forty to sixty percent of vulnerability to alcohol addiction is genetically determined. Social and psychological factors account for the remainder. It is reasonable to assume there is a similar vulnerability to other drugs.

The psychological vulnerability to addiction is based on the assumption that the addict is in pain, and the awareness of the pain is blocked by the addiction: alcohol, drugs, overeating, sex, excitement, etc. To give up the addiction is to experience the pain. The pain comes from the psychological abuse (and perhaps physical or sexual abuse) and abandonment— real or imagined—by someone very meaningful to the addict earlier in life. These experiences generate the belief that "I am not valued or wanted, I am an unworthy person, and no one could love me as I was." The addictive object is more available and more dependable than is looking for support and caring from another person.

YET TO COME

The considerations involved in making a re-commitment.

Section V
Recommitment

You two loved each other once. Hopefully you now have a good idea(s) of what went wrong and why. State your hurts and unfulfilled desires. Listen to your partner's hurts and unfulfilled desires. Repeat these to each other for verification. Consolidate your lists of what needs to be changed. Are the good parts of your relationship worth working for? Are you still attracted to each other?

There are three reasons not to try to reestablish an intimate relationship: (1) loss of respect, (2) an attitude—in feeling and thinking—of indifference toward the other, and (3) the fear to risk any additional hurt—there has been so much hurt that you simply can't be vulnerable to the same person again.

Make sure that both of you (1) agree on the prerequisites that make working on the relationship worthwhile, (2) stop ongoing hurts, (3) let go of old hurts, and (4) stop sexual relationships with any third parties.

Make a mutual commitment to help each other to change the patterns the two of you have used to deal with hurts and their transformations.

Rebuild with positives.

CHAPTER 21
YOU TWO LOVED EACH OTHER ONCE

Understanding what went wrong; agreeing on what needs to be changed.

Some activities expose your partner's value system to be grossly different from what you believed she/he represented. Examples include:

- Being physically abused by your partner.

- Discovering that your partner—man or woman—sexually molests children. This assumes there is little if any doubt in your mind about the accusation.

- Discovery that the partner—man or woman—has been engaging in criminal activity.

- Discovering infidelity despite vows of sexual faithfulness.

- Realizing one of you has an addiction. Consider the following example of gambling addiction that was used in the previous chapter:

  ■ *A woman discovers her husband has depleted their joint savings account and part of their children's college funds. She confronts him. He acknowledges the withdrawals to cover major losses from large bets at various casinos over a period of two years. He says it takes a large bet to give him the excitement of the adrenalin rush. She is fearful of losing their home and the remainder of the children's college funds.*

In other instances the hurts are less dramatic but cumulative: lack of consideration, chronic put-downs, and verbal abuse day after day for years— perhaps until the youngest child leaves high school or until someone says, "I've just had enough," or, "This is no way to live. I find myself not wanting to go home."

The reaction to these occurrences may be more important than the incidents themselves in determining the advisability of trying to work on the relationship. In the face of these, some couples might not perceive the hurts as so deep or dramatic. They might decide to try to pick up the pieces and make a go of their relationship.

Psychological Conditions That Seem
to Preclude Successful Rebuilding

Three psychological conditions seem to preclude the successful rebuilding of a relationship. To identify these situations, a person needs to look inside himself/herself.

1. **One partner's loss of respect for the other:** A vignette in "Respect for Partner," Chapter 8, discussed a husband who lost the couple's home to a con artist, even though the wife sensed the deceptiveness and tried to persuade him not to invest in the scheme. Loss of respect may occur in a sudden revelation, or by a slowly growing awareness.

2. **One partner's feeling of indifference for the other:** We do not mean the numb feeling that often follows a severe, unexpected hurt. Anger, even intense anger, can and often does suddenly flip to affection. Anger means the other individual is still important to you. Chronic unresolved and perhaps unresolvable anger may lead to separation/divorce, but anger is not as good an indicator that there is no hope for the relationship as is the presence of genuine indifference. Indifference usually doesn't appear for several weeks after a major unexpected hurt and sometimes only after the process of understanding what happened is nearing completion.

3. **One partner's unwillingness to risk being vulnerable and to be hurt again:** "The hurt(s) is so deep, so heavy, that I can't open myself to another hurt. I can't let myself love him/her again." This situation may be present after only one major hurt. It occurs frequently after a couple has re-established a loving relationship following a major hurt, only to suffer a recurrence of a similar hurt in the same category, e.g., a second affair.

Considering Separation

What kind of a support network do you have and are likely to have if you separate? What kind of support groups are available in the community in which you expect to live? You can make some inquiries quietly. How easily do you make friends with your same gender, with the opposite gender?

Do you contemplate being lonely after the separation? How difficult do you expect that to be for you?

What is your financial situation likely to be after a permanent separation? Many people contemplating separation or divorce consult an attorney for a knowledgeable estimate of the financial ramifications. Can you live on the available funds? Will you need to work? What are your marketable skills? Some of our patients put off separation until they acquired those skills.

If you are married, do you think your partner will contest a divorce? Do you have any idea how strongly your partner will contest the divorce? Are you ready to go through that legal fight? What would it take for you to get ready?

Assessing the Relationship

Each individual must weigh every factor for himself/herself in deciding whether to separate, try to make changes, or simply tolerate similar types of hurts in the future. Some of these factors include:

- How fulfilling has the relationship been for each of you? How fulfilling does it continue to be in other areas?

- Do you still love your partner? Realize you can love and hate someone at the same time. These emotions don't cancel each other out; they can exist side by side for a time.

- How good a parent has your partner been or is likely to be? Do the two of you feel close while parenting?

- What are you willing to settle for? Do you think you would be able to attract a better partner?

- If the relationship doesn't change, do you believe, overall, you will be better off and happier in the relationship or out of it? What is your level of anxiety about continuing the relationship as it currently exists?

- Do you need or require changes to be willing to continue the relationship long-term?

Assessing the Likelihood of Change

Usually the most difficult aspect to evaluate realistically is the likelihood of significant change(s) that would preclude a recurrence of hurtful behavior. One guide to the likelihood of change is your prior efforts to change and their results.

How long have each of you realized this (these) problem existed? Were you struggling alone to deal with it (them)? Was your partner struggling alone to change it (them)? Were the two of you struggling together? You may wish to answer these questions with quantification terms, i.e., "only nominally," "not much," "some," "in a major way."

- Did you get professional help, jointly or individually? How helpful was it?

- Does your partner know you are thinking of separating?

- Since you (or the two of you) have been thinking (or talking) about separating, have the severity and frequency of hurts been increasing or decreasing? If this is a change, what do you think the intermediate thinking has been?

Motivation

Perhaps the greatest determinant of successful change is motivation. The following may help you assess your partner's willingness to work at changing, and of your partner's assessment of your willingness to work at changing:

- Generally speaking, the more positive and fulfilling the relationship has been for each of you, the greater the motivation for change.

- If the precipitating hurt or series of hurts is one that has resulted in an apology by either of you, how sincere do you think your partner's contrition is? How sincere is your contrition?

Change is not likely to occur unless each of you is willing to look at yourself sincerely and honestly and be open with your partner. To do so takes courage. It is being vulnerable. Although you may be able to effect some change without your partner's active participation, having it would be extremely beneficial.

- How sincere are you about your willingness to look at yourself honestly and work to change the relationship?

- How sincere is your partner about willingness to look at herself/himself and to work to make changes? Beware of how convincing an addict can be one moment before resuming addictive behavior in the next.

If the problem is one of physical abuse or of addiction, we strongly recommend a 12-step program, and would advise you not to continue in the relationship without that help. These problems often grow progressively worse.

Tell each other how determined you are to make the relationship mutually rewarding.

Looking at Current Communication

Perhaps a major cause of hurts in the relationship is poor communication. The two of you can start your changes by reviewing, separately or together, how the two of you communicate:

A) Do each of you clearly state your desires? Do you use "I" sentences? Do each of you try to avoid inflammatory words and words that are easily misunderstood? Do each of you convey the depth and intensity of your desires? Does your partner acknowledge she/he received your messages? How do each of you respond? Do the two of you understand the repertoire each of you uses to respond to a request?

B) Do each of you communicate your feelings? Are they received with caring and respect? What are the ways each of you communicates the fact that you feel hurt? Do you each have a variety of ways to do so—a repertoire? Do you share the same perceptions about your communications of hurts? Do each of you clearly state the depth and intensity of your hurts? Does your partner acknowledge she/he received your messages? How do each of you respond? Are most hurts resolved by examining the first hurt either of you had since you were feeling okay toward each other?

If either of you answered "no" to any part of questions A or B, then reread Sections I and II (Chapters 1-9), pausing after each chapter to discuss it.

C) How do each of you transform your unresolved hurts? Do you and your partner have the same perceptions?

If the two of you are not clear about how each of you transforms hurts, then reread Chapters 9 and 15. If the two of you still have questions about how unresolved hurts are transformed, make a pact to call the next occurrence to your partner's attention.

If the two of you have answered these questions together seriously and without rancor, then you have already begun to work together to effect change. Congratulations!

Looking for Common Ground

Once you and your estranged partner have committed to saving the relationship, and have examined your current communications, continue with the following exercises:

Identify your hurts and unfulfilled desires verbally or on paper. List the items you think would be on your partner's hurt list. Similarly, your estranged partner needs to enumerate her/his (a) hurts and disappointed desires, and (b) concept of what is on your list.

Compare your two lists with those of your partner. Discuss these hurts and frustrated desires. Listen to each other with the aim of understanding the other's perspective. Listen attentively, with your eyes on the speaker. Ask questions— with a tone of curiosity— for clarification, completeness, and understanding.

Repeat to your partner what you have heard him/her say. This demonstrates the fact that you have heard, and gives your partner the opportunity to clarify, correct, or add pertinent details to what she/he intended to say. Accept any and all restatements as though they were originally intended. Of course, it is in your partner's best interest to listen to you and to demonstrate that fact by repeating to you what she/he heard you say. Again, doing so functions as a validity check. Listening demonstrates caring and a desire to understand each other's perspectives. Not listening demonstrates arrogance or lack of caring, and will increase animosity in the process of reaching a settlement in a permanent separation.

Each of you needs to identify the differences in (a) your understanding of your experiences of living together, including the hurts, (b) the interpretation of those experiences, and (c) the feelings generated by the experiences.

"I was really hurt when you got pregnant again after we agreed not to have more children. At best I took it as your indifference, at worst as a deliberate betrayal. I felt like I wanted to run— to get the hell away from you."

"I was really thrilled when you threw that surprise party for my birthday. I really felt loved."

Be on the lookout for insights that might be expressed as "I didn't realize you saw it that way." Be equally alert to your partner conveying any insight about your interpretation of event(s). Sometimes relationship problems seem to evaporate with such insights. Some couples can find common ground between their differences and, realistically, they don't expect to be hurt again in the same manner.

√   Sincerity, honesty, and completeness in communication are the basis for a satisfying, ongoing relationship.

If there is to be hope for reconciliation, the partner's feelings need to be acknowledged. If the individual can go a step further by acknowledging those feelings as reasonable—given the partner's point of view and understanding—it forms the basis for realistic hope for the relationship. From this position it is but half a step to empathy and caring, which will be expressed almost automatically.

However, in most all cases—certainly in cases of longstanding hurts and animosity—this process must be reciprocated. (See Chapter 16 for the "Sandwich Phenomenon") With mutual empathy, the couple will naturally move toward each other, however guarded and gingerly. Do not apologize unless you think you have been mistaken. Any apologies must be sincere. In common usage, the phrase "I'm sorry" can be an apology or a statement of sympathy. Usually the context makes the meaning clear. Ambiguity can remain, however, and the statement can be misinterpreted by the hearer. Clarity can be added by the expressions "I'm sorry that happened to you," or, "I sympathize (or empathize) with you." Or ask for clarification: "Are you apologizing or sympathizing?"

With your new joint understanding, you need to figure out together how to avoid a recurrence of the hurt(s). This may be a lengthy process. Professional help may be essential if the hurt has been obscure or displaced, either in target or issue. (Chapter 15 defines targets and issues) "Acting out" is a behavioral form of displacement.

For example, a man who could not fully represent himself to his wife—express his hurt or anger—may express that anger and compensate for feelings of inadequacy by visiting prostitutes. It could also be the woman who has an affair to get back at her husband, and who gets a message of intrinsic worth and lovability from someone else.

Another situation in which professional help is likely to be essential is a hurt that taps into a similar hurt from the individual's past. (See "Neurotic Anger" in Chapter 16) Often left over from childhood, this may be difficult to recognize. A "yes" answer to either of the following two questions is an indication of another issue intertwined with the current one, and therapy may be helpful:

1. Was there a time in your past life when you had a set of several mixed feelings that are similar to those you have (had) with this incident?

2. Did anything like what caused this hurt also happen to you earlier in your life?

When Children Are Involved

Our experience in the area of effects of divorce on children is with (1) adult patients whose parents divorced and (2) divorced individuals with minor children. We did hear horror stories, especially when the parents kept in constant conflict with each other, and particularly when children were one of the major issues of contention.

Both parents should reassure each child that she/he is not the cause of the divorce. Feeling responsible for the parents' divorce is too great a burden for a child to carry. Further, at most that concept is only partially true. Even in circumstances in which one parent devotes a great deal of time to a child—physically handicapped or not—with the other parent feeling chronically neglected, the divorce is not the fault of the child, but of the parents for failing to adjust to meet the needs of every member of the family.

Tell your children that the fact that the parents no longer love each other and are getting a divorce does not diminish either parent's love of him/her. This message needs to be a campaign rather than a one-time statement from each parent. The parents' follow-up behavior and attitudes need to confirm the message and convey their love.

It is important that the parent who is not living with the child keep visitation commitments—as a sacred duty. Whenever a parent cancels or fails to keep the appointment, the child almost invariably will take it as an indication that she/he is not loved by that parent. This hurt will be transformed by the child into unworthiness and low self-esteem or anger. It will be much easier and less expensive if the two of you can arrange the details of visitations without involving a third party. Try to be considerate. Talk calmly. Don't put your child in a bind.

Don't verbally tear down, ridicule, or belittle your (ex) partner in front of the children. Part of every child's identity is his/her view of each parent, so attacking your ex in the child's presence is indirectly attacking your child.

Children who had some awareness of parental difficulty prior to one parent moving out did better than those to whom the separation came as a complete surprise. The parents may tell the child they are having difficulty getting along. Often a child will overhear some parental arguments. However, the child should not overhear too much animosity, especially in the form of physical or psychological abuse as character assassination, especially sexual epithets.

There have been two excellent studies published about the effects of divorce on children:

1. Judith Wallerstein, *The Unexpected Legacy of Divorce: A 25 Year Landmark Study*, 2000, reported on in-depth interviews with 60 children who were in some difficulty. Her study spanned 25 years.

2. E. Mavis Hetherington (and John Kelly), *For Better or For Worse: Divorce Reconsidered*, www.wwnortonco.com, 2002, tracked 14,000 families and more than 25,000 children, many for 30 years. She found 20-25% of children of divorced parents had problems, compared with 10% of controls. That means that 75-80% were rated as doing "OK" to "well adjusted."

Our experience supports Hetherington and Kelly's findings.

There Is Hope

Generally speaking, the two of you can greatly improve your relationship, perhaps with a therapist or other forms of help such as a self-help group. Physical spousal abuse is treatable in group therapy with a competent leader when the group is comprised only of abusers. Today, almost all sexual problems are amenable to professional help: lack of sexual desire, being non-orgasmic, pain with intercourse, premature ejaculation, impotence, inability to ejaculate. However, in spite of many successes that have been reported, it is difficult to help a child abuser change his/her object of sexual desire. The helping professions see no need to modify adult-to-adult orientation like homosexuality.

Seeking Therapy

You two were close with each other once. If now it seems that separation is just over the next bump in the road, if one or both of you are not sure there is any hope for rebuilding the relationship, if you're not even sure you care if there is any hope, or if you are not clear in your own mind that the best action for you is separation, then we advise that the two of you seek counseling. Doing so will add clarity to your thinking.

Therapy is often essential after a major hurt and betrayal if the two of you are to be successful at a re-commitment effort. Alternatively, therapy will enable a permanent separation to be achieved more amicably. A therapist acts as an unbiased third person to help keep matters focused, and to assure a relatively productive discussion for you and your estranged partner. A therapist also brings experience, insight, and some guidance to the process.

If your partner refuses to go with you, then go by yourself. After several visits, you and the therapist may invite your partner to join the sessions, perhaps only to listen.

Divorce Attorneys

Attorneys function to prevent or resolve disputes. The dissolution of a marriage is a legal matter, and an attorney(s) will probably be involved. There are some attorneys who will function as arbitrator for a divorce when both partners jointly ask for help to reach an equitable settlement. If you and your partner don't foresee any major issues of contention, the two of you might consult an arbitrator.

However, when there is a significant disagreement about the settlement, each of you will probably need and want your own legal representation to protect your interests. Your attorney may be able to resolve the issues with your partner and his/her attorney easily and quickly, or the negotiations may become extremely adversarial, with entrenched positions and with the generation of a great deal of animosity. If negotiations reach this point, they can have substantial impact on the relationships of everyone involved, including the children both now and in the future.

From a therapist's point of view, the legal advice of some attorneys has a detrimental effect, like when they advise their clients to empty the safe-deposit box and close all joint savings and checking accounts. These attorneys are protecting their client's interests, creating bargaining chips to use later in negotiations with the other side, and demonstrating aggressiveness on the client's behalf. However, when this advice is followed, the partner may see you as devious, unfair, and attempting to maximize your own wealth without regard for fairness or any other considerations. This tactic destroys what trust and goodwill is remaining, and generates the desire to strike back at each other's most vulnerable points in whatever ways are available. Unfortunately, sometimes the most potent and available means of retaliation is through issues of child custody, their living arrangements, and visitation. Remember: if children are involved, you are likely to have some contact with your former partner at least several times a month. Remember, too, that the amount of child support the court orders is always open to either of you filing a legal petition for review.

Some attorneys are sensitive to the potential impact legal tactics can have on clients' relationships, so they may counsel against those that will inflame the partners and hurt future relationships. However, that is not their *legal* obligation, which is to represent only your legal and financial interests to the best of their ability within the law. It is your responsibility to be aware of potential damage to future relationships with your ex-partner, children, extended family, and friends. Make sure this is balanced against the advice of your attorney in regard to your legal and financial interests. You can exercise control of your negotiating position whenever you wish. If your attorney seems unwilling to consider all of your needs, perhaps you need to seek representation from one who will.

After a divorce is final, resist all impulses to use the children's visitation or anything else about them as a "club" to hurt your ex. You are very apt to hurt yourself or the children more in the long run. □

IN BRIEF

State your hurts. Listen to your partner and repeat to him/her what she/he said for verification. Consolidate your lists of what needs to be changed. Are the good parts worth working for?

Sometimes therapy is necessary to understand what happened and why. If it becomes clear that separation with divorce is the best solution, plan to accomplish it with as little additional hurts to any family member as possible. When children are involved, extra care must be taken to ensure they are protected, and that their best interests will be met by the future versions of your changed relationship with your ex.

YET TO COME

Looking for someone new.

CHAPTER 22
BEGINNING WITH SOMEONE NEW

Some considerations in choosing someone new.

After a Separation

Sometimes both partners arrive at the desire and decision to separate at approximately the same time. For most couples, however, one partner arrives at the decision before the other. Generally, the one being left suffers more pain than does the one initiating the separation. If you are the one who is left, there is usually a period of numbness and hurt with sadness, grief, and feelings of being betrayed. Particularly if your partner's decision comes as a surprise to you, the loss of the relationship can be more devastating than if your partner had died. At least death would have been involuntary—except for suicide. In a separation, the loss is voluntary on the partner's part. You will need to grieve the loss. These reactions are normal.

Don't become involved in a new relationship while these feelings are still strong. New relationships should create opportunities to accentuate positive emotions, not be used to cover the pain of prior loss. You will need to work through what went wrong—the "why of it all"—in your own mind, perhaps alone, with a confidant, or with a therapist. If you were involved with an addict, we suggest you reread the chapter on addiction, with special attention to co-dependency. The material on "Love as a need to give or to take care of others" is also important. (See Chapter 12)

Looking for a New Relationship

When the hurt has decreased, when you have a pretty good idea of what went wrong, and when you have worked through the majority of your anger and hurt, you are ready to seek a new relationship. You will need to meet a number of new people—on average about a hundred—of a suitable gender and age range and who are similar to you psychosocially and intellectually. This figure of a hundred is arrived at in the following manner: when you are with a group of people, count the number of people you are romantically interested in enough to meet again and the total number of people of that gender. We expect you will find one or two *possibilities* for every ten people you meet. This was the result graduate students and patients discovered for themselves. Further, 5 to 15 minutes of conversation was enough time to eliminate one of these. These findings were the same for men and women.

Recognize that if you are attracted to only one of every ten potential partner candidates, and if the other individual is attracted to only one of every ten, then in order to find a new acceptable partner you will need to meet a hundred new people, $1/10$ X $1/10 = 1/100$, of your preferred gender who are similar to you psychosocially and educationally.

In order to meet 100 new potential partners, you will need to put yourself into situations where you have the best chances of meeting the kinds of people you seek. Figure out what is important to you, and consider where those with similar values can be found. If religion is important, churches and groups that carry out religious missions are good places to start. If you are a single parent, organizations like Parents Without Partners, which is popular in many communities across the U.S., offers opportunities to meet with other single parents. If you have particular interests such as the arts or sports or music or hiking, look for groups or businesses or newsletters or websites that cater to these people. With some legwork, you should be able to find groups for gays and lesbians, older singles, divorcees, widows and widowers, cancer survivors, parents of handicapped children—just about any demographic that appeals to you.

Most communities also have more targeted opportunities to meet potential partners, ranging from singles bars and clubs to dating services and classified advertising. When your life is busy with career and other obligations, the opportunities to meet singles are not as easy as in high school or college, so do not be quick to discount trying new ways to find the right person—including going back to school, or at least taking a few classes. Don't be shy about asking for ideas, either. If you take a scuba class and see people paired off, ask the instructor after class if there are any events or other ways to meet singles also interested in scuba. The possibilities might surprise you. In our many years of practice, we have heard countless stories of people finding partners in many of the most amazing and wonderful ways. What matters is that you get out there and make the effort, target your approach, keep an open mind, and don't give up.

Before You Become Really Involved

Lead with your heart, not your head. But before you really become involved, when you sense you are on the threshold, have a serious talk with the other person about the previous experiences each of you have had in relationships. This is being vulnerable.

This should be followed, perhaps at a later time, by a discussion of goals, expectations, hopes, and dreams. Does your date support yours? Be wary if you feel belittled or ignored. Try to get a sense of the other's moral value system and spirituality. Are they compatible with yours? This does not mean that they have to be the same—only that they mesh comfortably.

Men and women who tend to become either verbally or physically abusive or overly controlling usually give clues of that tendency early in a relationship. We recommend that early on—after two to four dates perhaps—you suggest something for the two of you to do that evening or for the next date. Expect your date to take your suggestion seriously. Is she/he willing to do your thing once in a while, or is your suggestion dismissed?

As you become more involved, be alert to the other person trying to exert undue control. Are you allowed free rein to do your things and to see your friends without a lot of explaining or *guilt trips*? A major indication of trouble ahead is an attempt to isolate you from your friends and family. Take this as a flashing red light—stop! She/he doesn't have to accompany you when you see them, though that might be nice. Maintain your relationships with the people in your support network. Doing so should not be a threat to a new relationship.

Value Systems

Every adult has a sexual value system, which is everything that turns you "on" or "up," or "off" or "down." People also have value systems for other emotions such as humor, anger, and sadness. Some values are universal, others are cultural, and others are individualistic. People like different kinds of jokes, yet there is some similarity within a culture. Otherwise the film industry wouldn't be able to make comedies. Similarly, with sadness, they make tragic movies, yet there is individual variation. One person may be saddened to see a cat that has been hit by a car; the next person driving by may have no emotional reaction to the dead cat. Science is a long way from fully understanding how an individual happens to develop her/his particular attractions.

The next two sub-headings will help you look at your sexual value system. The first deals with early attractions. The second looks at your sweetheart history, which takes a deeper look and reveals the history of your sexual value system.

Sexual interest in another person is enhanced by recognizing those physical characteristics and personality traits that match positive aspects of your own sexual value system. For example:

■   *We asked our university graduate students to list the traits that turned them on (or up) and off (or down), and to indicate their own gender. For the first two or three minutes, most sat with only one or two items on their paper. Then a number of thoughts came to them. Year after year the men tended to focus on physical appearance, e.g., figure, pretty face, hairstyle. The women would have more listings of the environment and the ambience. Both genders had numerous listings of personality traits— kindness, sense of humor, intelligence, novelty.*

√   **Sweetheart histories reveal the history of your sexual value system.**

Sweetheart Histories

When people examine the traits and qualities of their past—since puberty—and present sweethearts, a pattern usually emerges. By identifying your pattern and that of your current sweetheart, and by the two of you comparing them, you and your sweetheart will gain additional insight about your potential long-term happiness.

We begin sweetheart histories by asking people how, as children, they saw the personality of each parent. Follow-up questions of dominance, kindness, willingness to listen, temper, methods of discipline, etc., help to adequately clarify these pictures. Next we ask about the sweethearts that each individual has had since puberty. Former spouses and significant others are included. Specifically, we ask, "What traits attracted you, romantically or sexually?" "How did this person stand out from others in your environment?" Sweetheart histories may be traced for gays and lesbians in the same manner.

When these descriptions are completed, the individuals themselves identified the pattern of their sweetheart value system. The most common pictures that emerged fell into several patterns.[20]

1. **Falling in love with someone who is seen as similar to the parent of the opposite gender.** Occasionally, this similarity extended to the projected lifestyle and occupation. For example, one woman whose father was a well-respected naval officer married a naval midshipman. Both her father and her husband were seen as being independent thinkers, very kind, and considerate of women. Both men assumed leadership roles in the relationships with sweethearts. Both were protective—her father, of his alcoholic wife; and her husband, of his own mother.

2. **Loving someone who is seen as possessing the characteristics of the parent of your gender.** Some women are attracted to the characteristics they saw in their own mothers, rather than their fathers. Or these women may be attracted to men with characteristics their mothers held up as ideal. For example, one woman saw her father as being away with his business most evenings, and saw how it hurt her mother. She chose to marry a man whom she thought would work 9-to-5 and be home most evenings. She did not see him as ambitious, but did see him as fun-loving.

3. **A combination of the first two patterns, based on specific traits.** Marshall saw Marguerite similar to his mother in being kind to others and animals, and capable of being devoted when committed. He saw her as different from his mother in being more fun-loving, less prone to worry, and—most importantly to him—being willing to express her own thoughts and desires rather than just

---

[20] Please note that an independent observer might well characterize any of these others by different traits.

going along with what he said he wanted, as he perceived his mother doing with his father.

4. **Teenagers may fall in love with someone who embodies all the negative prejudices of an over-dominant parent. This value system may carry over into adult life.** This is an example of adolescent rebellion against the parent. The over-dominant parent may be the same or opposite gender from the teenager. Typically, this parent is over-controlling, opinionated, and seldom willing to listen to the child's desires or arguments. This parent typically is also prejudiced against groups of other people. The prejudice may be based on ethnic, racial, religious, social class, or quasi-distinctions.

   The parents' diatribes against these people are usually something the child has heard since grade school, and they engender a sympathy and a "kindred spirit" with this group. This is an example of the dynamic "The enemy of my enemy is my friend." This affinity results in the individual being drawn to this group in his/her post-pubertal years. And the individual often finds some member of that group who is sexually attractive and who is sexually attracted to the individual. Of course, falling in love with someone of the group that the over-bearing parent disparaged also has major elements of autonomy and hostility toward the parent.

   These are also prejudices of admiration and the desire to be accepted in certain social circles. This rebellion may be against the groups an over-dominant parent praises, like refusing to consider the graduates of elite schools or devout adherents of the parents' religion.

5. **Sometimes a person is attracted to another who has traits that would compensate for self-felt weakness.** "My significant other is outgoing and makes friends easily. I am so reserved." Or, "I am often impulsive. It is fun most of the time, and I can count on my partner to keep me from going off the deep end in a detrimental way."

When these choices—conscious or unconscious—are traced through the individual's history of attractions, some will have the same dynamics with every sweetheart. Others will vary between sweethearts who have an opposite set of characteristics from their prior sweetheart(s). We see nothing untoward with switches of this kind. At most, it is an indication that the person found those with the prior characteristics to be somewhat lacking. These patterns are evidenced in everyday life by people who divorce one "undesirable" individual, only to become involved with or marry someone very similar, e.g., alcoholics.

Examining Your Patterns In Sweetheart Histories

When you and your prospective partner are getting serious enough to talk about moving to a deeper level, write out your answers to the questions of your own attraction history following the outline given below. Then examine the histories for a pattern.

Write out how as a child you saw the personality of your mother and father. If one of your parents changed significantly over your childhood years, or if you had a stepparent who was important in your life, focus first on the years you were age 3 to 8. Then consider the period from about 6 months before your puberty to age 16 or so. If one of your parents displayed either positive or negative bigotry toward a particular group or class of people in this latter time frame, note it. Next, recall your first sweetheart after puberty. What was distinctive about this person? How did she/he stand out from others? What was there about this sweetheart that you thought attracted you? Spend some time thinking about these questions. Seldom do more than one or two answers immediately come to mind.

Continue this survey by answering the same questions for each of your sweethearts, significant others, and former spouses. Conclude with your current sweetheart.

Now look for the pattern among those you have described. Your pattern may contain opposites.

What Attracted You to Each Other

1. **Write out on a separate page what attracted you to your current sweetheart.** It is important that this listing be as complete as you can make it. If there are no statements of positive sexual attraction among your answers, try to think of one, now that you focus on the issue.

    Later, you may elect to share your history with your partner, but unless you have already confided this information, it would be a distraction to share it at this point. It is not necessary for the purposes of this exercise. In either event, don't expect your current sweetheart to share his/her sweetheart history with you.

    The answer therapists would be concerned about is:

    Therapist: "What attracted you to this sweetheart?"

    Patient: "She/he liked me—chose me."

    Therapist: "You didn't do any choosing?"

    Patient: "No. It was just that she/he really wanted me."

    The implication of the answer is that the patient's self-esteem was so low that anyone of that gender who displayed that degree of interest would earn his/her commitment.

2. **Write what you think attracts your current sweetheart to you.** How did you beat out the competition? Again, give yourself some time to think of more than one or two immediate answers. Usually it is the set of traits that a person tries to accentuate when the individual feels in danger of losing the relationship.

    The answer we don't like to hear to this question, because of its implication for self-esteem, is: "I don't know. I don't have any idea what she/he sees in me."

Answers to the following questions don't need to be written. They are stimuli for discussion between you and your sweetheart.

3. **How close is the match between what attracted you to him/her and those your potential partner thinks attracted you?** Some traits should be the same; some are usually different. **Does your prospective partner value those traits in himself/herself? Are they likely to endure?**

4. **Compare the other set. What is the match between your potential partner's list that attracted him/her to you and those that you thought attracted him/her to you? Do you value those traits in yourself? Are they likely to endure?**

5. **Do these answers make sense to each of you, or is one of them illogical, oddball, or neurotic?**

    • "I really don't want to be attracted by that— sado-masochism."

    • "I really shouldn't be attracted by that."

    • "I really don't like that particular trait— always being the one to decide what we do together."

6. **Examine the activities the two of you enjoy together. Do these activities meet the needs of both?** If not, we suggest the two of you go exploring for additional ways to have fun together.

7. **Are the sources of your excitement compatible?** Excitement may be termed adventure or risk. It is an emotion that the helping professions are just beginning to address. **Are the forms of excitement and the degree of excitement compatible? If there is variation in these dimensions, can each**

person freely support the other's activities? Sometimes the less active partner really enjoys and admires the dare-devilish feats of the other. However, difficulties are likely to occur when one individual finds excitement by taking financial risks that are unacceptable to the other, or activities that the partner regards as way too risky in terms of injury or death, such as bungee-jumping or hang-gliding.

8.   **Are your desires, ambitions, and dreams for the future compatible? What do each of you hope for in the future? Do your desires include having children?**

Evaluating Attraction to Each Other—Projecting Activities

The implications of your and your partner's responses to the preceding questions are largely common sense. The questions and answers are intended to be taken as an indication of what the two of you need to discuss, rather than identifying future outcomes.

In the following examples we are picking only one item on a person's list out of four to eight items. Each of the items below must be viewed in light of the whole list, and of the depth and intensity felt by each person.

■   *The reason she may be attracted to him is that he is a stay-at-home kind of guy and she is also attracted by his witty comments as they watch TV. He may respond that he is working his way through school and doesn't have the funds to party like he would really like to.*

■   *Two gay men found each other as seniors in high school. One is very reserved and shy. The other is an athletic star and very popular. In part, it is this popularity and his friend's easy manner in dealing with it that attracts the shy one. The athlete pauses because he used to be shy, too, and he knows he is shy in other settings. The athlete knows his own popularity will fade after graduation, and he wonders if he will continue to be easy-going and friendly as his shy friend sees him now.*

■   *He is attracted to her because she doesn't put herself on display. She dresses conservatively, not sexy. In part, this leads him to believe that she would more likely to be sexually faithful. His mother left the family for another man. What he doesn't reveal right away is that he doesn't think he could be good or adequate enough to keep her from finding some other man more attractive and ultimately leaving him. Her father left the family, but she hasn't told him this yet. Her grandmother buys all her clothes for her, but only conservative ones. She longs for what she doesn't have: sexy clothes and admiring looks from the fellows. She says she thought he liked her because she was plain-spoken and didn't play games. Yes, he liked that, too. Together they realized they have the same vulnerability—fear of being abandoned. This results in them feeling closer, and makes them aware of their danger.*

■   *They met and related around the political campaign of staunch environmentalist candidates. Everything they find attractive about each other is a sub-item of their beliefs or activities in this campaign. Is that enough, they ask. Is that a major issue that they will be active about throughout their adult lives? Can they develop other interests together? A second item pops up: he wants children; she feels raising a child, let alone children, would be too time-consuming and be a distraction from her mission in life, which is working to protect the environment.*

■   *She is attracted by his kindness and consideration of her, which seems to come to him so easily. He will listen to her. She adds, "I'm very giving myself. He really lights up when I do something special for him. That lights me up." He says, "She is easy to be with. I don't have to guess or wonder where she is, either literally or figuratively. I usually like where she is. We can talk and work things out."*

■   *She wants to live in the country, raise animals, and have lots of friends drop in. He dreams of living in an apartment or condo in the city and being part of the cocktail circuit—where all the action is. □*

IN BRIEF

Give yourself time to work through most of your hurt and anger about the separation. Generally, you will need to meet 100 new potential partners to find a compatible relationship. Your own "sweetheart history" can be very revealing and can show what you found attractive in your partners. Do you know what attracted your partner to you? Does your partner know what attracted you? Ask each other. Discuss your answers. You may find compatibilities you didn't know you had, or you may at least become aware of potential troublesome areas.

YET TO COME

Letting go of old hurts that are not continuing. Check out three types of respect-attraction each of you has for the other.

CHAPTER 23
PREREQUISITES TO PUTTING
IT BACK TOGETHER

Let go of old hurts.

Discovering what went wrong is only part of making a serious commitment to re-building the relationship. There must be hope, a realistic expectation that together you two can re-establish what you have lost, that you can build an even more satisfying relationship. Your decision should not be made lightly. In most cases, you should explore what went wrong before the two of you make your decision. You both will have better understandings of what changes are necessary. The exploration can involve all the steps in Chapter 21. You may consult with a therapist individually or jointly to increase your understanding.[21]

Sometimes both individuals are certain they want to work things out even before they have explored what will be involved. It is important that you—and the therapist, if one is involved— not be stampeded into attempting to fix things without giving adequate attention to the underlying problems. Certain prerequisite agreements need to be part of the pact.

A major distinction is to be made between (1) old chronic hurts-angers based on past issues that are not recurring, and (2) hurts-angers based on recurring instances.

Stop Ongoing Hurtful Behavior / Nurture Trust

There must be a serious commitment to stop ongoing hurtful behavior. This may involve enrolling in a suitable 12-step program for those behaviors that have a compul-sive or quasi-compulsive element. For cases involving financial hurts, the chance of a recurring hurt can be reduced by the restructuring of financial arrangements, such as automatic payments of the mortgage, car loan, and utilities, and having only one credit card with a reduced limit. Other hurts may require different changes, perhaps a lower-paying job with better hours so you can create a date night that you both hold as sacred.

Don't try to re-establish a meaningful relationship while either of you has *one leg in bed* with someone else. This principle holds, even if the two of you have not re-

---

[21] If seeing a therapist individually, it is essential that the session be fully described to the partner—not an easy thing to do!

established a sexual relationship. Use masturbation for your sexual outlet, if it is not outside your moral value system.

√ *Don't try to re-establish a meaningful relationship while either of you has one leg in bed with someone else.*

Once a pact has been made not to be sexual with a third party, then be trustworthy and be trusting to the extent of giving your partner the benefit of the doubt. However, it is prudent to inquire about questionable behavior or circumstances that arouse your suspicions. To ignore questionable behavior tends to convey the message that it is acceptable. But don't accuse until the evidence is very strong. To accuse falsely is to damage trust and to provide an excuse for the very behavior you fear. "If I'm going to be accused of it anyway, I might as well do it" is an immature expression of righteous anger that is an all-too-common response.

Past Hurts That Are Not Continuing

Often the accumulation of old non-continuing hurts that were not resolved in a timely manner is grossly one-sided, piled high because one partner failed to express her/his hurt and anger with adequate depth and intensity at the time of the events. The injured individual must take some responsibility for this mismatch—perhaps for not standing up to the other's anger or not wanting to be confrontational. Often the other partner will say, "I knew you didn't like that, but I had no idea it bothered you that much!"

There comes a point when one needs to let go of old hurts—to write them off as bad debts and continue on a here-and-now or cash-and-carry basis. Often the injured individual will hold on to old bad debts as some balance sheet, to the detriment of the relationship. When this happens, a price tag—a compensation to settle the debt in full—needs to be named, requested, discussed, and negotiated. It often becomes apparent that what the individual really wants is to be given what she/he never received, i.e., making up for nine years of one-sidedness, or whatever. The naming of the price exposes the ridiculousness of the demand.

Letting go of past hurts is very hard for some people, especially those with righteous indignation who took solace in the feeling of being a martyr.

■ *A husband replies to his suffering wife: "Look, I'm sorry I did those things. I'm sorry you feel ignored and taken for granted. I thought I was working for both of us, but those years were hell for me, too. Maybe not as hard as they were for you, but your coldness hurt, and I didn't know why or what to do about it until just recently. I'm sorry, but I can't live the next nine years of my life with reversed roles. I want all the happiness we can have with what years we have left. If it will make you happy, I'll act as your slave, do everything and anything you wish for nine days or nine weeks, but then we have to start fresh."*

We call *starting fresh* letting go of the past. If, however, the same type of incident recurs, it needs to be dealt with as a current hurt. Make a joint commitment to let go of the past. A commitment of neutrality means you will not predict how the partner will react based on how she/he has reacted in the past. Holding yourself in a "neutral" position requires a significant effort. The result will be to give your partner maximal opportunity to change.

Attraction

Each of you needs to ask yourself and answer the question, "Am I attracted to my partner?" Perhaps you became involved with her/him just because she/he fulfilled the criteria on a parental checklist, or even your own checklist. Perhaps your partner has changed in some way that you do not find attractive. Or perhaps your tastes have changed, or you have a deeper understanding beyond attractiveness.

There are three ways you need to find your partner attractive:

1. **As a person:** What are the character traits that you find attractive in someone you live with? Is your partner someone who is intelligent, honest, trustworthy, good-looking, serious, fun-loving, neat and clean, reliable, kind and considerate, a homebody, unafraid to work hard? Is she/he someone who possesses a sense of humor, who can make commitments and stick to them, knows what she/he wants and goes after it, likes animals, believes in the same or similar religion as you, has the same value system, wants the same or similar lifestyle? Try to think of as many attractive characteristics as you can.

2. **As a man or woman:** Do you enjoy her/his expressions of masculinity or femininity? The male image of warrior, womanizer, and worker that the entertainment industry frequently portrays doesn't appeal to every heterosexual woman or homosexual male. Similarly, not everyone is attracted to the same aspects of femininity, whatever a particular woman may present to others.

3. **As a lover:** Are you attracted to your partner sexually? Does she/he turn you on? Is there chemistry?

   ■   *"I married my husband for all the right reasons except one. I was never turned on by him. Marrying him was a mistake. All the other aspects were so perfect for us, but they couldn't compensate for that lack of chemical attraction. I never told him. He thought I had some sexual hang-up. It wasn't fair to either of us."*

If the assessment of these three aspects reveals voids or gaps, do you think any of these attractions would return if the two of you worked through your difficulties? Was the lack of attraction in one or more of these categories a significant part of the difficulties in your relationship?

In the absence of significant attraction in any category, think carefully about whether or not you truly want to try to continue the relationship. This is especially important if the sexual attraction was lacking for one of you, and if that lack of attraction led to an affair. (See Chapter 26 for more on sexual attraction.)

We are talking about at least a significant amount of attraction, not your maximum attraction. It is not uncommon for people to realize they would not want to live with or have children with the type of person to whom they are maximally attracted. There is always the potential to meet someone who is more attractive or younger or who has a more appealing lifestyle.

There is a lot to be said for the ability to make a commitment and stick to it. It gives stability. It generates a common history. It gives a sense of self-identity. Happiness is not found in chasing everyone you find sexually attractive. Ultimately, the chaser will end up without anyone to love or to be loved by. That is loneliness and depression, if not despair. Commitment with the *right* person offers one of life's greatest opportunities to find true happiness. Whether putting an old relationship back together or starting with someone new, it will take serious effort, but the payoff makes it all worthwhile. □

IN BRIEF

As prerequisites to making a joint concentrated commitment to work toward re-establishing a loving relationship, the two of you need to:

1. *Make a commitment to stop ongoing hurts. This commitment may include a 12-step program and some restructuring.*

2. *Let go of old hurts and exercise neutrality when interpreting messages from your partner.*

3. *Look at the current status of your attraction to your partner, as a person, as a man or woman, and as a sexual partner. Is saving this relationship worth the effort?*

YET TO COME

How to change habit patterns of transforming hurts.

CHAPTER 24
CHANGING THE HABIT PATTERN OF TRANSFORMING HURTS

Make a comprehensive pact involving what each of you wants to change for the benefit of the relationship. Identify ways you want your partner to help you change your issues.

Changing the pattern of transforming hurts is not an easy task. Or, more accurately, it is not an easy series of tasks. Continuing efforts to change must be maintained until the substitute behavior has become habit. In therapy circles this latter process is called "working through."

This chapter is divided into three parts:

1. **Cooperative Efforts to Change** discusses the process of two partners working cooperatively to make a pact to bring about change in the dysfunctional patterns each has for transforming hurts.

2. **Resistance to Committing to a Pact** discusses what one determined individual might do to effect change when the partner is resistant to agree to work for change.

3. **Changing Patterns Successfully** deals with the creative identification of alternative, substitute behaviors that are both meaningful and acceptable, or at least tolerable, to the partner. Without this capstone, efforts at change will likely fail in the long run.

Cooperative Efforts to Change

Hopefully, by now the two of you have identified the troublesome patterns of transforming hurts that each of you need to change in yourself, plus those patterns each of you need your partner to change. (See Section IV) A positive way to initiate the cooperative action necessary to change dysfunctional patterns for transforming hurts is to make a pact. The elements of such a pact are:

• Statement by each individual of the changes she/he is committed to make.

• Endorsement by each partner of the other's goals in the way hurts are transformed.

• Agreement on the completeness of the stated goals for a happy relationship.

Don't leave a major issue off the table.

- Agreement to "alert" each other when an undesirable behavior is perceived to be unfolding or has occurred.

Inform your partner of the changes you are committed to make and get her/his endorsement for them. Ask if there are other changes she/he would like for you to make. Discuss the substitute behaviors you want to try. Get your partner's input. They may be vague in your mind. It is OK to acknowledge that the two of you will work out the specific details later.

√ **Your and your partner's motivation and commitment are the greatest determinants of successful change.**

Ask your partner for help in making those changes; be specific in exactly what you would like him/her to do. Specifically, how do you want to be alerted when, on occasion, you revert to behavior you have committed to change? Perhaps the alert could be tapping on the corner of your eye, meaning, "Look at yourself," or pointing to you chest with your thumb. If you use words, we suggest something like, "I see behavior that you have asked me alert you to." Later this might be shortened to: "Alert." The pact to change the habit pattern should include informing the partner of a hurt as soon as it is recognized—perhaps "Ouch!"

If the two of you have not addressed your partner's side of each of these steps as well as your own, then do so now. Ask what changes she/he is willing to commit himself/herself to make for the benefit of the relationship. The more balanced both agreements are, the better. However, they don't need to be mirror images, nor do the alerts need to take the same form.

Don't get hung up on language. The terms "hurts," "anger," "put-downs," "slights," and "insults" can all be responded to in the same way. If a different word is used, such as "irritant," let it pass. If your partner continues to call hurts or put-downs irritants, you can join her/his wording and call them irritants, too. Don't insist that your partner admit that it was a put-down. Leave room to save face. The benefit to the relationship will occur in the future.

On the other hand, if you are offended by a word your partner selects, let your partner know how you hear that term the first time it is used. If your partner responds in a positive way, good; if not, at least feedback was provided, and your partner got the message. Wait to see what term she/he uses next time. Let it pass once. On the following occasion you can judge the depth and intensity of your annoyance and decide to live with it, or you may raise the issue again.

The partner doesn't have to admit she/he fell back into unhealthy behavior to change behavior next time. Use all the communication tools discussed in the preceding chapters of this book to clarify the interaction and to back up the discussion to the first hurt either of you had since you were feeling OK about each other.

Initiating the discussion the first time after making the commitment to address— and, hopefully, to change—the patterns can be scary. Below are two alternative ways to begin, in addition to simply saying, "Ouch!"

- "I find I'm a little scared, but we agreed to look at our hurts together and to find a better way to deal with them. Remember? Well, here is my first hurt. I felt belittled by _____. Did you have an earlier hurt? Did you intend your statement to be hurtful? Please don't belittle my hurt."

- "My heart is in my throat. We made a pact to work together to change the way we deal with hurts. Now I see you are angry. Where was your hurt? I didn't mean to put you down."

Similar general statements could be made if the partner withdraws or shouts down further discussion.

Some couples find that a hand signal or gesture indicating a need or desire to interrupt the scenario is less provoking than words. Some couples find the "halt" sign comes across as a command rather than as an **I** statement. Other couples signal "This is crazy" by pointing one finger at their head and making a circular motion; after one or two turns they extend a second finger to signify "Both of us are acting crazy" or "We are going around again."

Hopefully, the partner will pause in his/her reaction to hear what was said and to begin to look at what has transpired.

√ *Under stress, people tend to revert to old established habits.*

Sometimes people will intensify their habitual behavior used to deal with hurts. Under stress, is it common to revert to old established habits. In this situation, it is usually better to wait until the hurt reaction has passed or cooled down before inviting examination of the interaction. A hurtful situation can be examined days or weeks after the incident. A delay of several days is customary in all once-a-week therapy.

■ *One couple lies stomach-down on the bed with their heads turned toward each other and with an arm on each other's back as they engage in discussion. Their touch is reassurance of their underlying affection and commitment as they talk of their hurts and resentments.*

Judging Progress

Progress is being made when the two of you can talk about the issues together. Don't necessarily expect to come up with all the right answers in the first several discussions. Progress is being made when each is clear on what can be done differently next time. Don't focus on the past except as a learning exercise, and don't focus on the difficulties of the first several confrontations. Such focus leads to feelings of inadequacy and blaming each other. Focusing on the next time leads to a sense of mastery, adequacy, and hope.

If the two of you are persistent, the "What we can do differently next time?" changes progressively. If the alerts result in hurts or put-downs, modify the messages and the manner they are communicated. If the alerts continue to cause grief after two or three efforts to modify the messages, then you might just walk away, which is an alert. Follow up with words later. If your partner is still unreceptive, revisit your agreed-on pacts to change.

If previous hurts resulted in anger and harsh put-down words, progress is being made when you have a less-heated discussion. Most importantly, progress is being made when the two of you can interrupt a habit pattern earlier than usual in the typical scenario. The sooner either of you realizes that you are in an old habit pattern and stops moving down the usual path, the better.

In the early stages of rebuilding, it will be important to recognize effort to change in yourself and, especially, in your partner. Generally, people use different criteria to give credit to themselves or to others. Credit is given to others who appear to do something with minimal effort, while we give credit to ourselves for achieving something that was difficult for us. If we need someone to hold our money, we will choose someone who we think will not be tempted to use it for her/his own purposes. Similarly, if we need our appendix removed, we prefer someone who is skillful, confident, and experienced. Yet the individual who struggles with possibly misappropriating our funds—but doesn't—will give himself more credit than will the person who never thought about spending the money. Similarly, the budding surgeon doing her first solo operation will exert much more effort and give herself much more credit than will the experienced surgeon.

√ ***Generally, people tend to give themselves credit for effort, but give others credit for doing things effortlessly.***

It is also important to recognize change and to give your partner credit in non-patronizing ways. Be guided by the responses to the appreciation you have expressed in regard to previous changes. Perhaps your partner wants the new responses to be assumed to be normal. Try responding with a smile.

Difficulty Expressing Even Slight Hurts

Some couples have difficulty mentioning *any* displeasure, let alone hurts or anger. However, hurts do disrupt the overall happiness of a relationship in ways that are usually not fully recognized at the time. This advice is contrary to most common thinking that goes something like: "We have trouble with anger; therefore I won't risk more bad feelings by trying to deal with the situations that are minimal, but instead will address only the major ones sparingly."

Our advice is to gain practice and experience with situations of minimal anger: "I find myself angry. It stems from my hurt about _____. Did I misinterpret what you said or did you intend for me to take it the way I did?" Remember, you are operating on the basic assumption that a hurt is either accidental-careless, a miscommunication, or retaliation for a prior hurt. This couple need not be concerned with the other possibilities. (See some of Chapter 7)

"I don't know how to hear that. On one hand it seems OK, but on the other, I hear a put-down in it. Which way would you like me to take it?"

Repeat this over several days or weeks as the opportunities arise. If these go OK, then you may shorten your statement, e.g., "How do you want me to receive that?" Then, "My sending can't be all that clear all the time, either. Do you sometimes have questions about my messages to you? I would like the opportunity to clarify it if you ever hear an ambiguous message or a put-down from me."

Constant Criticism, Anger, or Control

Other difficult patterns arise when one partner is constantly critical, angry, or controlling. Such patterns begin as a means to keep from being hurt. In time, the patterns may become more habitual than defensive. Even so, the approach we suggest is the same. To help change a situation, do three things simultaneously:

1. Identify any area in which there is no control, criticism, or anger—maybe with children, friends, or parents. Compliment your partner on dealing with an issue in one of these relationships. Be sincere, but look for instances to compliment. Later, say, "I wish our relationship could be more like _____."

2. At the lowest level of your partner's criticism/control/anger, be more assertive: "I would like to do this my way this time," or, "I don't think this task/job calls for that degree of perfection.[22] I want to do it my way." If you have a sit-down discussion, talk about your need for autonomy, identity, and self-esteem: "I thought this task was my responsibility; as such, I expect to be in charge unless I ask for you to take over."

3. Begin to challenge your partner's anger/control/criticism, e.g. (without sarcasm), "You see, I can risk getting into difficulty with this job because I know I can always call on you and you will be able to do it well. In the meantime, I

---

[22] When an auto or airline manufacturer places an order for a part, the precision required is specified, e.g., to a tolerance of 0.01 inch.

can get a sense of achievement if I do it OK." Again, "My love for you would have much more room to grow if I felt you were more vulnerable to my fouling up and would still love me." Or, "Hey, hold on to that anger, control, or criticism a bit. You can blow later, if you really need to. Right now, I need you to please just be helpful, patient, and vulnerable."

Resistance to Committing to a Pact

All too frequently there is significant resistance on the part of one or both partners to make a pact that is a commitment to change the self and to assist the partner in her/his efforts to change. Or the resistance may center around one— or several— particular patterns of transforming hurts being included in the set of goals to change. Yet the partners continue to stay together and to complain about their unhappiness.

Usually this resistance is more focused on making the verbal commitment to the pact than it is on participating in making the changes. Not surprisingly, individuals who have the greatest reluctance have a need to be in control, or at least not to feel controlled by the partner. Often they are somewhat put off by the idea of such a pact originating in a book or from a therapist instead of being their own creation. Secondarily, they don't want to be put in a position to have someone point out to them that they are not living up to their agreement to change: "If I don't agree to the pact, I can't be tagged out."

Assume you have a tentative pact if: (1) your partner listens attentively as you describe the changes you want to make and the help you would like from him/her in making those changes, and (2) the attentive listening persists—without objection— through your statements of the changes you would like him/her to make. The omitted element from a true pact is the partner's request for your help in her/his own changing by giving alerts when you perceive a detrimental behavior pattern beginning to unfold. Proceed on the assumption of a pact with all but this one element.

As you proceed, observe your partner's cooperation, however tentative. You will need to find some way to acknowledge her/his cooperation, but without giving praise or overt appreciation. For the person who needs to feel in control, receiving praise can trigger resentment. Parents and superiors give praise to children and subordinates. Hence, it is open to being perceived as usurpation of control, despite your intentions. Any immediate positive response, including the brief, knowing smile, may be too much.

√ *Being praised can trigger resentment for the person who needs to feel in control.*

Sabotage, another form of partner resistance, is insidious and often goes unrecognized. In some instances the sabotage is outside of the full conscious awareness of one or both partners. The sabotage begins when partner **A** recognizes the presence of a trigger that led to a habit pattern that partner **B** is committed to change, and **B** begins to act in the habitual complementary way to reinforce the old pattern. Partner **B**'s response may be exaggerated.

To effect change, it is important that the partner assumes that some change is underway and tolerates the ambiguity of what that change will entail. Not to expect change, and to respond as usual in the old scenario, is to stack the deck against any change being made. By changing her/his response, the partner sends the message that "This time, I suspect, something is already different."

This concept of not falling into the usual role in the old behavior pattern will be a constant, ongoing effort that needs to be updated and renewed after each significant interaction. This requires commitment, effort, and vigilance until a new behavior pattern has become established.

In the treatment of addiction there is a concept of the partner being co-dependent with the one who is addicted. (See "Co-Dependency," Chapter 20) Co-dependent means doing things that contribute to the addiction. These actions may be overt or subtle. They are usually not in full awareness, but rather are felt to represent being oneself, or some other rationalization.

> ■ *One substantially overweight woman announces to her husband that she is going to lose 80 pounds. When she has lost 20 pounds, her loving husband buys a large freezer and 57 gallons of her favorite flavors of ice cream. When confronted, he replies, "It was on sale. They are your favorite flavors. I thought you would like it. It is a loving gift." She understands his intent—he doesn't want her to lose weight. With some probing, he comes to realize that he believes that if she loses weight she will be extremely attractive, that other men will approach her, and that she will leave him for one of them.*

Less obvious examples include: (1) maintaining a supply of alcohol in the house "for guests," despite the fact the partner is an alcoholic, and (2) rescuing the partner financially when she/he chronically overspends.

√ *If one person in an intimate relationship is hurting or miserable and is not successful in hiding it, then both are unhappy.*

"Tough love" is an approach based on the concept of not aiding and abetting the very behavior that both people say they want to eliminate.

There are limits to the changes a person can achieve single-handedly, regardless of the amount of motivation. There is also variation in how easily and rapidly changes can be achieved. Hence, there is a great deal of difference in saying, "I'm willing to work to achieve what we both want because I think that, potentially, I can be happier with you than anyone else," as opposed to saying, "Well, I'm willing to see what changes." The first statement is full commitment; the second is passive, conditional, and weak.

Summary of Changing Patterns Successfully

A successful assault on the old hurtful patterns requires a two-pronged attack:

1. Talk about the hurt, and progressively back up the discussion/argument to the earliest and most basic issue(s).

2. Identify the habitual transformation of hurts and its detrimental consequence to the self or to the relationship, and identify and implement a substitute expression of that feeling or behavior.

Both prongs of the attack need to be pursued simultaneously. To pursue only one is apt to result in failure to change the habit pattern.

There are numerous ways to identify and implement a substitute expression:

- Define areas of autonomy.

- Find different means of generating and experiencing excitement.

- Break the rejection-control cycle by freely giving warmth (the opposite of rejection).

- Find different ways to feel adequate as a man or woman other than looking for someone new to confirm your attractiveness or sexual desirability.

- Walk out of the house and slam the door instead of hitting your partner. Work out at the gym or club; a vigorous game of tennis or handball will dissipate muscle tension. If necessary, call your partner to tell him/her where you are, and continue your approach to the issue(s) at a safe distance.

√ *Identify the habitual transformation of hurts, then identify and implement a substitute expression of that feeling or behavior.*

Back the discussion up to the first hurt either of you had since you were getting along OK. In doing so, remember that behavior can generate hurts. Under these circumstances, the first hurt is usually discovered to be a miscommunication, which is readily corrected, and the hurt is resolved. Try to be honest, which may entail saying harsh things.

■ *Partner A is later than expected in arriving home. Partner B is hurt by the lateness and the absence of a telephone call. B expresses hurt-irritation: "It's a frequent problem. I don't feel respected." A's honest reply might well be: "Coming home is not something I look forward to anymore."*[23]

Partner B: *"What would it take for you to look forward to coming home?" This is a far better response than a caustic, "Well if you got home on time once in a while it might just be a little more pleasant."*

Partner A: *"A warm greeting."*

Partner B: *"I have a hard time doing that when I feel demeaned by your lateness."*

Partner A: *"When I took this job I really was looking forward to getting home as soon as I could. Now I think I realize that the time I set to be home was optimistic and unrealistic. How would it be for you if we changed the expectation by half an hour or 45 minutes? I think I can make the half hour most of the time, and you could count on the 45 minutes. I hear it is not the time away, it is your demeaned feeling when I am late."*

Partner B: *"Let's try it."*

In time, and with practice, the two of you will catch the old hurt pattern earlier and earlier. □

IN BRIEF

Use a two-pronged simultaneous attack to change the habit pattern of transforming hurts. Find new and acceptable substitutes for other emotional needs for compound problems, and use all the communication skills to back up the hurt to the first hurt since you were feeling OK with each other. Be patient. Be persistent.

YET TO COME

Accentuating the positive.

---

[23] That's the honest part—no temporary excuses or explanations.

Chapter 25
Rebuilding

Be kind, considerate, and polite. Have fun together. Do the two of you look in the same direction when you consider something greater than yourselves?

Recreate the habit of being kind and considerate to each other. Do little things, as well as big things, for your partner. Such acts demonstrate you are thinking about your partner; they are acts of caring. Be polite to each other. The word "please" costs so little and means so much. "Thank you" is in the same category. There are many non-verbal ways to say it: a touch, a glance, and a smile.

The individuals in an ongoing committed relationship need first to be friends. Just being friendly is not enough; they need to value and enjoy each other. Friendship implies the absence of all major negatives as well as enjoying significant positives. In setting your goals for change, realize that elimination of negatives may be a prerequisite for building something positive, but it will never be sufficient to create something positive—just as the elimination of debt will not, by itself, build wealth.

The history of a couple's courtship contains many aspects that can be useful in re-building the positives. What interests have you shared and enjoyed? Have some of these activities fallen by the wayside?

If the two of you think you need more and different kinds of fun together, then explore new activities. You can take turns suggesting a joint activity. Recognize that trying out something might be a stretch for one of you.

The list of potential activities seems endless. The following categories of activities of potential enjoyment[24] include those of Masters and Johnson's sensual inventory:

- **Body Movement:** Moving your body through space, as in skiing, swimming, "working out," walking, and hiking constitute one group. There are also games that involve body movement, such as tennis and golf. Sailing and riding bi-cycles, motorcycles, and horses form another group. Dancing together—mov-ing your bodies in harmony and with physical contact—is worthy of serious consideration. Don't be put off by dancing lessons. Dancing also involves touching.

- **Touch:** Touch means "I am here with you." It can be very empathic. When your partner is feeling stressed or bored, a touch often relieves some of the tension. A squeeze intensifies the touch. Hug each other often, and hold the

---

[24] We recognize others may group potential pleasurable activities entirely differently.

hug slightly longer than you have been inclined to. There is enjoyment in both touching and in being touched. The sensuality of touching also includes touching animals and pets, and can be extended to encompass activities such as woodworking and hobbycrafts.

- **Travel:** Trips have several different aspects of enjoyment. They include considering where to go, anticipating what new experiences you are likely to have, and sharing souvenirs, photos, and stories with others when you return.

- **Intellectual Challenge:** A number of people find that intellectual challenges such as crossword puzzles, bridge, chess, and other mental activities are a meaningful way to relate. These challenges may be competitive or cooperative.

- **Creativity:** Creative endeavor is often a one-person activity, but it can be assisted and enjoyed by both.

- **Visual Stimulation:** Enjoyment from vision includes: bird watching, exploring museums, and enjoying nature and scenic wonders. Couples may become interested in art and sculpture, plays, spectator sports, or looking at each other.

- **Sound Stimulation:** Enjoyment of music, birdcalls, and other sounds of nature can be shared. Reading to each other can be enjoyable, for the reader as well as for the one listening to the sound of the partner's voice.

- **Taste and Smell Stimulation:** Some couples move to increase enjoyment from taste and smell. It can range from exploring the fragrances of perfumes and colognes, or the taste of various herbs and spices, to becoming gourmet cooks and wine connoisseurs.

A word of caution: Don't try to make all of your enjoyment joint activities. Everyone needs solitary activities and activities with a same-gender friend. (See "The Times of Your Life," Chapter 8)

Sexual Intimacy

Sexual intercourse is the height of physical intimacy. If a couple uses intercourse as the height of psychological intimacy as well, it takes on a dimension greater than the sum of the individual elements. The freedom to explore stems from the assurance that each of you can move to enhance your own arousal with your partner in a whimsical, non-goal oriented, spontaneous manner with full confidence that your partner will protect you from doing anything that is physically or psychologically uncomfortable.

Sexual arousal is "contagious." As your partner becomes aroused, your own arousal increases.

√ *Sexual intercourse is the height of physical intimacy. If a couple also uses it as the height of psychological intimacy, it takes on a dimension that is greater than the sum of the elements.*

Sex is also holding hands, snuggling, noticing your partner's appearance, and making complimentary comments. Sex is "drinking in" your partner's masculinity or femininity. It is doing thoughtful things for your partner. It is making and holding eye contact. It is spontaneous touches, sharing, and having sexual fun together.

Psychological sexual intimacy includes a healthy, lusty sexual exuberance between the two of you. Different couples enhance their sex by adding dimensions of romance and creativity. Some couples go one step further and play at their sex in a free, whimsical, and spontaneous way. Many couples view sexual exploration within their relationship—such as erotic clothing, environment, music, varying sexual positions—as enhancements that add variety and novelty to an already enjoyable encounter. (See Chapter 26)

Psychological Intimacy

Rebuilding love and affection is sending the message in little everyday ways that you value your partner's happiness almost as much as you value your own. This message is probably conveyed as much by attitude as by action, and it takes many forms:

- **Showing** happiness to see your partner, positive attitude, cheerfulness, consideration.

- **Informing**, as in verbalizing your feelings and thoughts, especially the whimsical ones; letting your partner into your mind.

- **Asking** your partner's feelings and thoughts on almost all issues that could have an impact on the partnership's daily living.

- **Responding** to your partner's request for help or moral support in his/her endeavors; sending a message that you are receptive to such a request.

- **Requesting** opinions, support, help from your partner without concern about how your partner will hear the requests.

- **Communicating** without fear of being misunderstood, knowing that if a misunderstanding does arise the two of you can readily resolve it.

- **Rejecting** a request or accepting a rejection of a request with understanding, grace, and love. (See Chapter 27)

- **Doing** little thoughtful things that ease your partner's day.

- **Romancing** with little things and big things that show your thoughtfulness, caring, attraction, and ingenuity.

Religion/Spirituality

When two partners are in concert about their religion and/or spirituality, it can function as a powerful uniting force for the relationship. For many people, religion and spirituality are synonymous; for others, organized religion is far afield from their spirituality. If differences in religious beliefs and/or spirituality have been a source of discord or something each has kept personal, find other kinds of common ground such as appreciating beauty while keeping arguments over other topics like evolution versus creation off-limits.

Some people experience their spirituality in the sacred depths of nature. They find the awe and wonder in the sea, waves on the beach, the sounds and sight of birds, lightning, mountains, the Aurora Borealis, the moon, sun, stars, and the vastness of the universe. Then there is the enjoyment, excitement, pleasure, and satisfaction of sharing your body with your partner. And, most especially, there is the wonder when one's child is born.

Wherever you find this, share it with your partner, and share your partner's awe and reverence, too, non-judgmentally. We all need something to remind us that there are things bigger than ourselves and our preferences. The closest thing you two have within your joint power to make greater than yourselves is a happy family.

You may benefit from rereading "Romance," Chapter 11. □

IN BRIEF

Have fun together. Explore all the forms of sensuality together. Can the two of you find wonder, awe, and greatness in the same places?

YET TO COME

Sexuality.

Section VI
Sexual Communication

Even if sex is enjoyable, it is only a part in the overall relationship. But if sex is lousy, it can dominate and spoil the whole of the relationship. This section is not so much about sex as it is about some sexual communication techniques for you and your partner.

Sex is perhaps the aspect that is the least likely to be fully integrated into one's personality and one's daily living. As a result, some people are free to express their preferences and hurts to the partner in every area except sex. Some people diminish their and their partner's sexual enjoyment by being overly concerned about pleasing the other at the expense of representing themselves and maximizing their own enjoyment. Both partners then miss out on the contagion of the other's sexual enjoyment.

Bear in mind that most sexual problems are correctable by therapy today. Also, people can overcome sexual inhibitions. What a person finds sexually attractive in another is very difficult to change, even when the individual's desire to change is great.

Sexual attractions are habitual. Orgasm is a powerful conditioner and reinforcer, especially when combined with the satisfaction of a psychological need.

The following statement of Sexual Intimacy is repeated for your convenience:

Sexual intercourse is the height of physical intimacy. If a couple uses intercourse as the height of psychological intimacy as well, it takes on a dimension greater than the sum of the individual elements.

Sex is also holding hands, snuggling, noticing your partner's appearance, and making complimentary comments. Sex is "drinking in" your partner's masculinity or femininity. It is doing thoughtful things for your partner. It is making and holding eye contact. It is spontaneous touches, sharing, and having sexual fun together.

Psychological sexual intimacy should include a healthy, lusty sexual exuberance between the two of you. Different couples enhance their sex by adding dimensions of romance and creativity. Some couples go one step further and play at their sex in a free and spontaneous way. Many couples view sexual exploration within their relationship—such as erotic clothing, environment, music, varying sexual positions—as enhancements that add variety and novelty to an already enjoyable encounter.

CHAPTER 26
UNDERSTANDING & MAXIMIZING
SEXUAL AROUSAL

Understanding some frequent sexual situations that can cause problems when misinterpreted.

In the broadest sense, this whole book is about effective sexual communication and one of its products, sexual arousal. These in turn are manifest by (1) representing yourself verbally and being assertive in other ways, (2) increasing your self-esteem, (3) respecting your partner, and (4) expecting, almost demanding, respect from your partner. Sexual arousal is an attitude of genuinely caring about your own happiness and sexual enjoyment, plus that of your partner. Further, it is communicating that caring to your partner and receiving, in return, indications from your partner of caring for your happiness, comfort, and sexual satisfaction. It is the freedom to be you, without any need for uncomfortable pretense for the sake of pleasing your partner. It is being free to be vulnerable to your partner by being free to be nude, to express your sexual attitudes and desires without any fear of sexual criticism or ridicule. It is resolving hurts with trust and respect, and together exploring ways to enhance your mutual sexual enjoyment.

Sexual Interest

A great deal could be written about self-esteem and sex. Individuals who feel that their appearance is sexy, feel sexy. Many people either consciously or unconsciously do things to increase or decrease their sexual feelings and their sexual attractiveness to others. The cosmetic and clothing industries are well aware of these facts. Fashions not only include chic clothes, but the "right" kind of blue jeans or cut-off jeans. Most men and women have greater sexual interest when they feel they are dressed in a sexual manner than they do when dressed otherwise. Others may dress in unflattering clothes or may use obesity to avoid sexuality: "Since I've put on 60 extra pounds, it is rare for a man to hit on me."

Doubts about one's sexuality can prompt a man or woman to engage in sex primarily to remove or confirm self-doubts. If the doubt sinks so low as to create a feeling that the individual can't be aroused, then interest drops significantly. Sexual interest is very low or absent in depression. On the other hand, "feeling like a million dollars" or "feeling on top of the world" enhances sexual interest.

Self-esteem has two major roots: (1) achievement, and (2) a sense of being lovable and loved, including receiving respect and recognition from others. Any significant achievement—solving a nagging problem at work, being victorious in a battle, winning a close game—will add to sexual interest. Anything that adds to a sense of being valued for the self alone will add to sexual interest: "I'm worthy because *I am*." Originally the sense of being valued usually came from parents and parent surrogates during infancy and early childhood. For adults, it often comes from a lover. The sense of being valued/respected can come from non-sexualized relationships. Regardless of the origin, there will be an increase in sexual interest.

Recognition, acclaim, and admiration add to self-esteem and sexual interest. The sense of being valued may often grow if it is nourished by the consistent attention of someone who meets the criteria of the individual's sexual value system. This may occur by one person (often the male) hanging around the places where the other is likely to be. It occurs naturally when two people work together. The sense of being valued is increased when admiration is added to the above-mentioned attention. The admiration can be grounded in work activities that are not of a routine nature. Compliments are a form of admiration, as are other forms of recognition and tokens of appreciation. Small gifts of flowers, candy, etc. are usually in the romantic realm.

Loss of Sexual Interest

Depressed people have little or no sexual interest. The deeper the depression, the less the sexual interest. Even mild depression, characterized by feelings of boredom and not having much to look forward to, likely will be accompanied by significant loss of sexual interest.

Mild depression can be very difficult to recognize, either in a partner or in oneself. The question "What do I (or my partner) do for fun?" is often revealing. Fun activities that are engaged in only three or so times a year are to be discounted; there needs to be some fun/enjoyment activities each week. Mild depression can be combated by having fun or by expressing hostility—or both.

√ *We all need fun and enjoyment activities each week.*

A chronic sense of guilt can cause depression. If the guilt is sexual in nature, guilt feelings may arise every time sexual feelings begin to occur and, in a more selective way, block sexual interest. Other areas of life may or may not be affected.

Anger often results in reduced sexual interest because angry people don't feel like being close. Most people recognize that acute anger creates distance. However, many people don't recognize that chronic unresolved anger can diminish or even eliminate sexual interest. Unlike the other causes of low sexual interest, the loss with anger usually is only in that particular relationship. This is assuming a person is not angry with all men or women, or the whole world.

√ *Love and sex tend to unite and to make two people one. Anger tends to separate and individuate.*

Anger can enhance sexual interest in three ways:

1. Individuals who are afraid of being swallowed up, of losing all of their identity or separateness. This is the autonomy issue in another form. Love and sex unite and tend to make two people one. Anger separates and individualizes. These people make passionate love only after a fight and having felt independent and autonomous. At other times their sexual interest often is quite low.

2. People who measure their self-esteem in terms of control over others. They put themselves up by stepping on other people's heads or sexuality. Some prostitutes value this control over their customers. At the same time, the customers may value their control over the prostitutes.

3. Some men who have fused anger with their sexuality seek out prostitutes and "screw my anger into the whore." The more extreme cases are sadists or rapists, who want to inflict physical pain. They may or may not experience guilt. The prospect of guilt may protect some of these men from acting or even thinking as a sadist or rapist. All or much of their sexual interest may be suppressed to avoid those thoughts and their associated guilt. For other men, their anger may jam or override their conscience and their awareness of risks and, therefore, result in an unleashing of these behaviors.

Fear and worry may reduce sexual interest. Usually the individual is aware of any fear, but minimal levels of depression or anger may go unrecognized. Acute anger and acute fear are emergency emotions. The body responds via many mechanisms to prepare to fight or run. These body reactions are the opposite of those needed for sexual arousal. The emergency emotions predominate. However, because the fear is not a sexual fear, the individual may not realize that her/his low sexual interest is due to the chronic fear.

In its response, the body does not distinguish the origin of the fear. It does not have separate body reactions to the fear of being burned, of making a fool of oneself, and of not being able to adequately perform sexually. The body's response to fear is always along the same path. The response varies only in the degree of fear.

Fatigue—whether mental, emotional, or physical—reduces sexual interest. The fatigue may be the result of an extended period of mental concentration, or it may be chronic, as with the individual who is a workaholic. Emotional fatigue may also reduce sexual interest.

Human beings vary in almost all dimensions. We vary in our level of sexual desire just as we do in height or intelligence. Humans also vary in tastes, including sexual tastes. Hopefully, the differences in sexual interest between partners is not too great.

Physical Aspects of Arousal

The physical aspects of sexual stimulation and arousal are better understood than are the psychological aspects. Without doubt, the body organ with the greatest potential of generating sexual arousal—in both male and female—is the human mind. Probably the second greatest erogenous zone for low- and moderate-level arousal is the skin, lips, and hair, considered together. The genitals rank third in low-to-moderate levels of arousal, but the genitals are secondary only to the mind at high levels of arousal.

Stroking of the hair and skin is a turn-on in all cultures, as well as among primates. Desmond Morris, in his studies of human sexuality,[25] points out that touching one's own hair or checking to be sure it is as one wishes is a sign of sexual interest. Direct eye contact that is held longer than usual is a message of sexual interest.

Sexual Fantasies

Because the psychological aspects of arousal are most easily seen in the process of masturbation, this will be discussed first.

Physical masturbation is almost always accompanied by sexual thoughts. Some people, especially during their teen years, feel guilty just thinking about sex. Some have guilt over masturbation since sexual thoughts accompany the act. Some work through their internal conflict and become, essentially, free of guilt. Others develop sexual fantasies that relieve them of the moral responsibility for being sexual, which is one origin of rape fantasies in women. Males can avoid the moral responsibility of being sexual by placing it on the woman or on some third individual who they fantasize is forcing them to be sexual.

√ *Sexual fantasies should be free of guilt, and should be something the individual can imagine doing as an adult without remorse.*

Masturbation and the accompanying sexual thoughts and fantasies tend to become habitual. That is, classical conditioning occurs between the levels of sexual arousal in masturbation and the content of the sexual fantasies. The sexual thoughts that habitually are in the individual's mind at the time of physical orgasm may become most sexually arousing and valued as an adult.

---

25 Morris, Desmond: *Sexual Interest*, Oxford Press, 2000

Some young people will masturbate to orgasm while fantasizing exclusively about romance and seduction. Individuals who have not extended their fantasies to include inserting the penis in the vagina, thrusting, and orgasm have not mentally prepared themselves for intercourse as well as those who have occasionally fantasized intercourse and orgasm. For some individuals, their first intercourse may be an anathema, even after an ongoing sexual relationship has been established.

Pornography

Individuals are not limited to their own imaginations for their mental sexual stimulation. A sexy novel is the published version of a sexual fantasy created by the author. Men often use picture pornography for mental stimulation while masturbating. Certainly, both visual and written materials are also enjoyed without physical stimulation, but often they are recalled during subsequent opportunities to masturbate.

The *Merriam-Webster's Collegiate Dictionary*, 1998 Edition, defines pornography as: "The depiction of erotic behavior (as in pictures or writing) intended to cause sexual excitement." This is an interesting definition for the following reasons:

1. It would include sexy and romance novels as well as pictures and movies.

2. It is not sexual behavior but rather its depiction. The definition excludes erotic dancing on stage, but includes pictures or movies of erotic dancing.

3. Pornography is defined by the intent of the producer, not by the effect on the user. Hence, a picture in a men's magazine of a woman in a negligee could be considered pornographic, while the same picture in a *Victoria's Secret* or *Fredericks of Hollywood* catalogue would not be pornographic because the primary intent is to sell negligees.

4. This definition would include a steamy love letter written with the intent of sexually arousing the lover.

We consider it normal for you and/or your partner to enjoy pornography on occasion. However, neither of you should be dependent on it for your sexual arousal. Your sexual interaction with each other should be preferred and should displace pornographic arousal.

For a broader discussion of pornography, see Appendix B. For the topic "Addiction to Pornography," see Chapter 20.

Sexual Arousal in Actual Relationships

In an actual sexual relationship, reality replaces fantasy as the mental sexual stimulation. This reality combines psychological, sensual, and physical stimulation. Most importantly, it includes both touching and being touched, doing and being done to. The partner's responses are not to be watched and evaluated, but to be enjoyed. "My partner is sexually aroused with me!" As the arousal of each partner increases, it increases the arousal of the other, bouncing between them to the crescendo of orgasm.

Another emotion, usually of caring and intimacy, is present in each partner in both actual and fantasized sexual relationships. These emotions are not necessarily the same for each partner. Sexuality can be linked with a sense of adequacy: "I am a real man or woman because I have intercourse." Intercourse can be used to reassure the self that she/he is not homosexual. Sexuality can also be linked emotions of both anger or domination-control.

Sexual responses follow sexual arousal, just as blushing follows embarrassment, and laughter follows humor. Each of these responses in turn intensifies its emotion. These feelings and responses are not learned. Children may be taught not to laugh during religious ceremonies, for example, but that teaching doesn't interfere with other laughter. On the other hand, children may be taught not to laugh too loudly or too long. If they take it seriously, the spontaneity of laughter is stifled. Hopefully your and your partner's sexual socializations were not too restrictive or inhibiting. Learn with each other and from each other. Within this relationship, consider yourself the world's authority on your gender, your own sexual desires, and your sexual responses.

Sexual Turn-Offs

Odors from poor oral or genital hygiene can be sexual turn-offs. Here an appropriate statement might be: "Hey, I'm getting distracted by how we smell. Let's go play in the bathroom and wash up, maybe break out the perfume and cologne." Bathing or showering together, washing each other, etc., are activities which will accomplish the hygienic goal with less likelihood of the partner feeling dirty, frustrated, angry, or loss of arousal.

There are some exceptions, but generally fear is the greatest turn-off: fear of what your partner will think of your body, fear of "not doing it right," fear of not pleasing your partner, fear of losing control. Hopefully, you can set control aside just as you do with a belly laugh. Fear is fear, regardless of the triggers. It is an emergency emotion. It takes priority over pleasurable feelings, but both may exist simultaneously at low to moderate levels.

There is a turn-off phenomenon we call "Too much, too soon, too fast." This turn-off occurs when one partner is somewhat aroused and touches the genitals of his/her non-aroused partner, who is not expecting such a touch and reacts with a startled response. Without a verbal explanation from the partner, this reaction may be taken as a personal rejection. Sometimes even with a verbal explanation, the partner fails to understand. Under these circumstances, the best way to get your message across is to reverse the roles—that is, to touch his/her genitals when she/he is not expecting to be touched. Usually the touchee responds automatically, as though she/he had been attacked. Both genders describe the touch as "grabbing at" or "groping for my genitals," while the toucher thinks of the touch as just a touch for sexual stimulation.

Excitement

The term "excitement" is generally used in two contexts. One is "suspense," such as the outcome of a ball game. Note the decreased interest in watching a delayed showing of an athletic event when the final score is known.

The second context is "sexual excitement." This use implies some element of suspense in each particular sexual encounter. Sameness leads to decreased enjoyment or boredom in sexual as well as in other areas. Most people will listen to their favorite records once or twice at a sitting, but then prefer to listen to a different one. Fear can generate or add to excitement. It is possible for some people to become sexually aroused in certain situations where fear predominates.

Novelty & Variety

Novelty is variety—but it can't be so novel that it is scary! With a trusted partner, anything suspenseful adds to the likelihood of sexual excitement. A shared sexual fantasy can add to variety, novelty, and excitement. If sexual encounters become routine, predictable, and without variation, the individual loses some sexual enjoyment during the encounter, and the anticipation of sameness reduces sexual interest. Novelty can be achieved by varying such things as the setting, preliminaries, the approach, clothing, sexual positions, music, or lighting. A distinction should be made between something that is enhancing because it adds to variety, and the same thing that is or becomes necessary and essential for arousal or orgasm. The latter, if it is an object, is called a fetish.

√   *Variety and novelty add to sexual excitement.*

Couples vary the setting—from their bedroom to in front of the fireplace, to out of doors in the dark or in the moonlight, to hotel rooms with their various types of décor, and to the office. Extreme forms of setting may include an element of chance of being observed, which for some couples adds to suspense and excitement, and which for others is a complete turn-off.

Both partners, men particularly, often are aroused by watching their partner undress or just by looking at the partner naked. Looking at your partner during intercourse is also often enjoyable. This means "lights on."

The invitation itself, whether verbal or simply behavioral, can be quite varied. A couple may remove minimal garments to have intercourse, or one or both may wear something sexy. They may undress each other rapidly or may prolong it, or even play strip poker. They may begin sex play in the shower together.

There are two pairs of variation of sexual attitudes and behaviors that a couple may explore for a given sexual encounter. One may say to the other, "Lie back and let me have at you." The active partner may then adopt a "giving" attitude, often with slow, gentle touching or a massage while the relatively passive partner is primarily "receiving." Or, alternatively, the active partner may "take" with more assertive behavior. The more passive partner then adopts the attitude of "I am yours; take what you would like," with the understood caveat that the more passive partner will protect both of them from the active partner doing anything that the other finds negative. This is the 2nd principle of problem-free sex. (See Chapter 29)

Making and holding eye contact without blinking occurs in two situations. One is hostility—a stare-down. "Who will blink first?" The other situation is sexual. Both mean "I want a piece of you." Protracted eye contact is often used as a pick-up signal. It can also be used by long-term lovers while holding hands to intensify intimacy. As time passes and the eye contact is maintained without a blink, the encounter takes on a different dimension, often deeper and much more spiritual.

Varying the positions for sex play and intercourse can greatly contribute to variety. The three major issues with positions are: (1) Can each see the other's face, even in the dark?— face-to-face seems more intimate to many couples than rear entry does, (2) Where is the weight of each partner? and (3) Which partner is in position to thrust, or are both in a position to thrust?

Both men and women enjoy the woman astride the man, which enables her to thrust the way she wishes on a moment-by-moment basis to maximize her sexual arousal. She is taking. In using this position, the penis is held at about a 45-degree angle toward the man's head, and the woman moves back as much as down to effect the insertion. If the woman holds the penis upright at a 90-degree angle to the man's body and sits down at the same angle, the penis will hit the posterior portion of the pubic bone and, with the woman's weight, can possibly result in serious injury. Once the penis is inserted, the angle can vary at will unless it slips out of the vagina.

Not all sex is penis-in-vagina, even with heterosexual couples. Hand-genital stimulation can occur simultaneously or in turns. A couple may also enjoy oral sex, sex with a sex toy, or anal intercourse.

The admonition to "relax" during a sexual encounter applies to mental relaxation, to be free of anxiety and fear. It also means to be free to move to maximize your enjoyment without thinking, "How am I doing?" or any other judgmental, self-evaluating, or critical thought. It does not mean absence of the muscle tension that accompanies excitement, regardless of its cause. For example, the excitement of watching the last moments of a hard-played ball game will generate muscle contractions, probably most noticeably in the hands and face.

At moderate and high levels of arousal and response, there is an involuntary tightening of the voluntary muscles throughout the body. Some women falsely believe that this muscle tension is interfering with their relaxation and, hence, with their further sexual response. This tightening may also be misinterpreted by the partner as stress or pain. The muscle tension at high levels of arousal or at orgasm does not produce a Mona Lisa smile. However, the smile may occur in the afterglow.

A considerate, but misguided, lover may ask his partner, "Are you getting close to orgasm yet, honey?" Her answer invariably will be, "I am not as close as I was before you asked me." Any thought that is not sexually stimulating will detract from, and sometimes halt, sexual arousal and response. We advise individuals never to ask their partners after intercourse, "Were you orgasmic?" Rather, ask, "Are you satisfied?" or, "Would you like more stimulation of some type?"

Orgasm may sometimes be precipitated by voluntarily tightening some of the pelvic muscles. These are the same muscles used to shut off urination in mid-stream or a bowel movement at midpoint. Sometimes orgasm can be precipitated by a psychological shift to a more assertive, driving, thrusting mode to get one more bit of enjoyment—not for striving toward orgasm.

After orgasm or multi-orgasm, each individual feels satisfied and physically relaxed. Sometimes this may be followed by a depressed feeling, perhaps in contrast. This can be dissipated by extra attention, perhaps a loving kiss.

A woman who is highly aroused and not orgasmic may have physical discomfort following cessation of sex play. Her pelvis is apt to feel heavy, as it does just before a menstrual period. There may be some cramps or low back pain, and in women who have delivered children, there may be pain down one or both legs. These symptoms are produced by pelvic congestion, tissues that are engorged with blood.

The male has a comparable phenomenon from prolonged periods of high arousal without orgasmic release. Pain in the testes, from congestion of blood, is sometimes called "blue balls."

Orgasms are the physiologic response of prolonged levels of high sexual arousal, regardless of the form or type of stimulation that produces the arousal. In other words, orgasms are all the same, whether they result from necking, petting, masturbation, partner-hand stimulation, intercourse, or pure fantasy—as some women can do. However, orgasms themselves vary in intensity, just as do belly laughs, so they don't all feel the same.

Masters and Johnson documented that the most physically intense orgasms—for both men and women—are produced by self-stimulation. That is, the greatest degree of muscle strength and contractions, highest blood pressure, etc., are produced this way. An intermediate physically intense orgasm is produced by partner-hand stimulation. The least physiologically intense orgasm is produced by intercourse. Both men and women said they preferred the orgasm resulting from intercourse as being more satisfying. Perhaps this would be a little like saying the most physiologically intense laughter is triggered by tickling, but most prefer laughter triggered by psychological interaction with another person.

√   *Orgasms vary in intensity, but an orgasm is an orgasm, regardless of the type of stimulation.*

Fantasy in Intimate Relationships

Sometimes in an ongoing relationship, fantasy may occur during intercourse. If the fantasy is only occasional, it is not a reason for concern. If it becomes common during intercourse, it can be understood as an indication of the need for less predictability and more variation during actual lovemaking. If the same fantasy persists over time, or if some type of fantasy becomes necessary, then the individual needs to look at the self, the actual sexual relationship, and the content of the fantasy. The individual may need professional help to do so, especially if the content violates or challenges an ongoing value system.

People tend to fantasize about what they desire but don't have. What would it be like for the individual to create some part (or all) of the fantasy with the partner?

If the fantasy is a romantic one, we suggest seriously considering discussing it. Playing out a caring fantasy adds novelty and excitement. If it is for oral or anal sex, we suggest the individual discuss it with the partner. If you object to getting semen in your mouth, you can play the penis as a flute rather than a clarinet.

On the other hand, if the fantasy involves even pretended humiliation or pain, not to mention the actual infliction of it, then we strongly advise against actualizing it. There is a real danger—not only of the effect on the partner, but more importantly, of the need for a steady increase in the degree of humiliation or infliction of pain. When any sexual fantasy is shared in detail, it may be embarrassing; it may cause a partner to lose respect or become fearful (of one's own reactions or of the partner's). In some instances, sharing sexual fantasies can result in the fantasy losing its attraction.

Before sexual fantasies are shared in a committed sexual relationship, there needs to be a great deal of trust and acceptance of each other. The Cardinal Rule for such sharing is *Protect your partner from continuing anything that results in your psychological or physical discomfort.* This means that either of you has the right—indeed, the obligation—to say "stop" at any and every point, whether in the discussion or in actuality, and for the other to comply without recriminations. With these safeguards in place, and with the confidence that either of you will not hesitate to use them if the experience becomes negative, then shared sexual fantasies can open new avenues of heightened sexual enjoyment and intimacy. □

IN BRIEF

The mind is the most erogenous organ in the body. Sex is a natural body function. Sexual arousal is contagious, bouncing between the partners to crescendo in orgasm. Go for mutual sexual enjoyment and sexual satisfaction, not for Grade-A large erections or intense orgasms.

YET TO COME

Responding to a sexual invitation when you don't feel up to intercourse.

CHAPTER 27
REJECTING AN INVITATION

Minimizing feelings of personal rejection.

Perhaps the most difficult communication to make in an intimate relationship is to decline a sexual invitation without hurting your partner's feelings. To lack an efficient and effective way to communicate—in both directions—is to severely limit the relationship. Some deal with this difficulty by not making clear sexual invitations. During therapy, we often learn from couples that both individuals want more frequent intercourse—much to their partner's surprise. They acknowledge that they are not being turned down but, rather, are not making clear invitations out of fear of being turned down.

> ■ *In one marriage each partner said she/he made 90−95% of all the sexual overtures. In fact, neither one was receiving three-fourths of the invitations being sent by the partner. The husband's sexual invitation consisted of sticking his head around the bathroom door and looking at his wife with his eyes half closed and a grin on his face. The wife, still in disbelief, asked him to show her the expression, then said, "Oh, yes, I've seen that many times, but I didn't know it was a sexual invitation. I thought you had gas or something."*

Yet, these were two professional people with exceptional verbal skills.

Other couples handle the problem by having only one partner make all the invitations and the other always accepting. Usually the wife is in the latter role. She will tell us proudly, "I have never refused my husband." One gets the impression she expects a gold star from the therapists. Our reaction is to realize she has never really given herself whole-heartedly to her husband, or to her own sexual enjoyment. The freedom to respond "No" to a sexual invitation is critical to enjoying the maximum potential sexual happiness. Usually both individuals have some resentment. Psychologically, the right to say "No" precedes the right to say "Yes." Logically, the two go together. A child of about 18 months will say, "No." Children won't begin to use "Yes" until close to the age of three. This period is called the "terrible twos." (See "Negatives," Chapter 3)

Much of adolescent turmoil stems from teens individualizing themselves from their parents. The teens are proving to themselves that they are not just going along with their parents' wishes, that they are not puppets or carbon copies of their parents. They are proving that they are their own persons and are establishing their autonomy. This process is similar in adults when one partner needs to say "No" on occasion just to experience his/her own autonomy. Or the motivation may be to make it clear to yourself and the partner that she/he is not just a sexual object.

Equally important to saying "No" is the need to add some other statement about what your position really is.

> ■   *"I don't want to be sexual when we are upset with each other. I often feel that the fact we are feeling hostile or even cool toward each other somehow triggers your sexual desire. On those occasions when I go along, I experience our sex as having a domination component that I don't sense at other times. I don't know whether that feeling is coming from you or from me. I know I feel it, and I don't like it."*

> √   **People cannot venture a tentative "Yes" to a sexual invitation unless they are sure they can stop without fear of recrimination.**

Lending Oneself

It is much easier to reject an invitation for a walk or car ride—or almost anything else—without hurting the partner's feelings than it is to reject a sexual invitation. With other invitations there is something else that could be objectionable. If there are no negative feelings, we suggest you "lend" yourself to the situation and see if sufficient interest or arousal is present or will develop, given the opportunity. This is not lending yourself to the partner as a martyr or sacrificial sex object; it is lending yourself to the situation to explore your own feelings. For example, a person might say:

> *"Right now, sex is the furthest thing from my mind, but I think I could enjoy snuggling. If things progress on from there and I become aroused, well and good. But if I don't get aroused and need to stop, that has to be all right, too. With either outcome, we will have enjoyed the snuggling."*

Again, people cannot venture such a tentative "Yes" unless they are sure they have the option to stop.

This course of events can run into difficulty if the partner gets hurt or angry by the individual's stopping. "Don't start anything you can't finish," is the admonition. This is a false position, and is one that even the person who makes the statement doesn't live by. For example, if a couple is interrupted in the middle of intercourse by a child or the telephone or some other event, they are usually disappointed. However, most people acknowledge that they enjoyed what they had together. They would have preferred to have gone on, but not climaxing didn't make the whole sexual encounter a waste of time or a negative experience. They are glad they had what physical and psychological closeness they experienced on that occasion, even though they had to stop, rather than not to have had that enjoyment.

If the above situation is true when precipitated by an outside influence, shouldn't it be equally true for a disruptive influence within the partner's head? Based on that assumption, aren't the partner's feelings of equal importance to the telephone or a knock on the front door from a stranger? In our experience, most everyone answers, "Yes, of course, if she/he really does have a change of feelings or can't become aroused on a particular occasion."

So, we are back to how to decline the individual's invitation without rejecting the individual. In thought, the fear is circular. In reality, the very act of lending oneself to explore one's sexual feelings goes most of the way in convincing the partner that she/he is cared for and loved.

By analogy, if one partner—say, the wife—prepares supper and calls her husband to eat, then he says, "I'm not coming," it is very likely she would feel rejection. However, if he says, "I'm not hungry now, but I'll come and sit with you, and maybe the sight or aroma will change my feelings," it is very unlikely she will feel rejected. Recall the earlier principle about not using a negative statement without adding a positive statement.

On the other hand, he might say, "My stomach is feeling queasy. I'm afraid the aroma of food might make me vomit." We doubt she would feel rejected. Of course, he can't say this every night without seeking medical help for his stomach, nor can he eat an hour after she does for more than about the second night.

Similarly, if a partner responds to a sexual invitation by saying, "My stomach is upset," or, "I'm too fatigued," or, "I have a headache," it will probably be accepted by the partner without him/her feeling rejected. But this type of statement must be very rarely used unless other steps are taken to reduce the frequency of fatigue or headaches—or at least to make other time available for sexual play.

√ *The very act of lending oneself to explore one's sexual feelings goes most of the way in convincing the partner that she/he is cared for and loved.*

Go For Sexual Enjoyment, Not Always Intercourse

There are other alternatives to a sexual invitation, some of which belong in every couple's sexual repertoire. After "lending oneself to the situation," one partner might say:

- "I'm not really getting turned on very much, but I do have an erection (or I am lubricated). Be my guest!" This must be done with the idea of giving—not with the idea of duty, obligation, or being used.

- "I don't really feel up to getting turned on, but I will be glad to stimulate you by hand or mouth or vibrator, if you would like me to." This offer can be made at the beginning of a sexual encounter or after lending oneself to becoming aroused. Again, it needs to be done with an attitude of giving, not obligation.

- "I'm not up to doing much, but I will hold you or snuggle while you stimulate yourself." This gives psychological closeness.

Because men tend to be sexual first and social second, they may initiate sex when what they are really looking for is closeness. For the woman to freely give the closeness, even without intercourse, is quite satisfying on occasion, often to the man's surprise.

Feeling May Change Unexpectedly

Sometimes the feeling of being rejected is a delayed reaction of three to ten minutes, which can catch either party off guard just as they are about to fall asleep. The usual history is that after the declining of the sexual invitation, they snuggle, then one of them rolls over and breaks the body contact with the result that the partner, or even the one who rolled over, begins to experience the feeling of rejection. Often just reestablishing body contact, such as a hand on each other, will dissipate the feeling.

There are times when one or both partners are willing or even eager to be sexual, but one falls asleep as they get started. There are other times when a couple feels very fatigued and can't wait to stretch out in bed and get some sleep, but as they settle in they find the slightest touch arousing, so they proceed to intercourse. In retrospect, they don't understand where that energy came from. Both of these occurrences need to be taken as normal, without recriminations.

Another normal situation that sometimes gets misinterpreted as rejection or not caring occurs when one partner delays going to bed together at their usual time. This may be motivated by the need to have some time alone. The other may feel rejected. "She/he doesn't want to be with me, doesn't even want to have the opportunity to be physically close. I am rejected." There is human need for some *Alone Time*. It is as much a human need as is togetherness, though not necessarily for an equal amount of time. The need is more likely to be by the one who has less *Alone Time* during the regular day. It behooves this partner to state the need for *Alone Time*, and it behooves the other to accept the need as normal, without recriminations. (See "Couple Time—Alone Time," Chapter 8)

Don't Make Sexual Promises

Never refuse a sexual invitation with: "Not now, but I will tomorrow night," or any other specific time. Invariably the clock rolls around, and almost as invariably there is a feeling of pressure and obligation triggered by the previous commitment, added to what might remain from the previous refusal. You are setting yourself up for the next sexual encounter to be work instead of fun. One can make a commitment to fix the screen door tomorrow night, but one would not say, "I will laugh tomorrow night." What if tomorrow night comes and nothing is humorous? Of course a person may say, "I'll go to the party tomorrow night and maybe I'll laugh. We'll see." Similarly, one may say, "I'll make time to be alone with you tomorrow night, and we can see how our feelings develop." Such a statement adds to the suspense.

In general, the word "excitement" has two senses—suspense and sexual arousal. This is not coincidental. It implies there is some suspense in what the self and the partner may do next in any sexual encounter.

Living moment by moment implies the right to stop at any and every time. A couple can leave the dance floor at any point. Did you ever see any device that would play recorded music without an eject button?

Sex play is fun even when it doesn't lead to intercourse or even to genital touching. Don't miss out on the little spontaneous touches that sometimes proceed to full blossom. □

IN BRIEF

Instead of an outright rejection of a sexual invitation, suggest some other form of sex play for which you might be in the mood. Don't issue invitations for intercourse; issue them for sex play. If your partner issues an invitation for intercourse, make it clear that you are accepting the opportunity to engage in sex play to see where it leads. Let arousal unfold as a bud unfolds into a blossom.

YET TO COME

Communication during sex play.

CHAPTER 28
SEXUAL COMMUNICATION

Sexual communication during lovemaking needs to minimize distraction and enhance the romantic-sexual mood.

There is implicit communication in every sexual encounter. However, more complex and explicit communication may need to occur in sex play, during intercourse, and afterwards. It behooves a couple to have these communication skills available, in case the need arises. A good lover is not someone who always knows what to do to arouse the partner, but rather one who is astute at picking up even subtle signals from the partner about what she/he thinks might be enjoyable at the given moment.

√ *A good lover is one who can understand the partner's signals and is able to incorporate their meaning in the ongoing process of making love.*

Many men and women expect their partners to become aroused from the same routine sexual approach year in and year out, just as people enjoy their coffee—cream, no sugar—the same way for decades. Sexual pleasure is not like that. Most people prefer some variety and unpredictability in their sex play, both in their own activities and in those of their partner. A sexual touch that on one occasion is highly arousing might on the next occasion—or in the next moment—be distracting or even boring. This desire for variation is also true for many other forms of pleasure. Someone telling a funny joke shouldn't expect the same response from the same audience three nights in a row. People don't eat the same foods prepared the same way night after night, regardless of how much they like them. At an amusement park, people don't repeat the same ride all day; they go from ride to ride. People like variety in the movies they watch and in the music they listen to. It is each partner's desire for variety and unpredictability that makes sexual communication so important.

Of course, there are some basics to learn, such as: "Where is the clitoris?" and, "Which are the most sensitive areas of the penis?" But this knowledge doesn't include what your partner likes or the dynamics of how much, how often, and how softly. For example: when women stimulate themselves sexually, they usually begin with mild pressure some distance from the clitoris. As they become aroused they move to a firmer and more direct touch. At high levels of arousal, they move to a lighter and more indirect touch. There is no way any partner could know the appropriate time of these shifts without signals.

Signals

Children use signals instinctively, but in growing up many lose that spontaneity and have to consciously learn signaling. If a child sitting on his parent's lap feels that the parent's enclosing arm is too tight, the child will loosen the hold. The child will also move a parent's hand from one place to another instinctively. Children understand the momentary nature of requests.

Children at play often change the play by suggesting the group pretend something else. It is almost always accepted. Another child may change the game with another "Let's pretend" suggestion at any time. The first child is also free to change his own prior suggestion.

Good lovemaking recaptures that child-like sense of play. It allows you to give yourself over to the activity and the mood, and progress in ways that enhance the mood. It is a right-brain activity, a purely emotional response. Analysis and self-observation evaluation, or evaluation of the partner that is too deep or more than momentary, can deflate the mood, resulting in an interruption of love-making. Analysis and evaluation are left-brain functions.

In lovemaking, it is important to communicate adequately while keeping left-brain activity—analysis and the processing of information—to a minimum. Consider the woman who says, "I would like a little more pressure on my breast, please. A little more. Oops, that's too much." At this point both partners probably have a lower level of sexual arousal or may have fallen entirely out of the mood.

Vocal Signals

All our lives we have learned to use vocal sounds for communication with or without words. Cooing back and forth with a baby is satisfying to both parties. Two teenagers in love can enjoy talking about nothing on the telephone, just for the pleasure of listening to the other's voice. Music with or without lyrics fits into this category. Some people, especially men, may become aroused by sexual street talk—just saying or hearing the partner say so-called "dirty words." By contrast, hearing "sweet nothings" may add to the feeling and intensity in many relationships. Spontaneous sounds, like movements, may have specific meanings, such as the sound of rapid deep breathing as one partner nears orgasm, which may be taken as a signal. The individual may accentuate these sounds to enhance the signal function, which is often intended and taken to mean: "Please don't change what you are doing."

Signals are deliberate acts to communicate a specific meaning to another who is expected to understand the sender's intent. Signals may be visual, audible, tactile, or body movement. Many signals, especially those intended to convey complex information, are best agreed upon ahead of time and even practiced.

Hand Signals

Touch, including "body English" and hand signals, is less disruptive than verbal directions. The woman communicating how she would like her clitoris stimulated could put her hand on top of her partner's and press to the exact degree of firmness she wants. The partner doesn't have to think; he simply maintains the pressure she demonstrated. The same signal can be used by a person who experiences a partner's touch as ticklish.

There are five basic hand signals:

1. **Heavier touch** is communicated by pressing the partner's hand to the degree of pressure or firmness desired.

2. **Lighter touch** is conveyed by lifting the partner's hand slightly to achieve the lightness desired.

3. **Change of rate** is conveyed by imitating the desired rate of stimulation anywhere on the partner's body. If that message is not clear, move the partner's hand at the desired rate.

4. **Change body area** is easiest understood when the partner's hand is moved to the preferred areas—hair, thigh, chest, breast—for that moment of time. If a touch is uncomfortable, don't just move the hand away—perhaps leaving it in mid-air—move it to an area.

5. **Change body position** is communicated by moving to that position or by a word, or if the move becomes regular, the two of you can create your own non-verbal signal. Three quick taps anywhere on your partner's body is a good signal that can mean whatever the two of you agree on.

√ *Using hand signals is like a dance where either partner can lead at any given moment.*

The hand signal is a non-verbal **I** sentence: "I think I would prefer this touch." The person receiving the signal does *not* need to know whether the partner is intending to eliminate a negative touch or accentuate a positive one. It is only important to register that, for this moment, your partner thinks she/he would prefer this touch to that one. There is no guarantee, even if the touch is delivered in exactly the way a partner hoped for, that it will be enjoyable. If the touch turns out to be neutral or negative, a second signal can be given. There is no need to remember the particulars of this touch for another time. Depth and intensity can be conveyed by repeatedly sending the same tactile message or by using words.

√ *One clear signal is a non-verbal I sentence: "I think I would prefer this touch."*

We call these actions "signals" because they are not orders or directions, nor are they begging or supplications. The intent is to increase the signal receiver's freedom of choice, not restrict it. Since neither you nor your partner is a mind reader, whatever choice is now made will be an informed one. Most of the time, you will want to touch your partner in the manner indicated, but not always. If it would be negative for you, don't do it.

Practice These Basic Signals

Each partner needs to feel confident she/he can send, and the partner can understand, any of the signals described. They may require practice. We suggest you begin by sitting side by side, with one person at a time in the role of toucher. The toucher starts by stroking the partner's thigh. The touchee then places his/her hand on top of the toucher's hand and sends each signal in turn. Use words freely to clarify the hand signals as needed in this learning phase.

When each of you feels confident about sending and receiving these signals, incorporate them in early sex play. You women can practice signals in the genital areas by moving his hand to and away from your clitoris. In moving his hand "away," be sure to indicate where you would prefer it: hair, breast, thigh, etc. Don't just drop his hand from mid-air. Remember, the message is: "For right now, I think I would prefer this touch to that one." Other signals in the clitoris area that need practice are for firmer and lighter touches, as well as for more direct or more indirect clitoris stimulation. For indirect stimulation, a circular motion around the clitoris is often most arousing.

You men need to show your partner which areas of the penis are the most sensitive. This information is analogous to the location of the clitoris. There are relatively few nerve endings near the tip of the penis. The most sensitive area is the frendlum, where the head or glans of the penis doesn't quite meet on the underside of the penis. The next most sensitive areas are the ridge around the glans and the entire length of the underside of the penis. Practice sending signals to your partner showing the desired rate and the area of the penis you prefer to have stimulated.

Partners can also have fun designing their own signals. These may be grunts, groans, or other verbalizations: "Oh," "Oooo," "Uh," or a single word. A signal for "Don't change what you are doing" is one many couples make spontaneously. The force of thrusting is another. Be creative. Be playful. In being spontaneous, you may send signals that the two of you have not agreed upon. Will this particular signal be understood?

Holding Eye-to-Eye Contact

Prolonged eye contact occurs in two situations in our society. One is "staring the other person down," which may result in a physical attack. The other is when someone is signaling sexual interest or attraction.

Sit on the bed nude with your lover. Face each other, thighs apart, genitals exposed, knees out, and with your feet together. Your knees or feet should touch your partner's. Hold both of your partner's hands. Stare into each other's eyes. Hold that stare. As you hold the stare longer and longer, your mood and thoughts shift and shift again and again. You will seem to reach a different and more meaningful emotion with and about your partnership. Some couples call it a spiritual experience. □

IN BRIEF

Verbal directions during love-making can be very distracting to one or both partners. Desired variations in touch can be communicated non-verbally and unintrusively so the partner receiving the message doesn't even have to shift to left-brain functioning.

YET TO COME

Three cardinal principles for freedom from psychological difficulties with and during sex.

CHAPTER 29
THREE PRINCIPLES

Follow these guidelines to remain free of psychological sexual problems.

Except for some rare examples involving neurotic reactions or child sexual abuse from the past, every couple we have counseled for sexual difficulty has been violating at least one of the following three principles. The order of the principles is not important, but all three are essential. The principles summarize and elaborate on points made earlier in this book.

PRINCIPLE 1.   **Move predominately to maximize your own sexual enjoyment, and expect your partner to do the same.**

Each of us has the best (most accurate) idea of what might be sexually arousing to us at any given moment. It behooves us to move to enhance our own sexual enjoyment without any more thought than is usually involved in deciding which food to put on the fork next. Of course, we all probably also know a few predictable things about our partners' enjoyable sexual repertoire, and it behooves us to provide those words and touches.

> √ *The partner's increased arousal is contagious and adds to the other's overall excitement. But at any particular moment even the most astute partner can't know the other's desires as readily as the other can convey them by simply moving to fulfill them.*

It is fun to give. However, in the scope of things, this type of knowledge would be analogous to knowing how your partner prefers coffee or tea. The stimulation that even a long-term sexual partner desires at any given moment varies widely. To assume what it is that your partner would prefer in this particular sexual encounter is analogous to assuming to know what she/he wants to eat the next time you are in a restaurant, and ordering it without consultation.

If one individual agrees to touch primarily for the other's enjoyment, then that individual has taken both the responsibility for the partner's level of arousal and response, including credit for the partner's orgasm or blame for its absence.

We have seen many women who feel it is their responsibility to arouse their partner. These women believe they have not done their job until they have been sure their partner has ejaculated. Similarly, they tend to give credit to their partner for their own arousal and orgasm. Some of these women feel pressure to be orgasmic: "He is trying so hard to make me orgasmic, and I love him so. I really should be orgasmic." The pressure either "to give" or "to respond" can become a major inhibiting distraction, which often precludes the wished-for response.

Similarly, we have seen many men who take it as their responsibility to make their partner orgasmic. They often have their self-evaluation as a lover dependent on the partner's orgasm. With this task in mind, many men don't allow their partners free rein to touch them as the partners wish. Usually the partners feel worked on, rather than enjoyed.

√ **Good sex is what a person does with the partner, not to the partner.**

Conversely, with a high level of resentment, a woman might inhibit her orgasm by thinking, "I don't want to give him that." If, however, she openly acknowledges the self-interest of moving with her partner to maximize her own enjoyment first, and if she has done this for herself with him, then her orgasm is hers and, similarly, his orgasm is his. The partner may have been (and may continue to be) a necessary part of an individual's arousal, but the partner didn't make it happen.

√ **Would you really want to have lunch (or sex) with a person who tried to present only what she/he thought you wanted?**

We often see couples who have hindered or killed their sexuality with kindness by trying to please their partner without thinking of pleasing themselves, e.g., (1) the man who is trying to turn his wife on, (2) the woman who is working on her sometimes-impotent husband for all she is worth. They watch for feedback—a move, a wiggle, a raised eyebrow. Invariably the partner says something like, "I feel worked on," or, "I feel like a bug under a microscope, my every move analyzed," or, "I feel I'm alone in the spotlight, and it's stifling. I have to be on guard not to send the wrong message."

Moving to get or take sexual enjoyment is analogous to the **I** sentence: "I want..." or, "I desire..." It is essential to communication. (See Chapter 2)

In the past, our society had a "petter" (usually male) and a "pettee" (usually female). Almost universally the petter got more aroused than the pettee. In Masters and Johnson's sex therapy, an artificial situation was created during which one partner would be passive and the other would be a toucher. Then the two partners changed roles. Most commonly each partner stated that she/he became more aroused in the role of toucher. The one exception to this situation occurred when the touchee role is one that had been very rare—but longed for—in that person's sexual past.

PRINCIPAL 2. **Protect yourself and your partner from anything that is negative for you, and trust your partner to do the same.**

If your partner is doing something that is negative for you, change it. The repertoire of changing it includes a change in your activity, body position, body English, hand signals or words, or stopping sex for that encounter. Do *not* just grin and bear it! We believe that eliminating the negative is a moral obligation to yourself and to your partner. Eliminating any activity that is negative is analogous to saying, "Ouch!" (See "Ouch," Chapter 7)

Taking responsibility to change or stop whatever is negative for you ensures that your partner's self-interest can never be selfish. For our present purposes, selfishness can be defined as "carrying one's self-interest to the point of not caring if your partner is hurt—hurt in its broadest meaning." (See Chapter 7)

√ *When you take the responsibility to change whatever is negative for you, your partner's free and spontaneous maximizing of his/her sexuality remains in the category of self-interest, and cannot be selfish.*

Eliminating whatever is negative for you also frees your partner from guessing or worrying about how you are receiving his/her actions. Your partner is relieved from the burden and obligation of having to be on the lookout for subtle signs of your discomfort. She/he can be spontaneous and can move to maximize her/his own sexual enjoyment—making *you* the beneficiary of the contagiousness of her/his increased sexual arousal.

Taking responsibility to eliminate the negative is also moral in terms of protecting the sexual relationship. Enduring significant physical or psychological discomfort while having sex makes anyone expect discomfort the next time. This results in a tendency to avoid sexual opportunity; hence, it deprives both you and your partner from the fullest sexual enjoyment.

The second part of this principle is the reciprocal of the first: "Trust your partner to protect you from doing anything that is negative for her/him." There is no longer any need to divert part of your attention to watch and read your partner. You can rest assured that your partner will let you know. If you should miss your partner's first message, you can trust that she/he will send it again more clearly. Trust that your partner will do whatever is necessary to eliminate the negative while exploring for sexual enjoyment. This mutual pact is liberating for both parties.

Please note we have used the word negative. This is a distinction from "I don't like it," which can mean, "I neither like or dislike it." It can be neutral as well as implying a negative. Being neutral about what your partner is doing is OK. One does not need to eliminate a touch that is neutral.

Sometimes people wanting to expand their sexual horizons will want to explore activities that may be psychologically negative to them in the beginning. Acquiring new tastes in many areas of life can be uncomfortable at first. Drinking beer, eating caviar, or wearing high-heeled shoes are activities in this category for some people. The same response may occur the first several times something new is tried sexually, e.g., oral sex.

Several points need to be noted here:

1. The individual is always exploring or pushing himself/herself *for* the self. Never push your partner. Never allow your partner to push you. Your partner can invite you to explore what has been or is negative for you, but should not push, pressure, cajole, or threaten you. Pushing is always negative. The human response to feeling pushed is to resist. Each of you is the world's authority on the fact that you feel pushed. You may feel pushed by your partner when in fact your partner is not pushing. Even so, do whatever is required to eliminate your feeling of being pushed.

2. When you explore activities that have been negative, keep the exploration minimal in degree and duration. As you become comfortable at a new activity, you can increase it in small increments of intensity or duration. To try too much all at once, or continue it after your feelings become negative, will turn you further against the activity.

3. With any new exploration there has to be the absolute right to stop at any time or any point, either to revert back to one of the tried-and-true secure sexual approaches, or to stop the sexual encounter altogether. The right to say "No" psychologically precedes the ability to say "Yes" whole-heartedly. True, the partner may be disappointed, but there is no need for the disappointment to be taken as a personal rejection any more than should an interruption such as a child's knock on the door or a telephone call be taken as a personal rejection.

PRINCIPLE 3.   Let each moment, each activity, be an end in and for itself.

Do what you do for the enjoyment of the moment. Enjoyment and pleasure can unfold one moment, leading on to the next. However, to do something one moment in order to enjoy the next is work, rather than play. This kind of working is the sexual technique of the too eager adolescent who kisses in order to touch the breasts (if female), touches the breasts in order to touch the genitals, and touches the genitals in order to have intercourse, in order to score.

√ *Scoring is not the same as making love, and it most often results in the partner being turned off or feeling used.*

Moment-by-moment judgment (almost non-thinking judgment) is a characteristic of fun and play as opposed to work. *Sex needs to be fun and play.* (See Chapter 10)

For most things that we categorize as pure enjoyment, it is perfectly acceptable to stop at any moment. It is okay to stop dancing at any point; one doesn't need to wait until the end of the number. Usually it is permissible to stop eating at any point. In fact, an eating problem is apt to develop if a parent continually insists the child consume a prescribed amount. The moment-by-moment approach allows people to lend themselves to holding and touching to see if feelings of sexual arousal can or will develop at this time. If they do, fine. If not, that has to be all right, too.

It is unreasonable to expect to be able to protect your partner from all disappointments. However, you should be able to offer protection from feelings of being personally rejected. With environmental interruptions, most people feel that what they had up to that point was enjoyable—better than not having enjoyed that activity at all, even though both may be disappointed. If one person needs to stop and the other has continued sexual need, then the alternatives need to be considered, including the "safety valve" of some form of masturbation, either by your partner or yourself. (See Chapter 26)

Most couples we see with a sexual problem have some form of a "commitment line." They can be free and spontaneous until they cross that line; then they take on an obligation to "go all the way," whether they feel like it or not. The line can be a lingering kiss, or an embrace that lasts longer than usual. Often the commitment line is genital touching.

■ *One woman recounts how she often feels like rushing up to her husband when he gets home, then giving him a big hug and kiss. But, she reasons, "If I do that he will think I'm interested in sex. Let's see, am I? I have supper to get ready, and the kids to put to bed while he does the dishes. With all the things I should do, I'll probably be too tired by bedtime." All the evaluation thinking lowers her level of arousal. The spontaneity of the moment has already been lost. So he gets an "Oh, hi dear" from across the room, even if she does decide she might be interested later.*

√ **The natural human response to feeling pressured is to resent it and to resist.**

Masters and Johnson found in their research that couples who had never had a sexual problem did not have a line of commitment. They were never committed to any particular activity beyond the one they were enjoying at the moment. They could let A unfold into B, C, M, or S and Z, or they could stop at L or D. Neither individual knew or thought of what they might do in some future moment.

Some people commit themselves to intercourse hours or even days in advance. This is usually done to escape a sexual encounter in the present. "Not tonight, dear; tomorrow night." This statement puts the sexual encounter in the work mode; something to be accomplished. And when tomorrow night arrives, the commitment itself is often felt as pressure, even if the partner has not mentioned it. This situation is entirely different from setting time aside tomorrow night to be alone together and be spontaneous. This attitude is in the play mode. The best sex is always a playing activity. □

IN BRIEF

An agreement to protect each other from any sexual activity that is negative is freeing and liberating for each partner. Then each is free to be spontaneous in moving to maximize her/his own pleasure at any moment in time. The result is a beautiful, highly arousing sexual concert between the partners.

YET TO COME

Sexual changes with aging.

CHAPTER 30
SEXUAL CHANGES WITH AGING

"Come, grow old with me! The best is yet to be..." [26]

The physical changes that occur in sexual functioning with aging are similar to those that occur in the rest of the body; primarily, sexual reactions are slower and muscle strength is decreased.

Males

As men age it takes them longer to get erections. It also takes them a little longer to ejaculate. They should expect this to be the case and accept it as normal—and, equally importantly, their partners need to accept it, too.

But what if the slowdown is not taken as normal? After three minutes of effective sexual stimulation, if a man does not have an erection, he may say, "What's wrong with me?" This can promote a self-fulfilling prophecy because he shifts his attention from being involved in the sexually arousing aspects of his partner to watching and evaluating his erection. As his level of arousal drops, his erection decreases. As soon as a man asks himself, "How am I doing?" the answer is always, "Not as well as before I asked the question."

On the other hand, he may accept the increase in time as normal, but his wife may not. Hence, she may wonder, "Have I lost my attractiveness? Doesn't he love me anymore?" She may also say, "I sense you are working on me or yourself. I would prefer to just snuggle right now."

An older man's erection is less firm than it was when he was younger, but is often ample for intercourse. There is a reduced volume and force of the ejaculate. The man may lose his erection right after ejaculation, which may occur so rapidly that the penis seems to fall out of the vagina. A physician may recommend using Sildenafil Citrate, which enables many men to have erections.

If the couple is using intercourse as a means of being close and intimate, the man may not wish—or be able—to ejaculate every time they have intercourse. He may feel satisfied without ejaculating. Many women who are orgasmic have always accepted that they can feel satisfied on occasion without being orgasmic. Both partners need to accept as normal the fact that the older male may not ejaculate with every opportunity.

---

[26] Browning, Robert: "Rabbi Ben Ezra" from George Benjamin Woods & Jerome Hamilton Bushley, *Poetry of the Victorian Period*, Scott Foresman & Co., New York, 1955

Females

Similar changes occur in the older female. It may take her three to five minutes of sex play for her to lubricate, whereas the same response occurred in 10 to 20 seconds when younger. And it may take her longer to be orgasmic.

After menopause, with decreased estrogen, there is a thinning of the vaginal wall. It remains thicker and more resilient in those women who continue regular sexual intercourse, as compared to those who significantly reduce the frequency of intercourse, which is a form of disuse atrophy.

In older women the muscular contractions occurring with orgasm are weaker, as are all other muscle responses. This effect is recordable and has been documented. However, older women report no diminution in subjective pleasure or release gratification.

There is also the loss of fertility, with its possible psychological ramifications. Women should realize that, physiologically, conception may be a realistic possibility for 18 months after the last menstrual flow associated with menopause.

Both Genders

One of the most important aspects of satisfactory sexual functioning in the aged—both male and female—is continuity of sexual functioning. If a person loses a spouse and is sexually inactive for a prolonged time until forming another relationship, the re-institution of sexual functioning may be difficult. This circumstance is frequently the underlying reason for older people seeking advice of sex therapists.

When intercourse is not a part of the older person's life, masturbation—if it is within the individual's sexual and moral value system—will minimize the difficulty in resuming full sexual functioning for both men and women. Clinical findings indicate that the vaginal changes are less with masturbation, even when nothing is introduced into the vagina, than with cessation of all sexual activity for a comparable time.

Most physicians are knowledgeable about geriatric sexual functioning and are willing to discuss your sexual problems and concerns. If your physician doesn't inquire, then you need to introduce the topic. If you sense reluctance to talk about these issues, or if you are uncomfortable talking with him/her, then you can ask for a referral to someone who is more willing to discuss sex, or you can seek out such a physician on your own.

The need to be held and to hold, to snuggle, to feel loved and loving, does not change with increasing age. In fact, the need often increases as a compensation for less sexual intercourse. □

IN BRIEF

Older people need to be patient with the slowed sexual responses of their own and their partner's bodies. Enjoy each other. It is only the sexual enjoyment that sustains sexual responses.

YET TO COME

We hope that the future holds greater security in your partner's love and that you two have a fuller, more enjoyable life together.

Appendix A
Homosexuality: Authors' Statement

The major difference between homosexuals and heterosexuals is that homosexuals prefer sexual activity with someone of their own gender, and heterosexuals prefer sexual activity with someone of the opposite gender.

Homosexuals are attracted to people of their own gender by the same range of traits that attract heterosexuals to people of the opposite gender. Homosexuals fall in love and have the same types of romantic behavior, and they are eager to enhance the happiness of their lovers. When apart, they pine for their love's company, and they suffer with the loss of a love in the same way as heterosexuals. Their love poetry is just as deep and heartfelt as any written by heterosexuals. Many enjoy committed, long-standing, monogamous relationships. Homosexuals can suffer deeply from unrequited love. Some homosexuals, like some heterosexuals, have a Don Juan syndrome—a need to seduce every potential lover they meet. Homosexuals can damage their relationships and their lives in the same ways as heterosexuals, including by miscommunications and by having an affair while in a committed, monogamous relationship. The partner is hurt and disillusioned. In our medical practice we have seen individual homosexuals and homosexual couples in which at least one member of the relationship complains of every variation we have seen with heterosexual patients.

In 1973, The American Psychiatric Association removed homosexuality from its official classification of diseases. The American Psychological Association took a similar stance shortly afterwards. Two facts were seminal in these professional organizations taking this position. First was the publication of sociological sex research done with homosexual communities whose members were content with their sexual life. These contented-to-happy homosexuals didn't resemble, in the least, those who defined themselves as patients by seeking professional help for various aspects of their lives. Prior to the publishing of those studies, many psychiatrists and clinical psychologists assumed that all homosexuals were similar to those who sought therapy.

The second seminal factor was the publication of an article by Richard Green, MD, entitled "Homosexuality and Mental Illness."[27] Dr. Green examined and *refuted* every pathological symptom that had previously been used to support the concept that homosexuality was a mental illness. Subsequent investigations and reports by many psychiatrists, psychologists, sociologists, and scientists of other disciplines overwhelmingly support Dr. Green's position.

---

[27] Green, Richard: "Homosexuality and Mental Illness," *International Journal of Psychiatry*, Vol: 10, No. 1, 1972, p77

These factors and the public's awareness of civil rights in general have contributed to the fact that many homosexuals have become more open about their sexual orientation. This has resulted in a lot of people realizing that some of their friends are gay. As a result, many people are increasingly changing their opinions about homosexuality rather than changing their views of their friends.

This book applies to all relationships in which each person values the other's happiness at or near par with their own. Reading, understanding, and working through the issues described in this book: the Spiral of Love, the communication principles, the problems, the challenges, and the solutions will help you and your partner—gay or straight—to create and enjoy a deeper and more loving relationship. □

Appendix B
Pornography

Many Americans are not sure what attitude to hold about pornography. Is it bad or wrong? If so, what makes it that way?

For your convenience and continuity, we will repeat the pornography description given in Chapter 20:

The Merriam-Webster's Collegiate Dictionary, 1998 Edition, defines pornography as: "The depiction of erotic behavior (as in pictures or writing) intended to cause sexual excitement." This is an interesting definition because:

1. *It would include sexy and romance novels as well as pictures and movies.*

2. *It is not sexual behavior, but rather its depiction. The definition excludes "erotic dancing" on stage, but includes pictures, movies, and other depictions of erotic dancing.*

3. *Pornography is defined by the intent of the producer, not by the effect on the user. Hence, a picture of a woman in a negligee in a men's magazine could be considered pornographic, while the same pictures in a Victoria's Secret or Frederick's of Hollywood catalogue would not be pornographic because the primary intent of the graphic is to sell negligees.*

4. *This definition would include a steamy love letter written with the intent of sexually arousing the lover.*

The Concern About Pornography

In 1967, Congress became concerned about obscenity and pornography. Perhaps the concern was due in part to the seeming proliferation of adult bookstores and the more open use of pornography by the generation of the so-called sexual revolution. Undoubtedly the clash of values between the sellers of pornography and some members of the general public, which gave rise to a number of court cases, contributed. The prosecution of many of these court cases foundered due to the absence of a clear objective definition for pornography that could be used legally. These concerns added to the "general" attitude or suspicion that pornography was harmful and, if true, government had a legitimate role in regulating it. Congress passed Public Law 90-100, which established a Presidential Commission to investigate and to make recommendations. The charge to the Commission was:

1. Analyze the current laws and make a recommendation for a legal definition of

pornography.

2.   Identify the nature and volume of traffic in pornography.

3.   Study the effects of obscenity and pornography on the public and minors, and its relationship to crime and anti-social behavior.

4.   Make recommendations.

President Johnson appointed the commission members. The Commission made its report in 1970.[28]

The commission solicited written opinions from approximately a hundred national organizations, held public hearings, and interviewed police officers, managers of adult book stores and their customers, prosecuting attorneys, psychologists, psychiatrists, and sociologists. They examined pornographic materials. They examined scientific studies, plus had other studies designed and carried out for them.

We will restrict our consideration of the Commission's work to the third charge: the effect of pornography on the public and minors and its relationship to crime and anti-social behavior.

The Commission found that the rationalization given over the years for continuing to have laws against pornography has been that these materials are harmful to the general public in that:

1.   Pornography arouses and can cause or contribute to sex crimes by its arousal effect on men and adolescents.

2.   Pornography degrades women.

3.   Pornography is used for stimulus in masturbation, which is viewed as wrong or harmful per sé.

1. Does Pornography Contribute to Sex Crimes?

The Commission cited a controlled study of delinquent and non-delinquent youths and found that they had similar experiences with erotic material, including the age of first exposure and the intensity of the exposure, and that the exposure had no impact upon moral character over and above the effects of their background (p. 36).

After ten years of the repeal of all laws against pornography, Denmark experienced a steady decline in sex crimes. Dr. Sven Ziegler

---

[28] Kemp, Earl, Editor: *The Illustrated Presidential Report of the Commission on Obscenity and Pornography*, Greenleaf Classics Inc, San Diego, CA, 1970, pp5, 35-37

of the Ministry of Justice stated, "There is no evidence that this liberalization is leading to any increase in the number of sex crimes." Dr. Anders Groeth, a psychiatrist at the largest mental hospital in Denmark has said, "The general fear has been that pornography gives rise to uncontrolled impulses or acts. If it did, there would have been a rise in sex crimes (as there has been in other crimes)... Pornography seems to give relaxation of passions rather than stimulate uncontrolled impulses." He continued, "Pornography may give some inspiration in some marriages where they were a little tired... It is very useful for grown-ups who have been too shy in their marriages to experiment a little... Pornography probably decreases the need for extra-marital experimentation and in the end perhaps makes divorce in some cases less likely." (p. 10)

Research has shown that sex offenders in the United States have had less adolescent experience with erotic material than other adults. The data suggests this reflects the sex offenders' more generally deprived sexual environment. Dr. K. Michael Lipkin of the University of Chicago and Dr. Donald Kerns of Northwestern University came to the same conclusion after surveying 3,400 psychologists and psychiatrists. After years of study, Dr. Paul Gebhard, et al., of the Indiana University's Institute for Sex Research ("The Kinsey group") stated, "Summing up the evidence it would appear that the possession of pornography does not differentiate sex offenders from non-sex offenders... We have found that men with large collections (of pornographic materials) of long standing lose much of their sexual response to the materials and while their interest in collecting may continue unabated, their interest is no longer primarily sexual." (p. 10)

The Presidential Commission found no evidence that exposure to explicit sexual material plays a significant role in the causing delinquent or criminal behavior in youths or adults. In general, established patterns of sexual behavior were found to be very stable and not altered substantially by exposure to erotica. When sexual activity followed reading pornography, it constituted a temporary activation of the individual's pre-existing patterns of sexual behavior. Extensive use of pornography over a five-day period of time resulted in satiation, boredom, and diminution of arousal.

Sex crimes commonly utilize sexuality in the expression of hostility. These crimes often are triggered—verbally or behaviorally—by some slight or insult, and reflect hostility to a representative of a group to be dominated in order to re-establish the individual's sense of adequacy.

This concept of a slight or an insult as a trigger is well presented by Robert Stoller's *Perversion, the Erotic Form of Hatred.*[29] This book is clearly written and is suitable for the general public.

We would modify the Commission's statement about the triggers for sex crimes to say that initially a sex crime is usually triggered by a slight or insult, and that as the transformation of these hurts becomes a habit, the crime can be triggered by opportunity and, later, boredom—or the desire for excitement. Further, various aspects of sexuality may become addictions; that is, the individual feels that she/he can't get through the day without the fix of the addictive sexual behavior. People may become addicted to pornography and other forms of visual images, adult movies, peep shows, and exotic dancing, as well as visiting prostitutes or exhibitionism, etc. (See "Addictions," Chapter 20)

We are personally unaware of any incident in which pornography contributed to a sex crime. With the exception mentioned in the preceding paragraph, we agree with the Commission's findings.

2. Is Pornography Degrading to Women?

The Commission concluded that only pornography that depicts intimidation, coercion, or violence against women had a damaging effect on the viewer's attitudes toward women, in that men were less sensitive and sympathetic and more aggressive towards women. They concluded that it was the violence, not the sexual aspects of the material, that produced these effects.

It is true that the women in erotic material are idealized. They are depicted as attractive women who seem to enjoy sex. It is difficult to infer other personality or character traits of a woman from only one or several sexual pictures. Personality aspects are developed in written fantasy material. Men tend to prefer pictorial erotic material, while women tend to prefer novels. This approach is consistent with the attitude that "men are sexual first and social second." However, men with imagination use the erotic material as a starting point and do attribute personality traits to the women as they develop their fantasies. Recognize that an explicit sexual novel depicts a sexual fantasy in story form just as any other novel depicts a non-sexual fantasy related as a story.

We presented pictures of women from covers and ads of common magazines to men who were socially inhibited around women. They denied any sexual fantasy life. These pictures showed only the head, face, and shoulders of the women. We spread 15–18 pictures on the table and asked the men to "read" how the woman was feeling.

---

[29] Stoller, Robert: *Perversion, the Erotic Form of Hatred,* Pantheon Books, a division of Random House, New York, 1975

The most severely inhibited men were unable to make any statement about any of the pictures. That is, they were unable to see the difference in a woman who was smiling from one who was being stern, or sad, or distraught, or provocative. We found that the more socially inhibited a man is around women, (1) the less he notices personality and character of the women in his life's space, and (2) the less he incorporates any personality in his fantasies about women, including those fantasies stimulated by pornography.

It is hard to read degradation of women into a pornographic image of a woman having enjoyable coitus by sitting astride a man who is on his back.

We concur with the Commission's conclusion that only pornography that depicts women being intimidated or physically abused has a degrading affect on the viewer's attitude toward women.

3. Pornography as a Stimulus

The 1970 Presidential Commission on Pornography reported (on page 35) that research cast doubt on the belief that women are vastly less aroused by erotic material than are men.

Women usually choose a romantic novel, complete with several explicit sexual scenes, to facilitate their masturbation. Men often use picture pornography for their mental stimulation while masturbating. Certainly, both erotic pictures and erotic writing are also enjoyed without physical masturbation.

Perhaps the most famous book to aid female masturbation is *Memories of a Woman of Pleasure*, attributed to John Cleland,[30] first published in England in 1749. It has been translated into many languages. It has also been published under the title *Memories of Fanny Hill*.

But it is masturbation per sé that has been so misunderstood. Havelock Ellis traces the general attitude toward masturbation.[31]

In the early 18th century, an Englishman (supposedly named Bekkers) published a book on the "evils" of masturbation entitled *Onania or the Heinous Sin of Self-Pollution, and all its Frightful Consequences in Both Sexes, Considered, with Spiritual and Physical Advice*. Later editions of the book contained advertisements for "Strengthening Tinctures" that were alleged to help both men and women resist masturbation. This book went through 80 editions.

This idea that masturbation was the cause of many different diseases was picked up by a Swiss physician named Tissot who, in 1760,

---

[30] Cleland, John: *Memories of a Woman of Pleasure*, Bell Publishing Co., New York, 1963

[31] Ellis, Havelock: *Studies in the Psychology of Sex*; Vol 1, Random House, New York, 1905 & 1942, p248–253

published an extensive medical treatise on maladies caused by masturbation. Both Rousseau and Voltaire wrote on the subject, furthering the misinformation. Lallemand, a French physician, added stress and confusion by his publication in 1836. The diseases attributed to excessive masturbation by these authors included dementia, insanity, eye disorders, epilepsy, pains, shortness of breath, heart murmurs, skin maladies, and many more. "Excessive" masturbation was not defined. As a result, many men and women believed that they were at the threshold of masturbating excessively.

People in French insane asylums were observed masturbating frequently, and this was taken as the cause of their insanity. Today we know that the idleness and boredom in those large, impersonal custodial-care institutions contributed to the frequent masturbation.

The false concept of masturbation as the cause of eye disease and mental problems persisted the longest. The medical records of 160 men in the Matteawan State Hospital in New York, during the period of 1875-1907, listed masturbation as the sole cause of their insanity.

Masturbation is very common. Alfred Kinsey found that 94% of men who had no education beyond grade school, as did 97% of men at the college level, masturbated. The longer an individual waits to begin an active sex life with a partner, the more likely he has enjoyed masturbation.[32] Those people who delayed beginning sexual relationships in order to attend college or graduate school spent many years during which masturbation was their only or primary sexual outlet. For most men and women, some masturbation continues even after the individuals enter into a committed sexual relationship. One reason for this is that it is continuance of a habit established over many years of adolescence and young adulthood. Also, masturbation acts as an outlet for sexual desire when the partner is not available. Further, pornography and romance novels extend the individual's imagination and add spice to her/his fantasies and life.

We believe pornography, pictorial and written, is a sexual stimulus. However, we see nothing wrong with masturbation. Masturbation does not transmit sexual diseases, nor result in pregnancies. Just as envisioning yourself performing some task is a means to help prepare yourself to perform that task at some future time, sexual fantasies—if they are realistic—help prepare the individual for sexual intercourse in the future. Pornography that depicts mutual caring and includes intercourse can be helpful to the adolescent in his/her later sexual life. (See "Fantasy In Intimate Relationships," Chapter 26)

---

[32] Kinsey, Alfred; Pomeroy, Wardell; and Martin, Clyde: *Sexual Behavior in the Human Male*, W.B. Sanders Co., Philadelphia, PA, 1948, p339

Subsequent Studies

There have been three studies of pornography since the 1970 report of President Johnson's Commission. Two were conducted in Great Britain: the Williams Report in 1979,[33] and the Howitt and Chamberback Report in 1990.[34] The findings and conclusions of both of these studies were similar to those reported by President Johnson's Commission. The other major study of pornography, known as the Meese Commission Report,[35] concluded that pornography "might" be harmful. □

---

[33] The Williams Report: *Report of the Commission on Obscenity and Film Censorship*, London, HMSO, cm nd 7772, 1979

[34] Howitt and Chamberback: *Pornography Impacts and Influences*, London, HMSO, 1990

[35] Meese Commission, The: *The Attorney General's Commission Report*, Department of Justice, Washington, D.C., 1986

Appendix C
Where To Find Help

There are three major sources for obtaining help:

Professionals You Know: These are experts you already know and who know the resources of the community. Examples include your physician or clergy. They probably have first-hand knowledge of other people who have sought similar help, as well as who helped them and the results of that help. Others who would be in a position to refer patients for help would be in the same category, including divorce attorneys.

Telephone Directory: Programs such as Alcoholics Anonymous (AA), Al-Anon, and Gamblers Anonymous may be found in the business section or Yellow Pages of most local phone directories. It might be easier to use the index, which will refer you to the exact page where you will find the information you seek. Categories such as "Mental Health Services" and "Domestic Abuse" usually have multiple listings. You can also call your local telephone service provider's information line (usually 1-555-1212) and ask for the "Crisis Hotline" in your community. The Hotline personnel should be able to help you or refer you to the appropriate places to find help.

The Internet: Try your favorite one or more search engines using key words that describe the kind of help you are seeking. You may want to start with broad categories, (e.g., "erectile dysfunction," "gambling addiction," "marriage counseling") then narrow them to specific issues and/or cross-reference it with your geographic area, marital status, age grouping, or whatever is relevant. Two organizations not listed in some phone directories that have information clearinghouses and more specific websites are: "Sex Addicts Anonymous" (www.sexaa.org) and Sex and Love Addicts Anonymous (www.slaafws.org).

It is important to be persistent. If the help you locate does not seem appropriate or satisfactory, do not give up. There are tremendous resources available, most of which can make a significant difference when you find the right match. □

About the Authors:

Highlights

- From 1964 through 1968, Drs. Marshall L. and Marguerite R. Shearer gave sex lectures, on invitation, to sororities and fraternities and other housing units on the campus of the University of Michigan. During that period they were booked once a week for entire academic years. These talks continued during 1969-70 as well, but to larger audiences. During that time Marshall was on the faculty in the Department of Psychiatry at the University of Michigan School of Medicine, and Marguerite was a physician at the University Health Service.

- In 1970, they were recruited by Dr. Masters and Mrs. Johnson as clinical and research associates. They saw a third of their patients with sexual inadequacies as a therapy team, and were paired with Dr. Masters, Mrs. Johnson, and other staff members for their other patients. In addition, Marshall was responsible for developing the curriculum and doing the initial training for professionals in regard to the foundation's newly described treatment for sexual inadequacies. Marguerite was in charge of the infertility clinic.

- In 1972 they returned to Michigan and continued doing sex therapy, jointly for a while, then Marshall on his own. Marguerite used many of the same principles in her day-to-day family medical practice, including obstetrics and gynecology.

- From 1973 to 1996, the Shearers wrote a sex-help column, answering readers' questions for the *Detroit Free Press*, which was also distributed over the Knight-Ridder wire.

- Marshall is a Board Diplomat of the American Association of Sex Educators, Counselors, and Therapists (AASECT). He is also Board certified in both Psychiatry and Child Psychiatry. Marguerite is Board certified in Family Medicine and also in Medical Management.

- Marshall and Marguerite have been married since 1961, the only marriage for each of them. They have three adult children.

www.DocShearer.com

About the Authors:

Expanded Narrative

Marshall L. Shearer earned his medical doctor's degree from the Medical College of South Carolina in 1958. After a general rotating internship, he came to the University of Michigan for psychiatric training. He met Marguerite Raft when she was a senior medical student at the University of Michigan. They married in June, 1961, after Marguerite had completed her general rotating internship at Washington DC General Hospital.

Marguerite took a year of advanced training in internal medicine at Wayne County General Hospital in Eloise, Michigan, then a year divided between obstetrics gynecology and surgery at Women's Hospital of Detroit.

Marshall continued his psychiatric residency, which included a year in research and certification in child psychiatry. For about 18 months in 1962-63, he consulted one day a week with the Michigan Department of Corrections. Part of his responsibility was to do psychiatric evaluations on men who had recently arrived in prison to serve life sentences.

After their marriage, they joined the Bushnell Congregational Church on Southfield Road in Detroit. Marshall taught Sunday school there for one year. Marguerite and Marshall were recruited by the Minister to Youth, William Straight, to be resource physicians for a sex education program sponsored by the church and put on by Mrs. and Mr. Ventor. The program was divided between the junior-high and high-school students; the pupils in each group were both male and female.

The following year, the Shearers moved to Dexter, Michigan. Marshall completed his psychiatric training and joined the University of Michigan School of Medicine faculty full time, first as an Instructor, then later as an Assistant Professor.

Marguerite took a position as a physician at the University of Michigan Student Health Service, where she saw many coeds as patients. She soon became aware of the problems that many college students were facing in regard to sexual issues, particularly after the university eliminated housemothers and made dormitories coed. She was the first physician at the Student Health Service to prescribe contraceptives to students.

Marguerite saw a number of female students who had engaged in intercourse without being fully cognizant of what was happening, sometimes resulting in unwanted pregnancies. She was alarmed by some of the stories related by women who had elected to have abortions, which was illegal in those years. They included being separated from the psychological support of people they trusted, sometimes even being blindfolded and led down an alley where the procedure was to be done by a complete stranger. Some women reported hearing rodents scurrying around. Marguerite was further alarmed by the potential for injury to the women's reproductive systems and for life-threatening infections.

This led Marguerite and Marshall to volunteer to give sex education lectures, on request, to students living in housing units at the University of Michigan.

Marshall became a diplomat of the American Board of Neurology and Psychiatry in Psychiatry, and later of the same Board in Child Psychiatry. Marguerite became a Diplomat of the American Board of Family Medicine and, later, Medical Management.

At Children's Psychiatric Hospital at the University of Michigan as Assistant In-Patient Director, Marshall began working with couples in regard to their hospitalized children. He also consulted for Dr. Hazel Turner of the Ann Arbor Public Schools for one-half day each week from 1965–69.

Marshall conceived the idea of bringing a dog into the hospital, believing that it would have a therapeutic effect on patients ages 5 or 6, up to 12. They could relate to the dog with a "fresh slate," presumably with little or no emotional hold-over from their pasts. The dog would respond to the children's affection, and would give the kids something to love without making demands on them. The affection returned by the dog would be directly proportional to the affection it received. This experiment was supported by Marshall's section chief, Dr. Stuart Finch, and the Department of Psychiatry chair, Dr. Raymond Waggoner. With the assistance of Mr. Cleveland, of Hospital Administration, the request was approved.

Some time later, the dog got loose while being exercised on the hospital grounds, and subsequently had puppies. This created some stir—not so much with the children or the child-care workers, but somewhat with the nurses and quite a bit with some of the psychiatric residents who struggled with how to deal with the issue and how to give sex education to their young patients and support staff. The experience with the dog in the hospital was published by Elizabeth Yates, one of the child-care staff.[36]

Dr. Raymond Waggoner was also a member of the Board of Directors of Masters and Johnson Institute. At that time the organization was known as the Reproductive Biological Research Foundation. The RBRF had just completed its study of the treatment of sexual dysfunction and was interested in hiring a medical couple who were comfortable talking about sex. They also wanted a psychiatrist and someone from academia who had experience in teaching. Dr. Waggoner recruited Marshall and Marguerite.

While with Masters and Johnson, Marguerite and Marshall each carried a load of three new patients every two weeks. One-third of Marguerite's cases were with Dr. Masters, one-third with Dr. Spitz, and one-third with Marshall. Marguerite also was responsible for the RBRF Foundation's infertility clinic. Marshall's caseload was

---

[36] Elizabeth Yates: *Skeezer, Dog with a Mission*, Harvey House, Inc., Irvington-on-Hudson, New York, 1973

similarly divided. In addition to treating patients, he was responsible for developing a curriculum with Mrs. Johnson, and for teaching the first group of professionals.

Upon their return to Michigan, Marguerite and Marshall opened a joint sexual counseling practice. Marshall continued with his general psychiatric practice and had a clinical assignment at the University of Michigan as Associate Professor of Psychiatry. Marguerite practiced Family Medicine.

Marguerite was elected president of the Washtenaw County Medical Society in 1980. In 1983, she was the first woman elected to the Board of Directors of the Michigan State Medical Society. She was on the Michigan Delegation to the American Medical Association from 1990 until 2002.

Together, the Shearers have 57 years working extensively with heterosexual and gay couples and individuals in relationships. They have taken thousands of detailed sexual histories on both men and women.

Marshall L. and Marguerite R. Shearer are now active members of the First Unitarian Universalist Church of Ann Arbor, Michigan. □

www.DocShearer.com

Index

A

About the Authors
  expanded narrative, *256–58*
  highlights, *253–55*
Abuse
  early cues of, *180*
  spousal
    treatable, *176*
Accept Me, *78*
Acting out, *175*
Addiction, *199*
Addiction to a Person, *162*
Addiction to Alcohol, *156*
Addiction to Excitement, *162*
Addiction to Gambling, *162*
Addiction to One of the Paraphillias, *161*
Addictions, *115, 155–65*
  12-step programs, *159*
  alcohol
    causes of, *158*
  co-dependency, *157, 163*
  dependency
    definitions of, *157*
    present when, *157*
  emotional denial, *155*
  excitement, *162*
  gambling, *162*
  object of, *157*
  paraphillias, *161*
    exhibitionism, *161*
    frotteurism, *161*
    transvestism, *161*
    voyeurism, *161*
  physical, is, *157*
  pre-addictive stages, *159*
  psychological factors, *158*
  sexual, *248*
  sexual and love, *160*
  some dynamics of, *164*
  steps you can take, *164*
    intervention, *164*
  support groups, *159*
    Adult Children of Alcoholic Parents, *159*

Al-Anon, *159*
Alateen, *159*
Alcoholics Anonymous, *159*
  to a person, *162*
  tolerance and dependency, *157*
  types, *155*
Addictions as a Transformation of Hurts, *115*
Addicts
  common life scripts, *158*
Admire Me, *78*
Adult Children of Alcoholic Parents, *159*
After a Separation, *179*
Aging
  sexual changes, *239*
Al-Anon, *159*
Alateen, *159*
Alcohol addiction, *156*
Alcoholics Anonymous, *159, 253*
Allergy, *134*
Always & Never, *18*
Ambivalence, *27, 91, 131*
American Psychiatric Association, The, *243*
American Psychological Association, The, *243*
Anger, *112*
  as a signal of a hurt, *113*
  clarity of communication, *120*
  communication of, *117*
  components, *117*
  compound, *139*
  depth and intensity, *119*
  emotional denial, *120*
  expression
    appropriateness of, *120*
    effectiveness of, *121*
    price to be paid, *121*
  feelings of, *117*
  gunny sacking, *118*
    cause of, *118*
    dealing with, *119*
  I sentences, *122*
  issue, *118*
  judging effectiveness of expression, *121*
  low self-esteem, *120*
  martyrs, *120*
  neurotic anger, *118*

U

CPSIA information can be obtained at www.ICGtesting.com
Printed in the USA
BVOW09s0447180214

345221BV00001B/17/P